Servants of
WAR

Servants of WAR

Private Military Corporations
and the Profit of Conflict

Rolf Uesseler

3 1336 08111 5645

Soft Skull Press
Brooklyn

Originally published in German by Ch. Links Verlag under the title
Krieg als Dienstleistung, copyright © Christoph Links Verlag, Berlin
2006.

The translation of this work was supported by a grant from the
Goethe-Institut, which is funded by the German Ministry of Foreign
Affairs.

Library of Congress Cataloging-in-Publication Data
Uesseler, Rolf.
  Servants of war : private military corporations and the profit of conflict / Rolf
Uesseler ; translated by Jefferson Chase.
     p. cm.
  ISBN 978-1-59376-202-5
  1. Private military companies—History—21st century. 2. Private security services—History—21st century. 3. Mercenary troops—History. 4. Paramilitary
forces—History—21st century. 5. Security, International—History—21st century. 6. Privatization. 7. Contracting out. I. Title. II. Title: Private military
corporations and the profit of conflict.

  U240.U43 2008
  355.3'54--dc22
                                     2008035783

Cover design by Gary Fogelson
Interior design by Neuwirth & Associates
Printed in the United States of America

Soft Skull Press
An Imprint of Counterpoint LLC
2117 Fourth Street
Suite D
Berkeley, CA 94710

www.softskull.com
www.counterpointpress.com

Distributed by Publishers Group West

10 9 8 7 6 5 4 3 2 1

CONTENTS

1 The Business of War   1
The New Mercenaries: On the Job Around the World   1
The Death of an Antiterror Specialist   2
A Military Pilot on Various Continents   4
The Inventor of the PMC   6
A Special Kind of Arms Dealer   9
A Soldier on a Humanitarian Mission   14
Recruitment of a Private Soldier   17

2 Private Military Companies: The New Service Industry   19
The Broad Spectrum of Services   21
Practical Realization   27
Attempts At Categorization   29
Size and Orientation   31
PMCs and the Abu Ghraib Scandal   37
Personnel and Cost Structure   39

3 The Clients: "Strong States, Corporate Masters, and Rebels" 45
Strong States: The United States and Germany   46
The Interests of the Private Sector   56
"Weak States" with Security Gaps   60
Rebel Groups and Freedom Fighters   62
The Security Dilemma of International Organizations   63
Private Individuals and Security   67

**4 Global Markets for Armed Force: Four Private Military
Companies in Action**   69
Military Professional Resources Inc. (MPRI)   70
Kellogg, Brown and Root (KBR)   75
Executive Outcomes (EO)   80
Blackwater Worldwide   84

Contents

**5 Globalization and "New Wars": A Short History
of the Private War Economy** 91

Biblical Bandits and Greek Hoplites 92
Rome's Popular Army versus Carthage's Mercenary Forces 95
Mercenary Bands in the Middle Ages 97
Companies, "Free Lances," and Condottieri 98
Swiss Guards and German Lansquenets 100
The Ascendancy of the National Standing Army 102
The East India Company 103
The French Revolution and the Decline of the Mercenaries 105

**6 The End of the Cold War: Different Conditions
for Military Services** 111

The End of The Cold War and Globalization 113
New Conflicts in the Third World 116
The New National Energy Policy 118
The Technology and Electronic Revolution 121
Radical Changes in Intelligence Services 123

**7 Clientele Systems and Shadow Economics:
The Development of New Security Needs** 129

The Rise of Markets For Violence 130
Problems with the Clientele System 132
The Rise of Particular Communities 134
The Illegal Global Network 138
*Shadow Economies: The Link Between Legal and Illegal
Moneymaking* 139

**8 Dangerous Consequences: Militant Cooperation–
Business and Private Military Firms** 145

Intervention in the Andes 148
The Security Strategy of Transnational Concerns 151
Unscrupulous Multinational Oil Companies 153

**9 Out of Control: The Questionable Legality
of the Privatization of Force in the West** 159

Private Soldiers in Iraq 160
Secret Contracts, Legal Chaos 161
Lack of Oversight and Accountability 164

Legal Immunity and Ambiguity for New Mercenaries 168
The Conflict Between Democracy and Privatization:
   A State Within a State 172

10 Deceptive Security: National Betrayal in the "Weak States" 179
Dysfunctional Relationship Among Military, State,
   and Civil Societies 181
The Quick Fix: Buying Security 184
The Loss of the Monopoly on the Legitimate Use of Force 186
Plundering of Natural Resources 188

11 Aid Organizations: In the Military Slipstream 193
Endangered Neutrality 194
Military Firms as Security Risks 196
The Need for New Protection Concepts 199

12 Conflict Resolution without Private Military Companies?
Markets for Violence versus State Monopolies 203
Violating the Democracy Imperative 206
Jeopardizing the State's Monopoly on Force 209
The Politics of Peace in the Military Slipstream 213
Crisis Management and PMCs 215

13 Preventing Crisis and Securing Peace 217
"Peace from Above" versus "Peace from Below" 218
The German Plan of Action 222
Criticism from NGOs 225
Conflict Resolution as a Concrete Challenge 227

Conclusion 231

1

The Business of War

The New Mercenaries: On the Job Around the World

In theaters of war and crisis regions across the planet, we encounter fewer and fewer members of regular armies. Conversely, the number of private soldiers is increasing dramatically. Seldom is it clear for whom they're fighting, or who pays them or has sent them into action. Often no one can say to whom they're responsible, if indeed anyone. Nor is anyone in any great hurry to inquire where they acquired their state-of-the-art military hardware, including tanks, attack helicopters, grenades, and missiles.

Soldiers for hire used to be called mercenaries. Today, they are employees of PMCs, "private military corporations," with evocative names like Blue Sky, Genric, Logicon, or Pistris, designed to conceal that they are in fact private firms in the business of waging war. Most of the soldiers who work for them have never been members of an official national armed force. It's impossible to tell from either a uniform or a passport whether a Croatian, Pakistani, Colombian, Irish, or Ukrainian fighter is a former soldier in a regular army, a mercenary, a rebel, or a terrorist.

In the past former soldiers or members of foreign legions who were in search of adventure and profit would hire themselves out to do battle on behalf of mysterious, behind-the-scenes clients. Today that role is filled by the well-trained employees of PMCs. These companies don't just employ people who know their military handicraft. There is also a demand for managers, arms dealers, weapons engineers, computer specialists, translators, experienced pilots, and experts in logistics and satellite communications. Today's mercenary only partially conforms to the gung ho Rambo model. Instead, the prevailing mentality is that war is a job. The handicraft and the whole range of activities associated with armed conflict have become normal, everyday services. Clients demand a professional attitude and, above all, results. Employees are primarily interested in getting paid.

Five case studies suffice to illustrate the broad spectrum of the new mercenaries.

THE DEATH OF AN ANTITERROR SPECIALIST

Fabrizio Quattrocchi was born in 1968 and, as an adult, lived with his parents, his brother, and his fiancée in the city of Genoa. He served in the Italian military, where he received Special Forces training. After a series of escapades and short-term jobs, he and a few friends signed on with Ibsa, a security company whose headquarters were also located in Genoa. One of those friends, Paolo Simeone, had a biography similar to Quattrocchi's. At the age of eighteen, Simeone joined the San Marco Special Forces unit of the Italian Army. After his military service, he signed on for five years with the French foreign legion, with which he was stationed in Djibouti, Somalia, and elsewhere. In 1997, he worked for a minesweeping commando in Angola. In 1999 he went to Kosovo and a year later he returned to Africa. By May 1, 2003, when George W. Bush declared major combat operations in Iraq to be over and the reconstruction period to have begun, Simeone—with the assistance of Italy's U.S. embassy—had established close contacts among civilian and military authorities in the United States. Previously, in the wake of the attacks of September 11, Quattrocchi had joined a group of volunteers from Germany, Canada, and other countries and undergone antiterrorist training at a secret military base in the Philippines. Before Simeone left for Iraq in 2003, he founded a company, headquartered in Nevada, called DTS Security, which gave him a respectable business address for his U.S. contracts. In November of that year, he recruited Quattrocchi and three other comrades—Salvatore Stefio, Umberto Cupertino, and Maurizio Agliana—from similar backgrounds.

On Easter Sunday, 2004, Simeone's four employees were kidnapped somewhere between Baghdad and Falluja by a group calling itself the "Green Phalanx of Mohammed." The next day, the Arabic-language television station Al Jazeera broadcast a video of the hostages in which the kidnappers made their demands. Among other things, they called for the withdrawal of Italian troops from Iraq and an apology from Silvio Berlusconi, the Italian prime minister, for allowing mercenaries to be sent to the country. The incident created a huge media stir. The Italian Parliament convened in special sessions to debate the hostage situation, and the Italian president issued an official statement. Even the pope got involved, asking the kidnappers to release their prisoners. After consultations with President Bush and over objections from left-wing Italians, Berlusconi choose to take a hard-line stance and refused to negotiate with the kidnappers.

A scant twenty-four hours later, Quattrocchi was killed by a gunshot to the neck. The execution was recorded on video. Al Jazeera declined to broadcast the images, but they were made available on the Internet. One entity that took an interest was the Italian state prosecutor's office, which was concerned not only about the murder, but also by suspicions that the four men had violated paragraph 288 of the Italian Criminal Code, which forbids Italian citizens to fight in and for foreign countries without express permission of the Italian government. According to the law, Quattrocchi and the others should not have been in Iraq at all.

Months later, after protracted negotiations, Stefio, Cupertino, and Agliana were released. What are often referred to as "postfascist" elements in the Italian government styled Quattrocchi a martyr, and he was given a state funeral. The prosecutors' investigations stalled despite or perhaps precisely because of the fact that there appeared to be far more Italian mercenaries in Iraq than previously thought. The affair made it clear that politicians in Italy were not at all interested in clearing up the dubious status of private soldiers. The same attitude prevails today, and Italy is not alone. Most countries prefer to play deaf, dumb, and blind on the issue.

A MILITARY PILOT ON VARIOUS CONTINENTS

Thousands of new mercenaries have been killed around the world in the past few years, and tens of thousands wounded. Yet they seldom make headlines, and even more rarely do their names become known. Even their own family members usually don't know where they are or what their mission is at any given moment. Private soldiers prefer to remain anonymous for safety's sake, often assuming a number of aliases, and their employers commonly encourage or force them to do so. A person who is identifiable can easily become a target for enemy reprisals and will be deemed "no good" for the next job.

In Iraq there are around thirty thousand private soldiers authorized to use weapons whenever they deem necessary. The new mercenaries thus make up the second-largest "army" in that country behind the U.S. military, outnumbering all the other coalition forces combined. And Iraq is by no means the only country where they are active. In Afghanistan, president Hamid Karzai's bodyguards are provided by the U.S. company DynCorp, while other firms are responsible for the security of government buildings and infrastructure. In various conflict zones in Southeast Asia and South America, private soldiers fight against rebels, drug cartels, and warlords. In Africa, they watch over oil fields and diamond mines. Private soldiers were active in 160 of the world's nations in the past few years, and their services are in greater demand than ever.

The jobs vary, as do the individual men and—increasingly—women who work as new mercenaries. Vladimir P. is one of them. Born in Ukraine in 1962, he is an experienced pilot, capable of flying everything from twin-engine Cessnas to helicopters, military transport planes, bombers, and fighter jets. Before the dissolution of the Soviet Union, he was a career soldier in the Red Army. Afterward, he faced unemployment until friends got him an engagement in the 1998–2000 war between Eritrea and Ethiopia. Today, Vladimir says he probably owes his life to the quick realization by him and the pilots sitting in the "enemy planes" that they were former comrades from the Soviet Army. From that point on, Vladimir P. reports, they avoided encountering and engaging one another in battle. For the rest of the conflict there was no aerial warfare in that region of northern Africa.

Vladimir's next mission was to fly transport planes from various western European airports to the West African countries of Mali and Burkino Faso. Later he learned from newspaper reports that the cargo consisted of weapons bound for the civil-war-torn countries of Sierra Leone and Liberia. Vladimir speculates that the Russian mafia was behind these deals since the contracts with Burkino Faso were signed in Moscow. He says he does not know the details—perhaps he simply refuses to share them. Vladimir spent most of the last ten years in Africa, but he currently he works for a PMC based on the West Coast of the United States. His specialty is surveillance, and his task is to gather information on opposition groups in the northern part of South America. The data he gathers is used in conjunction with a security umbrella that covers the activities of multinational oil companies in the region. It is supported financially by various Western countries.

THE INVENTOR OF THE PMC

Britain's Tim Spicer was the man who came up with the phrase "private military company," and he was one of the first large-scale entrepreneurs in this growing field. In his autobiography, *An Unorthodox Soldier: Peace and War and the Sandline Affair*, he describes coming up through the ranks of the Scots Guards and being trained as a member of the elite Special Air Service (SAS) at the renowned British military academy Sandhurst. As an officer, he was assigned to Northern Ireland, Cyprus, the

Rhine Army in Germany, the Falkland Islands, and Bosnia. In 1995, highly decorated at the age of forty-three, he left Her Majesty's Armed Forces and became marketing director for the Middle East at the London investment company Foreign and Colonial. He spent the next twelve months jetting between the African subcontinent and the British Isles, building up connections. He then founded his first military-services company, Sandline International.

One of the operations for which Spicer and Sandline became known was the so-called Papua New Guinea Affair. The island nation off the northern coast of Australia had gained its independence in 1975, but in 1989 a bloody civil war broke out between separatist rebels and government troops on the island of Bougainville, the site of a number of English- and Australian-owned copper mines. The war raged on for nine years, costing thousands of people their lives. In 1997, in a push to defeat the rebels, the government signed Sandline to a three-month contract worth $36 million. The company was to provide units of mercenaries and weapons, train special forces within the government army, and provide support in terms of both military and intelligence operations. Then prime minister Julius Chan said that there was no alternative to calling in the help of the "private military sector." The operation commenced in February 1997. But an indiscretion led to the contract becoming public, and Australia, which had strong economic interests in the island, intervened. The regular army of Papua New Guinea was also against being supported by Sandline. A military putsch ensued, Spicer and forty-seven other mercenaries (English, South African, and Ethiopian) were arrested, and their weapons, including four attack helicopters from Belarus, were confiscated. A scant month after their arrival, the mercenaries were expelled from the country. But Spicer and Sandline successfully sued the new government of Papua New Guinea for the remaining $18 million owed to them on the contract.

The affair created a major international stir. Journalists began talking about a new type of mercenary force sponsored by the state since, as Spicer revealed in his autobiography, the British government knew about Operation Bougainville. In 1998, Britain was rocked by another political scandal, and then foreign minister Robin Cook was almost forced to resign. At the center of the affair were once again Spicer and Sandline. They had organized the transport of thirty tons of munitions in a Boeing 727 cargo plane to Sierra Leone—in defiance of a United Nations arms embargo against the country. The goal was to topple the reigning government in favor of the country's former president, Ahmed Kabbah, who was living in British exile. Spicer was charged, but he maintained he had done nothing illegal and had in fact informed the British government about the plan to reinstate Kabbah to power. [1]

The scandal made Spicer famous, and he founded other PMCs, including Trident Maritime. The firm made the newspapers in 2001, when Lloyd's of London refused to insure commercial ships in the ports of war-torn Sri Lanka unless they were protected by Trident. After three days of negotiations, and against the backdrop of increased activities by Tamil Tiger guerrillas and the threat of major shortages due to disrupted supply lines, the government of Sri Lanka accepted the terms of what might be called an act of blackmail. Spicer's company was hired and began policing the flow of goods to and from the Indian Ocean island, which soon regained its public status as a safe vacation paradise. Currently, Spicer is the CEO of Aegis Defence Services, which he also founded. A world leader in the private military service sector, Aegis has $293 million worth of contracts related to Iraq—one of the highest volumes of any company involved in the conflict there.

A SPECIAL KIND OF ARMS DEALER

Arms dealers continue to occupy a central position within the new universe of privately waged war since military conflicts could hardly be fought without them. The arms industry was privatized relatively early on in the West, but like other forms of trade it was subject for most of the post–World War II era to state control. This remains the case today—but only on paper. In practice, the "privatization of war" has led to a fundamental shift in the arms-dealing sector. Almost two-thirds of the weapons used in the world's countless conflicts are sold by private dealers with little or no state supervision. They currently account for around 90 percent of the casualties of war. During the cold war, arms dealers may have plied their trade, but in the main—as in the cases of the Armenian Adnan Kashoggi or Germany's Ernst Werner Glatt—their activities were unofficially tolerated or tacitly approved by the various secret service agencies in the West since they were acting in the national interest. Military hardware that could not officially be imported and exported to and from the United States, for instance, was moved with the help of men like Glatt and Kashoggi. [2]

Today state institutions are seldom informed about where and how PMCs service their clients' needs for rapid-fire weaponry, machine guns, and grenades. The globalized market is gigantic, as is the supply of arms on offer. Buyers can choose according to quality, brand name, and price in what amounts to a virtual supermarket. Unofficial, semilegitimate, or illegal networks, often with ties to organized crime and various national mafias, ensure that the supply remains constant. Even the mode of payment has changed. As a number of UN studies have revealed, arms today are often bartered for other salable commodities—drugs such as opium or cocaine, tropical wood like palisander or teak, and mineral resources including bauxite, copper, or raw diamonds.

Leonid Minin is one of the central figures in the arms-dealing network and thus also a new mercenary. An Israeli industrial magnate who was born in 1948 in Odessa in the Soviet Union, Minin was arrested on the night of August 5, 2000, in a suburb of Milan called Cinisello Balsamo, after police received a tip about a "wild cocaine party" taking place in Room 341 of the district's Hotel Europe. At the station, the police didn't know what to make of this cosmopolitan and obviously very wealthy businessman. His personal effects included currency worth more than $30,000, fifty-eight grams of extremely high-quality cocaine, and a briefcase full of documents and cut diamonds valued at a $500,000. In response to questioning, Minin claimed that the cocaine was for his personal use, saying that he was accustomed to taking thirty to forty grams of the drug daily at a cost of around $1,500—which, as a rich man, he could afford. Minin said he had recently bought the diamonds with the proceeds from the sale of shares in a company in Mauritius, adding that he also owned various companies in Gibraltar, Bolivia, China, and Liberia. He claimed to have just returned from Sofia, Bulgaria, where he had concluded a major deal in tropical wood. Although the Italian police found Minin's explanations plausible, they did not immediately release him on bail because of the large amount of drugs found in his possession. They had never heard of Leonid Minin, so they kept him in custody overnight and forwarded on a charge of possession of illegal substances.

The local prosecutor knew nothing of Leonid Minin either. It was only when the report reached police headquarters in Rome that the authorities realized, much to their amazement, that one of the most wanted men in the country had fallen into their laps. Leonid Minin alias Wulf Breslav alias Igor Osols alias Leonid Bluvshtein possessed Israeli, Bolivian, Greek, and German passports. He had been declared a persona non grata by Switzerland and Monaco and was under investigation in France and Belgium. The Italian Servicio Centrale Operativo itself had compiled a voluminous report on him after a complicated, twelve-month investigation that went beyond Italy's own borders. It had tried to prove that he was the head of a criminal organization with close ties to the Russian mafia. It was thought Minin was engaged in illegal oil deals, money laundering, and international drug trafficking. The starting point for the probe had been the murky dealings of a company in Rome called Galaxy Energy in the oil production sector. The firm's owner was Leonid Minin.

But even in Rome, the authorities were unable to decipher the numerous documents that the police in Cinisello Balsamo had found in Minin's briefcase. Minin, while awaiting trial on the drug charges, told prosecutors that they were photocopies from magazines a friend had left lying around the hotel—they turned out to be letters; faxes and contracts with Liberia; arms catalogues and cost estimates; "end user" certificates from weapons deliveries in Ivory Coast; price lists for weapons, munitions, and other military hardware; and paperwork concerning the delivery conditions of numerous shiploads of tropical wood. "Poco credibile," or barely credible, noted the prosecutor. Minin was sentenced to two years in prison for possession of cocaine. During that time, the Italian police enlisted international help to make sense of the documents and fit together the pieces of the puzzle. The picture that emerged after months of work was horrific.

Space does not allow us to go into the specifics or the complex connections, but in a nutshell, this was what the police found. [3] In the late 1990s, Leonid Minin had supplied weapons to Sierra Leone for at least one side in the period's bloodiest ethnic civil war—Tim Spicer's Sandline had supplied the other side. Minin's main ally was the Liberian dictator Charles Taylor, who was for his part closely associated with the leader of the Revolutionary United Front (RUF) and the vice president of Sierra Leone, Foday Sankoh. Both the UN and the Organization for African Unity (OAU) had placed arms embargoes on both countries in order to force the warring factions in Sierra Leone to the negotiating table. Taylor and Sankoh had no money to buy expensive arms, but they did have access to their countries' natural resources. The RUF controlled the diamond mines in Sierra Leone, while Liberia possessed huge quantities of tropical wood that were in great demand in the French, German, and Italian furniture industries. In return for his services, Minin had received mining and forestry rights. In Liberia he had founded a company called Exotic Tropical Timber Enterprises (ETTE), which had become the country's largest exporter. The wood was sent to Marseille and Nice, Genoa and Ravenna. The diamonds went via Israel to Amsterdam. Minin also did brisk business with the neftemafija, the oil mafia in Odessa, and trafficked cocaine via a company he owned in Bolivia.

With the proceeds from the sale of diamonds, wood, oil, and cocaine, which even after the deductions of commissions and profits amounted to the hundreds of millions, he had paid for the huge arms purchases of the two African countries. These transactions were carried out via Switzerland and Cyprus. The arms themselves were purchased from former Warsaw Pact countries—for example from the state-owned Ukrainian firm Ukrspetseksport—or in Sofia, Minin's favorite place to do business. Because of the arms embargo, as well as bans on exporting wood and so-called blood diamonds, the weapons could not be delivered directly to Sierra Leone or Liberia. But with some political assistance, and the help of targeted commission fees and bribes, Minin had reached agreements with members of the governments in neighboring Burkina Faso and Ivory Coast. Together with the defense minister of Burkina Faso, Minin arranged for a company in Gibraltar to deliver the weapons to the Burkina Fasan capital Ouagadougou, where they were immediately sent by air transport to the war zones. The contracts with Ivory Coast were signed in Moscow. The Ivorian embassy in Russia had been directly ordered by then Ivory Coast head of state Robert Guei to finalize the arms sales. The weaponry received was then transported from Abidjan to Monrovia.

Minin's businesses continued to function while the civil wars raged on the African continent and Minin himself was sitting in prison. Italian prosecutors' attempts to convict him of illegal arms trading and violation of the UN embargoes failed despite the weight of evidence on their side. After deciding that the deeds of which Minin was accused did not fall under its jurisdiction, Italy's highest civil court ordered his release on September 17, 2002. The "Israeli industrialist" was once again a free man. There was and is no adequate judicial instrument for combating these sorts of new-mercenary business deals.

A SOLDIER ON A HUMANITARIAN MISSION

Zlatan M. is also a new "mercenary," but it would be hard to imagine a crasser contrast than the one between him and Leonid Minin. One of the most unusual figures in the new business of private military service providers, Zlatan lives in a comfortable but by no means luxurious house on Croatia's Dalmatian coast. The small villa to which he retires between missions is crammed full of electronics. He gets his assignments via especially secure Internet addresses, and the incredibly detailed knowledge he uses on the job is also drawn largely from the Web.

Zlatan was born in Bosnia in 1978, but he seems much older—like a man in his late forties who has seen, experienced, and endured a lot. When asked about his nationality, he insists on calling himself Yugoslav, although Yugoslavia officially disbanded in 2003 and hadn't really existed as anything more than Serbia and Montenegro since 1991. His forefathers include Macedonians, Croats, Serbs, Slovenes, Herzegovans, Bosnians, and Kosovans— some followed the Eastern Orthodox faith; others were Catholics and Muslims. That's why Zlatan says he is a "born Yugoslav."

Zlatan is calm and reserved and tends not to say very much even at social gatherings with friends. But two things tend to get him agitated. One is the noise of fireworks, which remind him of bombs, and the other is words associated with America. The tension spreads across his face when he hears either one, and the effort it costs him to stay calm is palpable. These are symptoms of a trauma he suffered in his youth during the U.S.-led NATO bombings of Belgrade during the Balkan wars. Despite having received psychological counseling, he's never been able to fully get over his experiences of that conflict. Nonetheless, he later joined the military. It was, as he puts it, "shock therapy for a pacifist."

After his military service, he became a reserve officer and

hired on with a variety of Italian security forms, watching over golf courses in winter and campgrounds in summer. Then he received an assignment he had long coveted and often tried to get in his spare time—accompanying a humanitarian mission to a conflict region in central Africa. He saw it as his chance to help people who were being abused by warlords, rebels, militias, and mercenaries, to fight against war itself in all its forms. His experiences, when he hesitantly relates them, paint a hellish picture: orgies of murder; massacres of invalids in hospitals; villages full of the corpses of old men, young women, and babies with skulls shattered, bellies ripped open, and throats slit; refugees missing hands, feet, ears, and noses. The humanitarian aid workers who risked their lives in the ever-shifting war zones were terrorized and desperate. It was his job, he says, to protect them against the "genocidal marauders."

Zlatan can't say how many missions he's had in central Africa—he says he hasn't been counting. But he knows a lot about the backgrounds of these wars, which have cost more than four million people their lives, and the underlying causes, which he has painstakingly researched with the help of friends at nongovernmental organizations (NGOs). Of course, he says, the conflicts are about land for grazing and planting crops, access to water and power, tribal pride and ethnic rivalries. But he also says that this is a superficial media view that explains little. On the contrary, he says, the reasons for armed conflicts in central Africa—as is the case all over the world—go far beyond access to water and ethnic cleansing. The wealthy nations in the United Nations Security Council, he says, are far more interested in what's beneath the soil over which black Africans massacre one another: oil, gold, diamonds, and vast reserves of other natural resources such as high-quality copper, silver, magnesium, zinc, tungsten, cadmium, uranium, sulfur, beryllium, and coltan. Because they benefit from the chaos in central Africa, Zlatan claims, the large nations of the West are only willing to deploy some six thousand UN peacekeepers for an area the size of Europe, while around two hundred thousand troops have been sent to Iraq to democratize the country. One of the many examples he cites is the illegal trade in coltan, also known as columbite-tantalite. This trade is organized with the help of the intelligence offices in the Rwandan government. Coltan is in high demand in the West because of its extreme resistance to heat. It is used in the atomic energy industry as well as for building spacecraft, fighter jets, and missiles. It is also an essential component in the most recent generation of mobile phones, video cameras, computer chips, and game systems. In light of his experiences in Africa, Zlatan no longer primarily regards the conflicts there as "tribal wars." On the contrary, he sees them as proxy wars to determine who gets political hegemony over a region where, in his estimation, "all the world's big powers are becoming involved." In essence, he says, it's a battle to divvy up economic resources among global corporations.

Zlatan sees no conflict between his job as a for-hire security provider and his pacifist beliefs. He says that no one would be there to help the civilian populations, who suffer most under the armed conflicts, were it not for organizations like Doctors Without Borders, the Red Cross, German Agro Action, and the United Nations Children's Fund (UNICEF). And who, he asks, is going to protect the aid workers from the warlords, tribal militias, and marauding soldiers? If the international community cannot or doesn't want to provide protection, he argues, private soldiers have to take over the job. Zlatan M. is a man of conviction and, as such, he personifies a dilemma of today's globalized conflicts and the world's new class of mercenaries.

RECRUITMENT OF A PRIVATE SOLDIER

The following is an excerpt from a letter sent by Paolo Simeone to Fabrizio Quattrocchi. The letter was reprinted in a number of Italian newspapers.

The job entails the following:

We protect the personnel of a U.S.-based, multinational corporation involved in the reconstruction of Iraq's bureaucracy. We are considered a BG/CP (body guard/close protection).

Equipment

Weapons: Our employees are armed with a Beretta 92S pistol or Glock 17 with four magazine clips or with an smg HK MP5 A3 with six clips.

Coms: Motorola 380

Bulletproof vest

Pay

[Pay is] $6,000 a month, payable in cash and on site by the tenth of every calendar month.

You will receive the exact wording of the contract as soon as your travel dates are set.

We pay for your room, board, and travel.

At the moment, you are responsible for your own life and accident insurance, but we are currently trying to reach an arrangement with an American and British insurance company.

A separate contract will be drawn up for the more difficult assignments which you will likely receive (personal protection of American and other politicians and managers).

For such assignments, the pay will be $8,000–$9,000 a month, and we will be given accommodation in a house . . .

IMPORTANT: The job requires the utmost discretion. All weapons must be carried concealed . . .

Unfortunately the equipment cannot be acquired on the market here. Therefore, we ask you to make the necessary acquisitions in advance. The weapons store in San Luca or the stall in Shanghai can assist you—just tell them what is in this letter. YOU WILL BE COMPENSATED FOR ALL EXPENDITURES UPON PRESENTATION OF A WRITTEN RECEIPT. THE SAME APPLIES TO TRAVEL COSTS.

Travel

One-way ticket to Amman, Jordan

We will pick you up at the Hotel Paradise Suite (room and board not more than $50). At approximately 1:00 am a taxi ordered by us will arrive and take you to the border. Someone hired by us will meet you there and take you to Baghdad (we will ensure you have a pistol for the journey).

Amman-Iraqi Border: 5 hours

Border-Baghdad: approximately 6-7 hours

2

Private Military Companies
The New Service Industry

There are people who believe that everything
done with a straight face is rational.
—GEORG CHRISTOPH LICHTENBERG

Andy Melville is in his mid-twenties. A former British soldier, he is currently the head of the English PMC Erinys, which is active in Iraq. The U.S. Defense Department has given the firm a contract worth more than $50 million to protect its vanguard units and technical troops. In an interview with PBS on April 21, 2005, Melville said: "What we do is classified. We don't wish [others] to know what our clients are, where we're operating and how we're operating." Jason McIntosh, spokesman for Science Applications International Corporation (SAIC), a PMC based in San Diego, California, is likewise tight-lipped: "We refrain from talking about things our customers don't want us talking about. That's just good policy."

In 2004 Sanho Tree of the Institute for Policy Studies in

Washington described the frustrating points about trying to research private military companies. They carry out state functions, Tree wrote. They receive money from U.S. taxpayers, fly planes that belong to the U.S. government, and use American military bases—they carry out all their activities in the name of the American people. But when you try to get information from them, Tree wrote, they just say "Oh no, we're a private company—we don't have to talk to you."[1]

These statements underscore the difficulties of trying to find out exactly which services individual PMCs have been contracted to provide. Along with the companies' inherent reluctance to divulge their secrets, the problem is a legal one. Because they operate as private businesses, they are under no legal obligation to provide information to third parties—or even lawmakers. Thus, the Bush administration was able to refuse to respond to a request by the U.S. Congress for a comprehensive list of PMCs. There is no way of knowing exactly how many PMCs have been contracted for work in Iraq, for instance, or what sort of individual contracts for which sorts of services have been concluded. The government is not required to disclose contracts with a volume of less than $50 million to Congress. Only agreements above that amount are officially publicized, and they represent a minority of the contracts that have actually been signed—precisely because it is common practice to split up contracts into subagreements so that they do not exceed the $50-million mark.

Nor is easy to glean information from the companies' profiles on the Internet. However stylish and expensive their websites may be, descriptions of the activities of the firms concerned are usually restricted to generalities like "personal and property protection," "risk analysis," "crisis management," "education and training," "strategic planning," and "air transport." Only the images of often heavily armed men in military action indicate that the services on offer are not of the usual civilian sort. Some firms are so specialized that the services they provide are largely incomprehensible to the lay person. SAIC, for example, includes in its list of services on offer "Battle Management," "Electronic Combat/Warfare," "Information Warfare/Information Operations," and "Mission Planning Systems."

Generally speaking, PMCs provide the full range of services and hardware normally associated with the mandates of national armies, defense forces, and foreign intelligence agencies as well as police forces, customs officials, border guards, and internal intelligence agencies. PMCs have, however, concentrated their offerings on four areas; security, training, intelligence, and logistics.

THE BROAD SPECTRUM OF SERVICES

Security is a relatively broad area, encompassing the protection of individuals, property, facilities, and institutions. PMCs are hired to ensure the well-being of politicians, businesspeople, and VIPs who are under threat. They conduct area searches, draw up security plans and risk analyses, and provide specially trained bodyguards. In the form of sky marshals, they help protect airplane passengers and crew members, and they consult with the airlines as to how to avoid risks and combat the danger of terrorist attacks and acts of sabotage. In the realm of international shipping, they help develop security strategies to prevent hijackings and piracy and provide specialists to watch over major shipping vessels and deliveries. They offer security surveillance for land transport in all its forms and for state buildings and private companies. Other specialties include kidnapping-protection and hostage-release services; resistance to organized crime, money laundering, and human trafficking; defense against infiltration from "hostile" persons or groups; security surveillance of foreign embassies; and safeguarding facilities like power stations or oil refineries.

Services are frequently offered in packages. The U.S. PMC Trojan Securities International, for instance, advertises that it provides security and armed protection in crisis situations on land, in the air, and at sea. Under the heading "Maritime Security," the firm proclaims: "International trends are alarming. Today, maritime or waterborne terrorists are better equipped unlike the traditional pirates who used knives, sword[s], revolvers and pistols. Groups today are using machine guns, rocket propelled grenade launchers, radar and high speed boats." To combat this threat, Trojan offers the following services: "security consultancy, anti-piracy situations, maritime counter-terrorism, anti-smuggling operations, vessel escort protection, vessel & asset recovery, and maritime security training."

The area of education and training encompasses an equally broad spectrum of activities, including both basic and highly specialized training for domestic police and armed forces as well as services in foreign countries. Many of the techniques taught, such as the use of pistols and other weapons, are ones that could be learned at a standard police academy. But clients can also learn how to operate a tank or pilot an aircraft. Increasingly PMCs are specializing in using newly developed weapons and weapons systems, ranging from electronically networked ground weapons to computer-guided missiles. In the military area, the training is divided up into specialized army, navy, and air force units (comparable with the Green Berets, the Navy Seals, and the Delta Forces). In the civilian realm, PMCs train police and security personnel.

Many companies maintain their own boot camps, which are most frequently used for highly specialized training. The U.S.-based PMC International Charter Incorporated (ICI) runs one such camp in northeastern Oregon. There, trainees are instructed in skills such as unconventional warfare or parachuting onto uncertain terrain.[2] The French company Secopex specializes in training surveillance and security personnel for oil-producing regions and facilities. Trainees receive instruction at a forty-thousand-acre facility in Belarus, which includes an oil tower, aircraft, accommodations, and transport vehicles. There recruits get practical training in how to deal with some fifteen hundred types of emergency situations. Some firms offer simulations of armed ambushes on vehicle convoys by guerrillas and rebels; others specialize in hand-to-hand combat for fighting terrorists. PMCs also employ computer simulators to train clients in the latest methods of waging war. The San Diego–based firm Cubic is known for its "combat simulation centers" in which soldiers can practice for war under realistic conditions. One such center is located at the military parade grounds in the town of Hohenfels near the southern German city of Nuremberg.[3]

Whether the location is Uzbekistan or Peru, Sri Lanka or Nigeria, most PMCs that specialize in training maintain "neutrality" in fulfilling their contracts. They do not intervene in ongoing conflicts, remaining instead powers behind the scenes. Nonetheless, many companies do check up in theaters of battle as to whether their trainees are employing the capabilities they learned.[4] In contrast to the mercenaries of previous eras, today's private soldiers often let others do the shooting for them. Their efforts are aided by the fact that electronic networks are so advanced that they can follow an "automated battlefield" on their computer screens and inform themselves in real time about the status of combat halfway around the world. In some cases, they can use this technology to intervene in battle, make corrections, and issue commands to the front lines.

Parallel to the state military academies of the official national armed forces, PMCs have created private universities to train new elites for the military and civilian security realm. In Germany, for example, a private university in Freiburg called the Dukes School collaborates with EUBSA—a subsidiary of the PMC Paladin Risk—to offer degree programs to become a "Professional Protection Officer" or "Risk Manager." Practical instruction is carried out at pseudomilitary camps in England, Israel, the United States, and France.

A third emphasis of modern military companies is the area of intelligence, which includes everything from information collecting to outright spying. In the wake of the electronic revolution, many firms have developed techniques for information gathering and analysis that only they are able to master and offer as a service.[5] According to the nongovernmental organization Corporate Watch, around one half of the annual U.S. budget for its various intelligence agencies goes to private companies.[6] That includes intercepting or eavesdropping on electromagnetically based signals, both terrestrial and satellite. Conventional and mobile telephones, radio transmissions, radar, and laser- and light-based radio as well as Internet and e-mail communications are also affected. Furthermore, PMCs are involved in the entire sector of pictorial data and information, whether it be photographic, electronic, infrared, or ultraviolet in nature, and whether it is generated and transmitted on land or at sea, in the air or in space. The processing of such data into briefings and the analysis of the information for intelligence purposes makes up a large part of PMCs' service offerings. But companies also offer intelligence-gathering services based on the employment of individual covert operatives. The offers apply to both the military and civilian arenas—PMCs make their information available in equal measure to government and private-sector clients. The British firm AKE Group, for example, advertises on its website a comprehensive package of "real-time risk consultancy" services. They include location security audits, evacuations for personnel in high-risk areas, a 24-7 emergency hotline, and "Probable Maximum Loss (PML), Estimated Maximum Loss (EML) and Realistic Disaster Scenario (RDS) planning," custom tailored to the needs and ambitions of individual clients—be they governmental or private.

What this amounts to is a twenty-four-hour, private intelligence service that customers can rent in order to advance their interests. Companies like AKE Group advise, watch over, and protect their clients, analyzing dangers and risks and developing strategies for combating potential perils. The FBI is only one of the many government institutions that make use of such services, having engaged the PMC DynCorp to develop the bureau's new computer network Trilogy.[7]

Finally, PMCs offer a bewildering variety of services in the logistics sector, encompassing everything from the procurement of toilet paper to the organization of diverse types of transport vehicles. Clients can choose among catering of various qualities (from simple to gourmet), cleaning services for clothing and buildings, and accommodation (from tents to villas with swimming pools). Private firms offer a complete range of services to assist the military in constructing roads and bridges. They build airstrips and airplane depots, military bases and command centers. There is hardly an area of troop maintenance today that is not seen to by PMCs. They take care of the procurement of weapons, ammunition, and fuel. They operate complex refilling units, including the ones used for the midair refueling of warplanes, and they run their own shipping-container and transport companies—much of whose equipment is available for leasing. They maintain storage facilities and operate telephone and radio centers. No matter how remote the theater of operations, they provide the military with barracks and power stations and drill wells to supply troops with water. PMCs are so successful in the realm of logistics that they have established a near-monopoly on the area in the Anglo-Saxon world. National armies have outsourced everything from facility maintenance to clothing supply, from procurement to provisions.

Maintenance represents a huge portion of this spectrum of services, be it the upkeep and repair of motor vehicles, transport vans, helicopter warships, or other types of military aircraft. The maintenance personnel for the latest bombers and fighter planes—which, too, are made by private companies and bought by armies—are mainly provided by PMCs. Likewise, electronic military facilities and information-technology-based weapons systems can often only be maintained by the companies that built them. Increasingly, the military needs private employees even to operate such hardware, which includes both unmanned drones and networked missile systems. The American PMC Fluor, for example, boasts of having constructed a base for the U.S. intercontinental missile defense system on the Aleutian island of Shemya and installing the ultrasecurity, multiple-weapons system Milcon and an antiterrorism weapons system. In addition, Fluor also claims to have set up an ultrasensitive electromagnetic early-warning system and an antiseismic system to protect the facility from earthquakes.

PRACTICAL REALIZATION

This brief sketch of the spectrum of services offered by the private sector suggests how far PMCs have encroached upon a territory that used to be subject exclusively to the sovereign power of the state. But little—far too little considering the importance of the topic—is known about the specifics of how these firms go about providing such services. The information that becomes public after scandals come to light is fragmentary at best. In the majority of cases, critics are forced to use indirect methods to construct an overall picture—the actual overview emerges from a mosaic.

In September 2004, the public research institute British American Security Information Council (BASIC) published a study suggesting that, in Iraq alone, no fewer than sixty-eight PMCs had been officially hired under various contracts and for a variety of tasks. (Unofficial estimates put the figure at more than one hundred.)[8] According to the study, AirScan, for example, carried out "night surveillance of the pipeline and oil infrastructure, using low-light television cameras." Erinys was responsible for guarding petroleum pipelines and refineries. Blackwater Worldwide provided security for officials, including the then head of the provisional government Paul Bremer, and provided mobile security teams. The ISI Group handled bodyguard duties within the Green Zone and guarded several government buildings outside it. Cochise Consultancy and OS&S watched over VIPs, and Centurion Risk Assessment Services trained members of international and humanitarian organizations "mentally and practically for dangerous work in extreme conditions."[9] Triple

Canopy was hired to provide armed protection of convoys and other transportation. Titan and WorldWide Language Resources (WWLR) were contracted to take over translation and language training. CACI International and MZM provided people with language skills for use during interrogations. The Vinnell Corporation was charged with building up and training the new Iraqi Army, while DynCorp reorganized and trained the police forces. Ronco Consulting was "tasked to come up with a plan to disarm, demobilize and reintegrate the Iraqi armed forces."[10] Group 4 Securicor (G4S) was contracted to provide bodyguards and security personnel including air marshals. Combat Support Associates assisted the U.S. Army and its rapid response units in combat operations. ManTech maintained a forty-four-person-strong telecommunications center for American troops in Baghdad. Kellogg, Brown and Root (KBR) was responsible for logistics across Iraq and employed some fifty thousand people as carpenters, mechanics, electrical engineers, and so forth. Most of those workers came from third world countries, with a disproportionate number hailing from the Philippines.

PMCs are not only active in Iraq but also practically everywhere on the Arabian Peninsula. In Saudi Arabia, for example, because of the ruling family's mistrust of its own populace, a handful of U.S. companies handles almost all of the tasks normally associated with national armies and police forces. These tasks include antiterrorism activities, strategic and tactical planning, security consultancy, military training, intelligence procurement, information gathering, propaganda, and military logistics. Vinnell trains and advises the National Guard and provides security for "strategically sensitive facilities." Booz Allen Hamilton runs the country's military academy. SAIC provides support for all aspects of air and sea security.

O'Gara-Hess and Eisenhardt guards the Saudi royal family and trains local security forces. Cable and Wireless is responsible for training security forces to fight terrorism and carry out internal military operations.[11]

Though most prominent in the Middle East, PMCs are active on five continents. Wherever there is oil on the planet, new mercenaries guard the petroleum facilities and pipelines. Examples are the Hart Group in Somalia, Defence Systems Colombia (DSC) (ArmorGroup), AirScan in Sudan, and Military Professional Resources Inc. (MPRI) in Guinea-Bissau. PMCs have trained military personnel in more than 130 different countries, and they provide daily security plans and risk analyses for at least as many nations.

ATTEMPTS AT CATEGORIZATION

Many academic observers have tried to systematically categorize this new service industry, and the firms in question, concerned about their public image, often describe themselves as *security* rather than *military* companies. One commonly used classification distinguishes between security and military firms insofar as the former provides "defensive" or "passive" services in contrast to the "offensive" and "active" character of the latter. The argument is that PSCs typically protect people or property, while PMCs are directly involved in the conduct of war.

Another commonly used classification model is oriented on the military spearhead principle, envisioning PMCs as a triangle with a broad base whose numbers, both in terms of companies and their respective personnel, shrink as their activities draw closer to the front lines of battle. In today's high-tech armies, the ratio of front line soldiers to supporting personnel is roughly one to one hundred. That means that one hundred people—everything from cooks to risk analysts—are needed for every single individual fighting with a weapon in his or her hand. Correspondingly small, even if not quite so tiny, is the proportion of PMCs, known as military combat support firms, who directly engage in battle. One step back from the front lines is a second category, so-called military consultancy companies. They are responsible for everything from training to the strategy and organization that allows combat soldiers to be deployed. Still further removed from the front is the third category, military suppliers. Their responsibilities include the entire realm of logistics, from procurement to transportation.

Other analytic models stress the realm of a firm's activity as a criterion or distinguish between companies based on whether the employees are armed or not. But regardless of which system is used, the dividing lines remain blurry. Activities that may seem to be defensive from one perspective can also be interpreted as offensive. Classroom instruction in tactics for waging war can have much more far-reaching impact than the actions of an individual combat soldier, and the import of a private security company's interception of sensitive information can greatly outweigh an overtly military firm's procurement of toilet paper for military bases. Even a functional analysis does little to clear up the opacity. One reason is that the activities of the firms in question, in relation to their end objectives, are a matter of perspective. What may appear in one light as simple property protection can also be seen as the defense of a strategic facility from an economic or military enemy. The industry itself has done everything in its power to ensure the situation remains hazy. Those companies that specialize in security offer their services to both military and civilian clients, and the same applies to firms concentrating on training and education. To PMCs, the question of whether protecting the Red Cross in a conflict region is a military or a security action is a merely academic. They're far more interested in calculating the risks involved and quantifying them into bills to be paid by the client. Likewise there is a general lack of interest in the issue of whether fighting terrorists or protecting facilities from terrorist attacks is an internal or external affair—that is, a task for the police or for the armed forces. In the past decade, the main interest has been in how to privatize the public commodity of "security," for whose maintenance the state is ultimately responsible.

In light of the increasingly blurry lines separating PMCs from PSCs, the well-respected Stockholm International Peace Research Institute (SIPRI) has concluded that it is impossible to distinguish between the two. And the present book has chosen to use the term PMC to focus readers' attention on the international security implications of this issue.

SIZE AND ORIENTATION

PMCs are based primarily in industrial societies, where military know-how and supplies, as well as the need for security, are the greatest. However, the firms are rarely active in their home countries. The total number of people who work worldwide for PMCs is currently estimated at around 1.5 million. (An equal number of people, more than half of them "child soldiers," are involved in mercenary activities outside the PMC context.) The turnover in the industry in 2005 was approximately $300 billion.[12] The largest companies in the field are frequently among the top one hundred firms on their respective national stock markets. Industry leaders regularly post income reports of $1.5–

$9 billion annually. The world's second-largest PMC, Group 4
Securicor (G4S), for example, reported an income of $7.5 bil-
lion for the fiscal year 2004. The incomes of most military service providers, however, remain below the billion mark.

The size of PMCs varies enormously—from one-man operations to large concerns with tens of thousands of employees.
(G4S claims its staff numbers three hundred sixty thousand.)
Differences in size are reflected in the firms' organization. Some
are freelance endeavors, some limited-liability companies, and
some publicly traded corporations. Many of the most successful
PMCs have become subsidiaries of gigantic holding companies
with wide-ranging tentacles. MPRI, for instance, belongs to the
largest U.S. military company, L-3 Communications (Lockheed
Martin), which produces both high-tech machinery for fighter
jets as well as the "black boxes" used in commercial airliners.
Vinnell—a company that manages just about everything that
can be managed in the security and military industry—is part
of another giant of the U.S. arms industry, Northrop Grumman
Corporation. DynCorp, which focuses on electronics, is owned
by Computer Sciences Corporation (CSC), which does most
of its lucrative business with the Pentagon and the U.S. Army.
Kellogg, Brown and Root is a Halliburton subsidiary and one of
the largest logistics companies in the United States. (Halliburton
was, of course, formerly headed by Dick Cheney, after his term
as secretary of defense under George H. W. Bush and before
he became vice president under George W. Bush.) Takeovers
and mergers have benefited all sides of the transactions. Giant
conglomerates have expanded their portfolios to include the
increasingly important military services industry, and the PMCs
gained access to international capital and financial markets. In
a 2001 interview, Ed Soyster, a retired U.S. military general and

spokesman for MPRI, boasted that, because MPRI's parent firm L-3 was a publicly traded corporation, "anyone with a 401(k) retirement plan is probably an investor in our company."[13]

Managers of retirement funds are encouraged to invest in this sector because the returns yielded by military firms and their subsidiaries are often greater than those yielded by other stocks. For example, in the lean 2003 fiscal year, L-3 stocks increased in value by 64 percent. The managers of the Californian retirement funds CalPERS and CalSTRS—government employees and teachers respectively—put massive amounts of money into CACI and Titan. An unpleasant surprise followed when the two firms were discovered to be connected with the torture scandal at the Abu Ghraib prison in Iraq. The moral scandal was accompanied by financial damage. Investors had to swallow losses of 16 percent after the role of the two companies at Abu Ghraib became known.[14]

In their publicity, PMCs often present themselves as ideologically driven firms promoting peace, and tireless in their humanitarian efforts to end conflict and improve conditions around the world. But the behind-the-scenes marketing is done by one of the most powerful lobbyists in the world, the International Peace Operations Association (IPOA), which represents all the major players in the military services sector. Blackwater's company motto reads: "In support of freedom and democracy everywhere." To distance themselves from the negative image of the traditional mercenary and the illicit soldier of fortune, PMCs are at pains to stress that their activities are legal, that they respect national and international law, and that they only accept contracts from clients with good human rights records. But internally, PMCs are governed by the standard business philosophy, which stresses increasing turnover, expanding markets, reducing costs, and raising profits. In their leadership and management style, in contrast to old-fashioned mercenary troops, PMCs are scarcely distinguishable from other types of businesses. Aside from the occasional images of military combat on the walls, the interiors of their offices resemble those found in other high-tech industries. Bosses organize and direct their companies as complex systems, applying the latest economic and market theories, employing aggressive lobbying to ensure contracts and reaching decisions with an eye toward shareholder value.

Today, a number of PMCs have become global players, working for many different clients and governments, maintaining headquarters in various parts of the world, and carrying out their activities internationally. But one special characteristic distinguishes them from other global firms like insurance companies or banks. A significant number of PMCs have three or more separate headquarters. The reasons for this are varied and include the occasional need to avoid various national and international rules, regulations, and requirements. Such firms typically have a "lobbying headquarters" which is located directly in the national capital and/or decision-making center and which is responsible for acquiring lucrative contracts. Then there are the "operative headquarters," which are scattered across the globe to maintain proximity to their customers and to allow the firms to carry out their tasks more efficiently. Finally, there are the "legal headquarters," located in tiny countries and tax havens, which serve both to reduce tax expenditures and shield the company from the prying eyes of regulators and state prosecutors. By splitting their headquarters, PMCs protect themselves from civil-law claims such as liability and from state prosecution for their not-infrequent violations of criminal law. PMCs are far safer if their legal headquarters are based, say, in the Bismarck Archipelago in the Pacific, rather than the United States, and those headquarters can be quickly relocated to prevent being held liable or criminally responsible for a given action.

PMCs are only bound by the contracts they sign and the commercial laws that apply where they do business. Unlike state institutions, they need neither respect national or international military agreements nor fulfill any premandated public purpose. Their own publicity notwithstanding, PMCs obey only the rules of the market—that is, supply and demand. Globally active and servicing various parts of the world, they can evade national requirements, restrictions, and regulations at any time. Such companies have no particular interest in violating laws, but since legal restrictions do mean added costs, they prefer to sign contracts in places where their hands are left untied. This freedom allows them to develop customer-specific products and solutions. One could almost say that their services are disposable. They are discarded after a single use, and the next customer receives a different, "tailored" solution. Extreme customer orientation is one quality that makes PMCs so attractive to clients. The solutions they offer may be drastic, but they are also quick and efficient. The message to clients is: If you've got a problem with armed rebels, rebellious parts of your population, foreign militias on your territory, terrorist attacks, or even striking unions, then write us a check, and we'll take care of the rest, quickly and nonbureaucratically, satisfaction guaranteed. That is exactly what the president of the IPOA lobbying organization, Doug Brooks, said in the title of a 2000 *Conflict Trends* article: "Write a Cheque, End a War."[15] The quality of the solutions offered reflects what the customer is able to pay. If a state, an organization, a company, or an individual has enough money, they receive a luxury security package. Those who can't afford the deluxe version have to make do with reduced, noncomprehensive protection. PMCs are bound to carry out certain tasks by the agreements they reach. But they are also free to nullify those agreements, should they get a better offer or if the risks involved turn out to be greater than they anticipated. The only potential punishment they face is a preagreed fine for nonfulfillment of the contract.

In line with the logic of commerce, the guiding principle of PMCs' economic activities is that the income from the sales of their services should not only exceed their expenses but also yield the highest possible profit. Military firms are in this respect no different than other companies. Their aim is first and foremost to minimize expenses and maximize earnings; achieving a certain quality of security is at best a secondary concern. This is shown by numerous examples from Kosovo, Afghanistan, and Iraq. Regular army soldiers have reported that fuel supplies were insufficient, food quality low, and the cleaning of uniforms unsatisfactory. Recruits have complained that they received poor training, leading in one case to a private company being fired in favor of state instructors. The U.S. media reports on a weekly basis about overpriced goods and services. KBR, for instance, charges the Pentagon $2.27 for a gallon of gas, even though it only costs a dollar at Iraqi filling stations. A case of soda water costs $45 and a laundry bag $100, while internal Pentagon audits have shown that the company charged for ten thousand more meals per day than it actually delivered.[16] Such reports led Congress to step up their inquiries to the Department of Defense, and the Government Accountability Office has repeatedly complained about unjustifiably inflated expenditures.

PMCs and the Abu Ghraib Scandal

On April 28, 2004, the CBS television network broadcast images that shocked the world—photographs from cellblock 1-A in the Abu Ghraib prison near Baghdad. In one of them, an Iraqi prisoner with a sack over his head was shown being forced to stand on a crate of food rations. His arms were spread, and cable leading upward had been attached to them. Prison guards had told him that if he fell from the crate he would receive a lethal jolt of electricity. Another photo showed a military policewoman pulling a naked Iraqi prisoner on all fours behind her like a dog on a leash. A third image featured a pyramid of naked men with laughing U.S. soldiers posing in the foreground, with upturned thumbs.

In early May, the *New Yorker* published more details about the torture scandal at Abu Ghraib. The magazine extensively cited the fifty-three-page Taguba Report, a document originally intended for internal Pentagon use that described conditions in the prison. Cellblock 1-A was where American specialists interrogated Iraqi prisoners. The interrogators were prohibited from directly hurting the inmates, but they were allowed to break prisoners' wills by using "moderate discomfort" techniques, such as creating states of fear, shame, disorientation, and psychological and physical exhaustion. Public outrage was focused on Lynndie England, the military policewoman in the "dog" photo, and specialist Charles Graner and sergeant Ivan Frederick. Frederick later stated that the various methods used to break prisoners' wills were extremely effective, with the captives giving up all resistance after a few hours. England, Graner, and Frederick were subsequently court-martialed, together with three other military police officers, and sentenced to varying prison terms.

England and Graner are fairly well known from the media. But the name Steve Stefanowicz, which also came up in the Taguba

Report, largely evaded public scrutiny. Stefanowicz was the one who issued people like England, Graner, and Frederick their orders, such as, "Loosen this guy up for us; make sure he has a bad night." Sergeant Jarval Davis testified to the Taguba commission that "the [Military Intelligence] staffs to my understanding have been giving Graner compliments on the way he has been handling the MI holds. Examples being statements like, 'Good job, they're breaking down real fast.' 'They answer every question.' 'They're giving out good information, finally,' and 'Keep up the good work.' Stuff like that.'"

Stefanowicz, nicknamed "Big Steve," was not a regular soldier but an interrogation specialist employed by CACI International of Arlington, Virginia. The Taguba Report concluded that he should be fired and reprimanded, finding that he had "allowed and/or instructed MPs, who were not trained in interrogation techniques, to facilitate interrogations by 'setting conditions' which were neither authorized [nor] in accordance with applicable regulations/policy. He clearly knew his instructions equated to physical abuse."

The report also details a handful of other civilians, employed by the Titan company, who worked at Abu Ghraib. One of them, Torin Nelson, claimed in an interview in March 2005 that half of the thirty interrogators at the prison came from private contractors. With respect to the role of PMCs in the torture scandal, the Taguba Report concluded: "In general, US civilian contract personnel (Titan Corporation, CACI, etc. . . .), third country nationals, and local contractors do not appear to be properly supervised within the detention facility at Abu Ghraib. During our on-site inspection, they wandered about with too much unsupervised free access in the detainee area. Having civilians in various outfits (civilian and [desert combat uniforms]) in and about the detainee area causes confusion and may have contributed to the difficulties in the accountability process and with detecting escapes."

> But while the soldiers involved in the Abu Ghraib torture scandal were swiftly punished, the Titan and CACI employees who issued orders to the likes of England or Graner have yet to be prosecuted.

PERSONNEL AND COST STRUCTURE

There are more generals sitting on the boards of several military firms than currently serve in the armies of their respective home countries. Likewise, some PMCs have more analysts, computer specialists, and information gatherers than the intelligence services of entire countries. The level of specialist knowledge and specialized capabilities is so high that some regular armies admit that they are not up to the task and must therefore depend on private contractors. This applies most obviously to small- and medium-size military powers, but even the world's most powerful armed force has become dependent. In late 2004, journalist Barry Yeoman wrote in *Mother Jones*: "Pentagon officials say they can no longer fight a war without private contractors."[17]

The service personnel the Pentagon use to wage war possess a broad range of skills. In the Afghanistan War, some fought in covert paramilitary units against the Taliban regime and operated the Global Hawks, the U.S. Air Force's state-of-the-art reconnaissance planes. Interrogation specialists were active both at Guantanamo Bay and in Iraq. In the Philippines, they serve as specially trained antiterrorist soldiers. In Russia they protect oil fields, and in Colombia they fight against the drug cartels. Above all, the transition from traditional mercenaries to private soldiers working for military contractors has meant a change in status. Some eighty private soldiers, for instance, fought on both sides of the Angolan Civil War in the 1990s. They were recruited from around the world—from the Green

Berets, the French foreign legion, the British Special Air Service, South African Special Forces Brigade, Nepalese Gurkhas, and so forth. Although they basically served the same function as old-school Belgian, English, or French mercenaries, so-called soldiers of fortune, these men were employees of companies that not only paid them a fixed salary but also protected them, via the conclusion of binding contracts with recognized nation-states, from legal prosecution for their deeds. Their status as employees meant that they did not fall under the various conventions and rules of the UN, the OAU, and individual nations that had criminalized mercenary fighting. Today, so it is said in private-soldier circles, anyone convicted of being a mercenary should demand his money back from his attorney—or suggest that his lawyer find a new line of work.

The personnel employed by PMCs are as varied as the parts of the world where they ply their trade. They include various nationalities and races, people aged eighteen to sixty-five, and virtually all social classes, from the illiterate to university graduates. PMCs boast that they only employ highly specialized and individually trained experts—a claim that underscores the idea that the qualifications on offer are well above the standard level of state-run security organizations. But this is only partially true. PMCs are known not only for employing excellent specialists but also for keeping costs low. Because they work on a contract basis, the companies are kept going with a relatively small core of permanent employees. Depending on the size and volume of business a firm does, this core group can vary between a couple dozen and several thousand staff. Even sums in the hundreds of millions can be earned by a relatively small staff. One of the world's largest PMCs, ArmorGroup, for example, has fewer than eight thousand permanent employees—most of the work is done by freelancers. DynCorp, for instance, boasts of an index of fifty thousand freelancers that can be called upon at any time to do jobs around the globe. Wages range from $10 to $1,000 a day, and in the interest of flexibility, regular monthly salaries are seldom agreed to for nonpermanent employees. Highly specialized freelancers often enjoy the same pension benefits as permanent staffers and have the opportunity to buy company stock. The result is that some career members of official armed forces have quit state service because they can make more money as private soldiers.

To save on wage costs, PMCs recruit most of their personnel in the areas where their services are needed. The ratio of highly specialized experts—for instance, a trained staff sergeant in a special unit of a Western army—to native security forces is often one to twenty or even lower. Since the third world has no shortage of unemployed former soldiers and police officers, PMCs have little difficulty finding cheap personnel. Yet people in this category are most often badly trained, and the quality of service generally goes down when they are employed. In many cases, professional soldiers reject them as completely unsuited to and incapable of the task at hand. But cost isn't the only reason that PMCs employ people in the countries where they are engaged. The lack of language barriers and the familiarity with local customs ensure an easier and deeper penetration into the social structures and infrastructure of conflict regions. It is often difficult, if not impossible, to distinguish between an Iraqi PMC employee and Iraqi member of an insurgent group. The same holds true for covert agents in Colombia or intelligence personnel in Congo as well as combat units in both those countries.

The fact that the end of the cold war meant unemployment

for millions of professional soldiers provided the private military service sector with a surplus of labor of which the rest of the economy could only dream. It was simple for PMCs to find qualified specialists for almost every imaginable sort of task. Available personnel can be found for even the most delicate and risky of missions, and the costs and conditions are extremely favorable. Private military contractors don't have to worry about labor taxes, preset wage scales, unions, supervisory government offices, or auditors—and that is one reason the privatization of security seems to many governments like the cheaper option. Standing national armies and PMCs have completely different cost structures.

The first difference in cost structure applies to personnel. What makes a regular soldier in intelligence, logistical, or technical areas so expensive is not his or her salary. It's the cost to the government of finding the correct individual for the job amidst a mass of personnel. State armies recruit hundreds of thousands of soldiers, check their suitability, form them through more or less lengthy training regimens, and test the quality of the skills they have acquired in diverse sets of circumstances. All of this has to be paid for. PMCs have no such costs. They exploit the time and money states have spent in training specialists, simply luring them away from national armies with lucrative offers. If PMCs were required to compensate the state for the training of their employees, they would be no longer able to balance the cost-benefit equation. In addition, national armies can't just send their soldiers home, without pay, when they are not needed. By contrast, PMCs can calculate their personnel needs on a project-to-project basis and employ freelancers to work on specific jobs on fixed-term contracts.

The second difference is overhead. Aside from the costs

caused by their relatively small core staffs, PMCs have few running expenditures. Unlike governments, they don't need to invest huge sums of money in weaponry. They don't have to maintain and repair planes, helicopters, and tanks, or administrate and pay for depots, barracks, training grounds, or landing strips. PMCs either leave it to their clients to procure the necessary weapons and infrastructure for a mission, or they do the procurement and pass on the costs in their final bill.

Although they engage in unusual activities, PMCs are still pure service companies. The contracts they conclude with their clients fall under civil law and are subject only to commercial legal restrictions, whereas in the traditional military all transactions are supposed to be transparent and open to various forms of public auditing. These and other overhead costs weigh heavily on the state's wallet. Functional transparency and effective checks on the military cost taxpayers a lot of money, regardless of how beneficial they might be to security by preventing the abuse of military power. PMCs have hardly any overhead in this area. They only need to keep accurate books in case of an audit. The only people to whom they are ultimately accountable are their shareholders.

The divergent cost structures between state armed forces and private military contractors belie the idea that the privatization and outsourcing of service saves governments money. The scope of service varies and cannot be compared. Likewise the quality of the service is seldom the same and cannot be checked. And the costs for auditing and transparency are not included in the calculations. If the state forgoes checking on PMCs, from the awarding of the contract and actual delivery of the services agreed, it can save on its own personnel costs, and outsourcing will be cheaper. But if it maintains the same auditing procedures that are mandatory by law for national armies, outsourcing is more expensive—in part because the state no longer has to deal with one single institution, but dozens of very different companies.

Based on a number of empirical studies, the U.S. Government Accountability Office (GAO) has concluded that inadequate data renders any cost-benefit analysis of military outsourcing impossible. In addition, the GAO says that false projections of Defense Department costs and the omission of costs for the implementation of various security programs hinder any valid calculation of potential savings. Both GAO and academic examinations criticize claims that outsourcing saves money because those claims do not include the actual costs of implementation. In other words, the calculations of money saved are based on promises, not results. For this reason, German security policy expert Herbert Wulf has concluded: "It's astonishing what meager empirical basis is used to reach far-reaching decisions, which have not just economic, but serious social consequences for the world as a whole."[18]

3

The Clients
"Strong States, Corporate Masters, and Rebels"

Mors tua, vita mea.
—ROMAN SAYING

The spectrum of clients served by private military contractors is extremely diverse. Viewed on a scale of ascending morality, they range from brutal warlords and dictators to rebel groups and unscrupulous drug cartels to sovereign states, respected business enterprises, and international human rights organizations.

Viewed in terms of trade volume, the largest clients of PMCs are the so-called strong states—nations that possess fully developed and functional legal, auditing, and security systems both at home and abroad. Such countries are not only capable of defending themselves militarily against external enemies but also solve internal conflicts by peaceful means. The second largest client is the private sector, which includes both global players and medium-size enterprises. The third-largest group are so-called weak or failing states, especially in conflict regions. Weak states are ones that are insufficiently able to guarantee their own internal security or defend their external borders. Failing states are those that are incapable of maintaining one, several, or all of the various types of security a country needs. Fourth on the list in terms of trade volume are parties in civil wars, terrorist networks, and liberation movements. The fifth group is made up of international institutions and alliances such as the UN, the OAU, and the North Atlantic Treaty Organization (NATO), which are increasingly using PMCs in their peacekeeping and nation-building missions, together with nongovernmental organizations, which are being forced to take over more and more of what were previously state responsibilities. Private associations and individual civilians seeking to protect themselves against, for example, kidnapping and violence represent the smallest group of PMC clients.

These groups differ drastically from one another both in terms of their security needs and the interests and motivations that underlie the contracts they conclude with PMCs. Moreover, they are very different in how they exploit the chance to buy security on a market that has been opened up by private military contractors and the broad palette of services on offer.

STRONG STATES: THE UNITED STATES AND GERMANY

Among the strong states with an active global presence, the United States and Germany are particularly well suited to serve as examples of how private military services are employed. Several hundred PMCs make their homes in the United States, the largest number in any one country. They get most of their contracts from governments, chiefly from the U.S. federal government in Washington and specifically the Department of Defense. By 2001, Donald Rumsfeld had already taken a process that had been initiated, to various degrees, by his predecessors in the United States and colleagues in other countries, to its logical conclusion, saying that all tasks that were not part of the military's core activities should be outsourced.[1]

Since then, the political debate on this issue has focused almost exclusively on where Rumsfeld's "core" begins and ends, and how the outsourcing process can be handled most quickly and efficiently. Career U.S. military officers say that PMCs have established themselves in nearly all of the activities carried out by the armed forces, receiving contracts even in such sensitive areas as surveillance and intelligence.[2] The military intelligence departments—including the world's largest spying agency, the National Security Agency (NSA)—have outsourced jobs such as data collection, maintaining network technology, and managing security.[3] The desire to save on costs has played a role in this process, but so too has the information revolution in the digital age. State institutions now find themselves in a situation, despite the emphasis they place on research and development, of lagging behind the private sector in terms of the latest technologies. Governments are forced to buy services. An NSA report from early November 2005 concluded: "In the past, the majority of NSA's acquisition needs were based on government developments. Today the Agency relies more and more on the commercial marketplace for its solutions."[4]

During the 1990s, the reduction of U.S. military personnel by approximately one-third and cuts to U.S. military budgets created a major headache for the Pentagon. Above all, military leaders had to confront the question of how the United States could maintain its military presence in more than one hundred countries with the means at its disposal drastically restricted. The only solution was to buy additional capacities from the outside. To relieve soldiers of nonmilitary duties, PMCs were enlisted to supply and maintain U.S. military bases. One of the first firms that got involved in this area was Halliburton. Dick Cheney, who was then head of the company, boasted that his firm was the first to greet soldiers at their bases, and the last to say good-bye.[5]

Outsourcing became a mantra for the heads of the Defense Department, who believed they had found a way to extend the capacity of the armed forces with fewer personnel so as to meet the growing military challenges of the new millennium. Tasks previously performed by the military itself would be farmed out to private service providers. The first areas to be outsourced in the 1990s were provision, distribution, and supply as well as the building and maintenance of infrastructure, and the military leadership soon realized that the same could be done with education, training, and intelligence gathering.

Paying for such services still remained a problem, but the political leadership responded with a remarkable degree of ingenuity. Leaving aside the major acquisitions bills passed to pay for Operation Enduring Freedom and Operation Iraqi Freedom, two methods were used to raise money for the military. On the one hand, military costs were transferred to the budgets of other departments such the Departments of the Interior, Justice, Social and Family Affairs and the EPA. That was why, in the wake of the torture scandal in the Abu Ghraib prison in Iraq, congresspeople and journalists were unable to find any contract between the Pentagon and CACI, the private company specializing in the interrogation specialists who were active at Abu Ghraib. CACI was in fact on the payroll of the Department of the Interior, from which it had received a million-dollar contract to provide "translators."

On the other hand, lawmakers also created congressionally approved "special programs" and increased the budgets of those already in existence. In the global "war on terror" in the immediate aftermath of 9/11, previous outsourcing initiatives were given additional funds. "The war on terrorism is the full employment act for these guys," said D. B. Des Roches, spokesman for the Pentagon's Defense Security Cooperation Agency, in 2002 in reference to PMCs.[6] Stock market experts were hardly surprised then that share prices for such companies shot up dramatically after the attacks on the World Trade Center and the Pentagon, while most other stocks declined. With the help of private firms, the United States could secure and promote their geopolitical and geostrategic interests despite a reduced number of troops.

After 9/11, Washington set up thirty-eight military bases in additional countries and currently has a global military presence of more than five hundred thousand soldiers in more than 130 nations.[7] Military bases were established, for example, all along Russia's southern flank, from Ukraine and Georgia in the west, across Kyrgyzstan and Kazakhstan to the Chinese border in the east. This swath of territory is sometimes referred to as the "oil belt" because it is so rich in petroleum. In fact, the new bases were set up primarily to secure the interests and investments of U.S. oil companies. Billions have been pumped into the Baku-Tbilisi-Ceyhan pipeline, which runs from Baku, Azerbaijan, via Tbilisi, Georgia, to the Turkish Black Sea port of Ceyhan. Exxon-Mobil, Total Fuel Service, and ConocoPhillips have invested billions in Kazakhstan—in particular to exploit the resources of the Kashagan oil fields.[8] And PMCs such as DynCorp and Vinnell have been hired to advise, educate, and train the armed forces in all the above countries. The Pentagon also awarded lucrative contracts for building as well as maintaining and supplying these military bases to private firms. KBR, for instance, received a contract for more than $22 million to "supply" Camp Stronghold Freedom near Khanabad, Uzbekistan, while in 2003 Fluor got a "development contract" worth $2.6 billion for work in Kazakhstan.[9]

A wide range of special programs has enabled the United States to maintain a military presence around the world. One of the most prominent special programs is the International Military Education and Training (IMET) program. It had been handing out contracts to private firms since 1996, but the government under George W. Bush drastically increased its budget.[10] The program is aimed exclusively at foreign "students," who are trained to become military officers. Its budget for 2003 was $80 million, and its offerings have been expanded to include 133 countries.

The Foreign Military Financing and Foreign Military Sales programs are primarily targeted at helping foreign militaries and governments abroad get weapons, services, and supplemental training in the United States. These programs amount to de facto subsidies for the U.S. arms industry, which is paid to train military leaders and to provide and maintain new weapons systems. Large arms manufacturers often have their own subsidiary PMCs—such as Lockheed Martin's MPRI and Northrop Grumman's Vinnel—that are responsible for this area. The budget for the Foreign Military Sales program in the fiscal year 2001 was more than $381 million.

The phrase "antiterror assistance" is often used to describe the provision of military hardware and training for Washington's perceived allies in its global campaign against terrorism. The assistance can take a variety of forms, but it is targeted primarily at countries in South and Southwest Asia and the Middle East. There, regional centers have been set up to teach and coordinate antiterrorism strategies under the auspices of the Regional Defense Counterterrorism Fellowship Program. The program was a way of getting around congressional prohibitions against providing military training to countries, such as Pakistan and Indonesia, whose militaries have committed proven human-rights violations. It also served to conceal the fact that government funds were going to the PMCs that did the training.

The Plan Colombia, which was set up in 1999, has thus far received $7.5 billion dollars from various government sources.[11] The money goes toward stabilizing the government of Colombia, one of the Americas' largest oil suppliers, and making it a "reliable partner." In order to avoid having to intervene openly in Colombia's civil war, Congress limited the number of U.S. troops that could be sent there to a scant five hundred, while allowing PMCs, currently numbering around thirty, to operate unfettered in the Andean nation. Washington also supports the government in Bogotá with intelligence, education, and training programs, most of which are carried out by private firms. Developmental institutions such as the United States Agency for International Development (USAID) and funds from the "war on drugs" are used for the programs—together with money from the Departments of Defense and State. Thus some of the private soldiers in Colombia officially work as "developmental aides" and "antidrug campaigners" but in fact are deployed by PMCs to fight FARC guerrilla units and the Marxist National

Liberation Army, or ELN. In November 2004, the Colombian journalist Hernando Calvo Ospina remarked in the French newspaper *Le Monde diplomatique*: "Nowhere other than Iraq does the United States pursue such a varied policy of using mercenaries as in Colombia."[12]

The Africa Regional Fund is used to secure U.S. interests on the world's largest continent with its vast natural resources. Together with the U.S. military's Special Operations Forces, private military companies are at work in a growing number of African countries building up, educating, advising, and training local armed forces. More than ten thousand soldiers in Senegal, Uganda, Nigeria, Rwanda, Equatorial Guinea, Malawi, Ghana, Mali, and Ivory Coast have undergone military training—ostensibly so that they can participate in peacekeeping missions.[13] Plans are to expand operations to countries such as Guinea, Kenya, Tanzania, and Botswana. In Ghana the training courses have been run exclusively by private companies, including MPRI, Program Analysis and Evaluation (PA&E), SAIC, DFI MSS, and Logicon.

There are numerous other government programs from which private military companies are paid. The Joint Combined Exchange Training (JCET) program is a military exchange service allowing special forces from foreign countries to be trained in the latest American fighting techniques. Discretionary funds available to Combatant Commander-in-Chiefs (in military parlance, CINCs) represent a kind of slush fund for bankrolling regional military commanders, and the CIA Training Program is used to bankroll covert and semicovert military operations. All of these programs are exempt from congressional scrutiny, and those who run them have no responsibility to provide information to the public. Such programs allow the U.S. government to maintain the appearance of not interfering in foreign conflicts. Cases of potential embarrassment, for example failed military operations, can always be dismissed as a covert action carried out by a PMC, not as the work of Washington.

The United States and Great Britain usually outsource directly, with their respective governments themselves concluding contracts with private companies. Many European countries, including France and the Netherlands, take an indirect path, while still pursuing the goal of increasing their room to maneuver in both a political and military sense beyond their own borders. Their national armies are being transformed into a set of core forces, advance and combat troops, while all other military tasks are being handed over to military service providers. In addition, costly special services and ones that are only needed in unusual circumstances are being entrusted to PMCs. In order to realize these ends, countries like France and Holland form public corporations, which are then charged with transferring tasks associated with state sovereignty to the private sector. Such public-private partnerships also bring a financial advantage since they enable the executive branch to award contracts outside the constraints of Parliament-approved budgets for the military and the police. This approach allows for a quicker utilization of new technologies and weaponry and urgently needed services. Yet similar to leasing and installment-plan arrangements, it also defers payment to the future, in which the next generation will be left footing the bill.

Germany may not rely on PMCs to anything near the extent that the United States does, but it, too, is exploring the possibilities of military privatization. The German Defense Ministry has transferred the task of privatization to a Cologne-based, limited-liability company called the Society for Development,

Procurement and Operation, or GEBB (Gesellschaft für Entwicklung, Beschaffung und Betrieb), which began its work on August 22, 2000.[14] The mission of this company, a 100 percent subsidiary of the Defense Department, is "to relieve the Bundeswehr [the German Army] of the greatest possible number of tasks that do not belong to the core duties of the military"—a statement that could have been written by Donald Rumsfeld. The Bundeswehr calculated that some €10.5 billion or 45 percent of its total budget of €24.4 billion were for so-called nonmilitary tasks. In the context of modernizing the armed forces, the GEBB says it is pursuing a strategy of contracting civilian personnel to provide services, of creating room for investment, and of dramatically reducing operating costs and fixed capital. The company examines "nonmilitary tasks" with an eye toward determining whether privatization is "possible, economical, and sensible." The focus is on public-private partnerships, which "should be encouraged to come to the forefront." The GEBB conceives of itself as a mediator between the Bundeswehr and the private sector. The core areas of its modernizing efforts are the personnel and location structure of the territorial military administration, clothing, motor vehicles, accommodation, and food as well as the equipping and network connection of all "nonmilitary" departments with modern information technology.

The first areas to be privatized were transport and clothing. In the summer of 2002, responsibility for them was transferred to the newly founded companies Vehicle Fleet Service Limited (75.1 percent owned by GEBB and 24.9 percent by German Rail) and Clothing Society Limited (74.9 percent owned by the private consortium Lion Apparel and Hellmann Worldwide Logistics and 25.1 percent by GEBB).

Other projects in the areas of training, logistics, and information technology include pursuing the explicit goal of "transferring the operative support of the Bundeswehr with so-called service tasks to private partners." Training courses in the realms of motor vehicles, submarines, and the air force, as well as training via correspondence, are being examined to determine whether they are suitable for partial privatization. In the case of the air force, the GEBB has already developed a cooperative business model, focusing on basic and advanced training for technical air force personnel at what is currently the German Air Force Technical School 1 in the town of Kaufbeuren. The GEBB says that "the successful implementation of this pilot project would set a precedent for the entire training landscape." In the area of logistics, which costs around €3 billion, the privatization drive is less advanced and remains in the planning stage. A GEBB press release from October 25, 2005, states that "work is continuing on a plan for reorganizing a segment with a volume of around 800 million." The GEBB says it is aware that optimization can only be carried out if there is sufficient transparency over the entire supply chain, from planning to operation to checking on all flows of material services and information. But the company has also determined that such transparency cannot "be achieved presently or in the near future since it is dependent on the successful implementation of SASPF [information technologies and programs]." Since 1998, the U.S. computer and armaments company CSC, the parent of DynCorp, has been involved in this area. For a €7.2-billion reorganization and modernization initiative, which was dubbed "Project Hercules," by the year 2015 the Bundeswehr cooperates with a consortium including Siemens and IBM. The company that resulted, BWI Information Technology, is 50.1

percent privately owned, while 49.9 percent remains in public hands. Project Hercules has been characterized as the largest ongoing public-private partnership in Europe.

Generally speaking, "strong states"—and especially those in the Anglo-Saxon world—publicly justify the transfer and out-sourcing of responsibilities to PMCs with the idea that they are improving security standards while saving money. But primarily they are interested in expanding their own military capacities. National armies are gradually replacing the personnel they lost with the end of the cold war in the 1990s with private firms. In fact, the United States has more than compensated for the reduction in troops during the 1990s from 2.1 to 1.5 million soldiers: With almost a million private soldiers currently in its employ, the Pentagon has actually increased its strength vis-à-vis the cold war era.[15]

THE INTERESTS OF THE PRIVATE SECTOR

The private sector was quick to recognize the advantages of not relying on national and international institutions to protect its property and activities. As early as the early 1990s, the multi-national diamond consortium De Beers was already employing a PMC called Executive Outcomes to carry out covert operations relating to diamond reserves in southern Africa, specifically in Botswana and Namibia.

Private businesses have become the second most important source of clients for military contractors, engaging new mercenaries for various tasks in all corners of the globe. The private sector gives PMCs a considerably free hand in choosing the best means for advancing their economic and security interests. Cases of violence and disregard for human rights have become frequent and drastic enough that they have called forth protests. One could fill shelves with reports by organizations such as Human Rights Watch and Amnesty International, as well as groups such as unions, the International Labour Organization, and the International Labor Rights Fund about the illegal activities committed by PMCs in the service of private businesses. There have been cases of murder, intimidation, rape, abduction, illegal incarceration, and psychological terrorism. In July 2000, such criticism led international firms from around the world to come together under the auspices of the United Nations to reach a "global compact" to set general guidelines for cooperation between businesses and PMCs.

But there has yet to be any firm evidence that the statement of principle made by global players in 2000 has yielded real improvement in practice. Part of the problem may be that the compact failed to tackle the alliance of economic enterprises and private military contractors head-on. Without concrete sanctions for specific offenses, self-regulation efforts usually remain ineffective. In addition, multinational corporations— unlike nongovernmental organizations—have no problem with the blurring of lines between economic, political, humanitarian, and military activities in their dealings with PMCs. In any case, the leaders of the global economy have not yet made any such worries public. Nongovernmental organizations that have researched whether multinational firms and other business enterprises are adhering to the 2003 UN Norms for human and labor rights have come to negative,[16] often depressing conclusions.[17] In May 2007, the EarthRights organization concluded: "Nearly four years after the UN Sub-Commission on the Protection and Promotion of Human Rights adopted the Norms in August 2003, they have all but disappeared . . . The lack of widespread acceptance and any form of monitoring or accountability mechanism, makes such efforts futile if not damaging to the overall goal of prevention of human rights abuses by corporations."[18]

With a view toward stock indexes and investors, it can nonetheless be counterproductive for firms to attract public attention to the issue of security and risk in commercial enterprises. The private sector has taken care not to publicize the "security tax," varying between 2 and 8 percent, that it imposed on itself in 2001. That was the percentage of their running budgets devoted to maintain firm security, and the "war on terror" has brought new costs that have to be borne nearly across the board. Nowadays international businesses commonly spend between 3 and 15 percent of their budgets protecting themselves.[19] Airline consumers, for example, pay more for incidentals like airport surcharges and taxes than they do for transport on a plane. The primary economic sector—agriculture and raw materials—has to bear particularly steep security costs, although they vary dramatically according to which part of the world companies do their business in. But significantly, the parts of the world where risk is the greatest are also those in which the highest profits can be made.[20] Security costs, which in some sectors even exceed personnel costs, are not carried by companies alone. They're passed on. Petroleum corporations, for example, charge the countries from which they've received concessions for security services. A portion of the costs is also passed on to taxpayers since the state directly or indirectly cofinances security expenditures for companies doing business abroad. Moreover, a large proportion of the costs are borne by consumers since oil and gas concerns raise prices in accordance with security outlays. And corporations of course also write off security costs from their taxes.

So-called export processing zones, also known as maquiladora industries, represent a specific problem in the cooperation between commercial enterprises and PMCs. Having spread rapidly across the globe, these zones are industrial districts located in what amount to extraterritorial security areas, where duty-free, half-finished wares are imported and then exported in finished form. In 2005 there were more than three thousand such zones in more than 116 countries—around fifty million people worked in them. A third of the zones were located in Latin American countries. The zones are used both by medium-size companies and by global giants such as Nike and Philips. [21]

The states on whose territory the zones are located offer firms producing there a fully deregulated labor market, largely cost-free infrastructure, and enormous tax advantages. Within an industry zone, the state in question has ceded most of its sovereign rights to the private sector—the state, for example, is only responsible for external security. Official police forces are reduced to the role of doormen or security guards. What happens inside a zone is almost exclusively dictated by the firms producing there—usually in conjunction with private security contractors. Forced to submit to this arbitrary rule, employees dependent on the zones see the normal protections afforded by labor, criminal, and constitutional law suspended. There are frequent complaints about broken contracts, unpaid wages, dangerous and unhealthy working conditions, unjustified firings, and sexual harassment. The extreme low-wage sector (50¢ an hour or less) is the only source of income for the population that lives outside the "private business sovereignty zone." Nonetheless, conflicts continue to arise with companies and private security firms. The general manager for Vogue garment company in Mexico has been quoted as saying that his firm doesn't like unions and wants to have nothing to do with them.[22] Black & Decker also forbids its employees from organizing into unions. Workers from five countries sued Wal-Mart in front of a Californian Superior Court for unpaid wages and illegal working hours that ranged from ninety-hour weeks to 365 days without vacation time.[23] Disney's children's books are manufactured by young Chinese women who receive $25 a week for working fourteen hours a day, seven days a week, in unhealthy conditions.[24]

In countries such as Pakistan, India, China, and Jamaica, unions are officially prohibited in economic protection zones, and elsewhere workers run serious risks if they try to organize. The International Trade Union Confederation has almost daily reports of workers being fired as well as attacked, physically abused, and sometimes even killed by private security forces and paramilitaries.[25] The PMCs involved are sometimes located in the countries—often, though, they are American and European firms specializing in "protective security" services. In 2007 dozens of unionized workers in Bangladesh, Sri Lanka, Burma, Cambodia, India, and the Philippines were killed by private security forces. The situation is much the same in many Central and South American countries as well as in almost all African nations.[26]

The maquildora industries offer a particularly clear example of why the private sector contracts its security from private companies. With the help of PMCs, firms can pursue their economic goals and break potential resistance from employees without having to make compromises with labor organizations.

"WEAK STATES" WITH SECURITY GAPS

"Weak" and "failing" states normally hire PMCs to compensate for their own security shortcomings and to plug holes in their own security apparatus. Wealthier nations often force poorer ones, with reference to their dependency on the foreign capital invested in export processing zones, to spend money on private contractors. The weakness or indeed lack of adequate security in these countries, most of which are located in the third world, can be traced back to their colonial past or the cold war. The absence of legal procedure, transparency, and responsibility to the public lead to corruption, political nepotism, and judicial uncertainty, and continually increase the potential for conflict. In emergency situations, in which those conflicts threaten to turn violent, the fragility of the whole security system becomes apparent. That's when such countries ask strong states for help, and PMCs are called in to take care of the problem. With the assistance of private contractors, numerous coups d'etat have been prevented, corrupt regimes kept in power, and bloodbaths averted. But the fundamental problems remain and continue to boil just under the surface.

Africa is full of examples of armed conflicts in which PMCs have been hired by the countries' own governments to train or militarily assist its troops. Ronco has worked in Rwanda; Defense Systems Limited and Saracen International in Uganda; Iris and SafeNet in the Democratic Republic of Congo; MPRI in Liberia; Omega Risk Solutions, Stabilco, and MPRI in Angola; Executive Outcomes, Sandline, PAE, and ICI in Sierra Leone; Ronco in Mozambique; and Executive Outcomes in Botswana, Lesotho, Ethiopia, Zambia, and Namibia. Yet in none of these countries have PMCs been able to establish peace and solve conflict by military means. On the contrary, when "weak states," following government interests that are frequently inseparable from oil-company interests in richer nations, replace their own security forces with PMCs, they make themselves even weaker—in three respects. The illusion of stability is created, but it is of extremely brief duration. Military security is unevenly distributed throughout society and is employed only to protect state institutions and political elites. (Even Doug Brooks, one of the leading PMC lobbyists in the United States, writes: "For many African citizens in the years since independence, security has been the exception, not the rule.")[27] Bringing in PMCs undermines the legitimacy of state security organizations and gives rise to fears of a kind of imported neocolonialism. Ultimately, the foundations for conflict resolution are destroyed since there is no longer any generally acknowledged state authority that could mediate between the parties who disagree. In any case, and even in the best situations, the civilian population suffers most. Almost invariably, humanitarian considerations are ignored as the conflict is settled, one way or the other, and human rights are trampled underfoot. The deployment of PMCs does not serve the interests of weak or failed nations, but particular interests within those states—be they political elites or business lobbies that profit from the economy of war.

REBEL GROUPS AND FREEDOM FIGHTERS

Nonstate actors who use violence—rebel groups, warlords, liberation movements, and so forth—are interested in obtaining weapons, getting advanced military training, receiving strategic advice, and learning to use modern war technology, especially with regard to intelligence. Because of the controversial nature of many such groups, it's usually only smaller PMCs that agree to work with them. In cases where more powerful interests are also at play, however, the larger private contractors become increasingly willing to get involved. Situations have arisen in which all of the warring parties have secured the services of PMCs. In Zaire, for instance, French-backed private soldiers tried to protect the Mobutu government, while PMCs and rebels with the support of the United States tried to overthrow that government—eventually with success.[28] The conflict was the beginning of one of the bloodiest battles the continent had ever seen. Some commentators have referred to it as the First World War of Africa.

In the annual reports filed by UN Commission on Human Rights Special Rapporteur Enrique Bernales Ballesteros, the United Nations expert on mercenaries has repeatedly drawn attention to the ever-greater role played by PMCs in facilitating the sales of weapons and military services in the deregulated global market.[29] Often, they do this not directly, but in the guise of subsidiaries, sometimes self-owned ones, to which the transactions are subcontracted out. In cases of especially controversial missions, the subsidiaries may pass on the contracts to even smaller companies so that in the end it's difficult to tell exactly who was responsible for selling weapons to, say, a guerrilla group or terrorist network. The public rarely learns which PMC was hired by this or that rebel group or warlord. Some of the few exceptions were the news that Executive Outcomes had supported, then later fought against, UNITA rebels in the Angolan Civil War of the 1990s, that Omega had advised and armed the Kabila rebels in Congo, and that the Revolutionary United Front in Sierra Leone had procured weapons from Israeli firms.

THE SECURITY DILEMMA OF INTERNATIONAL ORGANIZATIONS

The needs and interests of the fifth group of PMC clients—international, regional, and humanitarian organizations—are very diverse. Thus far, the UN has only awarded contracts to military service providers in exceptional situations. Because of the value the organization places on its reputation and credibility as a kind of world government, it has shied away from hiring private companies for this sort of task. In 1979, after decades of tough negotiations, the UN succeeded in passing a convention against "the recruitment, use, financing and training of mercenaries." It came into force in 2001. An Office of the Special Rapporteur was set up to monitor adherence to the convention and to observe developments on the world's various continents. Handing over UN responsibilities to PMCs would have been tantamount to legitimizing modern mercenaries through the back door—in an all too apparent contradiction of official UN policy.

There are several reasons for the isolated instances, for example the peacekeeping missions in East Timor and Somalia, in which the UN has engaged PMCs. Politically motivated, public criticism of UN peacekeeping missions is growing louder and louder since the IPOA, the main PMC lobbyist, has gotten more aggressively involved in such discussions. The IPOA accuses the UN, among other things, of wasting money and being incapable of achieving peace.[30] In early 2003, IPOA head Doug Brooks was cited as saying that, by contrast, private military companies could end all the wars in Africa for $750 million.[31] One reason the UN sometimes fails to live up to its responsibilities is that member states are slow to pay their contributions. That situation makes the UN susceptible to offers by PMCs to carry out peacekeeping missions at a tenth of the usual cost—and the UN is all the more receptive when the international press lists the UN's failed missions in recent years and calculates the number of lives that could have been saved had the peacekeeping troops not been so low-quality and inefficient. Numerous other flaws could be added to that list, but what's been lacking thus far is an analysis that details how and why mistakes were made. Ad hoc solutions using PMCs are not sufficient to turn the situation around, no matter how unavoidable or logical military interventions might seem at first glance. Events in Somalia, Afghanistan, and most recently in Iraq show that the military option is not always the best one. The UN is caught in a dilemma. On the one hand, in places like Sudan, Haiti, Burundi, Burma, and elsewhere, the demand for peacekeepers is growing. On the other, none of the strong nations are willing to provide additional personnel or take over the financing of peacekeeping missions. In this situation, the UN has restricted itself to hiring PMCs to advise and protect subsidiary organizations such as UNICEF, United Nations Development Programme (UNDP), and the World Food Programme (WFP) as well as officials like the United Nations High Commissioner for Refugees. One of the main service providers is the British firm Defense Systems Limited.[32]

Other transnational organizations, such as the OAU and NATO, are in a very different position. In general they have far fewer problems, both in terms of legitimacy and finances, handing out direct or indirect contracts to PMCs. The OAU, for example, uses military contractors in western and central Africa, while NATO—in particular, the United States and Britain—employ them in the Balkans and Afghanistan. These organizations have no scruples about including private soldiers in their overall strategy, even though the transfer of state security responsibilities to private military entities not only legitimizes the latter but also undermines the state's monopoly on the legitimate use of violence.

Many nongovernmental organizations are very hesitant about or even strictly opposed to using PMCs for protection. Their reasons are varied. The International Committee of the

Red Cross, for example, is worried about blurring the lines between humanitarian, political, and military actions.[33] But in some cases, NGOs have no choice but to avail themselves of PMC services. In Iraq, for instance, they couldn't otherwise get permission to be active in the conflict regions. In Rwanda, NGOs need private security providers to be able to stay in the country and continue their work. Thus despite the critical stance of most NGOs, they are increasingly using modern mercenaries, all the more so as the number of aid workers killed in conflict regions now exceeds that of regular soldiers.[34] The Red Cross enjoys armed protection in Congo, Afghanistan, and Iraq. Medico International has hired firms to guard its installations in Angola. DSL—a subsidiary of ArmorGroup— offers a number of humanitarian organizations armed protection in a variety of crisis-ridden countries. Respected research and political consulting groups such as Toronto's Centre for International Studies and London's Overseas Development Institute have recommended that NGOs consider privatizing their security needs in the interest of humanitarian goals.[35] The IPOA has gratefully passed on this recommendation and lobbies worldwide for aid organizations to use PMCs. In a 2003 interview in German, IPOA president Doug Brooks argued: "Hundreds of thousands of innocent civilians die every year in wars that could be stopped, if the West would deploy reliable peacekeeping troops. Private companies are preparing to meet this need, more transparently, responsibly and professionally than UN troops. People who describe private enterprises and their employees, who risk their lives to stop such wars and protect civilians, as mercenaries are badly informed and callous."[36] The absolute resistance among humanitarian groups toward PMCs has been breached, and critical voices are becoming more isolated. Conversely, private military providers hope to expand their business in the humanitarian sector.

PRIVATE INDIVIDUALS AND SECURITY

Private associations and individual civilians make up the smallest part of the market for military service companies, but it's a growing market. The ongoing social conflicts in poor countries, as well as many wealthier ones, are leading to a fragmentation of society, which can also be seen in territorial terms. Numerous causes, including but not restricted to financial shortfalls, mean that state security services are inequitably distributed. The results are various zones with a divergent quality of security. These are more visible in densely populated cities than in rural regions and reflect the distribution of wealth within a given society. Private sector areas such as production facilities and factory grounds enjoy the highest security standards—along with semipublic spaces like airports, train stations, and shopping malls, which are run by public-private partnership enterprises.[37]

Since the terrorist attacks of September 11, 2001, a diffuse climate of threat has spread throughout Western countries and has led, among wealthier social groups and individuals, to both an increased need for security and an increased demand for professional protection services. Highly specific risk analyses and armed protection have become standard among the contracts received by PMCs like ArmorGroup, Rubicon International Services, and the Steele Foundation, when they are hired to accompany individuals to crisis regions or protect the children of diplomats. More and more civilians avail themselves of such services. Teams of consultants analyze their clients' security situations at home and in the workplace, check their daily routines (visits to the post office, routes typically taken by car, and so forth) for risks, and draw up contingency plans for emergencies.

4

Global Markets for Armed Force
Four Private Military Companies in Action

Travel the world, enjoy the adventure,
meet interesting people, and kill them.

Armed conflicts on the international stage have changed. Nations are no longer the entities that most often wage war upon one another. Instead, violent confrontations commonly occur in the form of what experts call "low-intensity conflicts," and even those campaigns carried out by wealthy nations—for instance, in Iraq or Afghanistan—more closely resemble police or punitive actions than classic wars.[1] Today's conflicts are, on the one hand, increasingly denationalized and, on the other, more and more international. In conjunction with this shift, a market of global dimensions has arisen for military force. The provision and acquisition of military might has become a business. Transnational sources of violence, such as terrorist networks, and private actors like warlords and arms dealers have growing influence on local, national, and international conflicts. PMCs play a larger and larger part in this constellation. Four examples illustrate the range and variety of their activities.

MILITARY PROFESSIONAL RESOURCES INC. (MPRI)

MPRI is a subsidiary of Lockheed Martin, the largest arms manufacturer in the world, and enjoys superlative relations with the Pentagon. The company got its first domestic contract in 1996 from the U.S. government as part of a pilot project revolving around the training of reserve officers in fifteen military academies. After a successful trial period, MPRI took over responsibility for training soldiers at two hundred such institutions. Today the Reserve Officers' Training Corps, or ROTC, is completely in the hands of private companies. In addition, MPRI does training work for the Civil Air Patrol (the civilian arm of the U.S. Air Force); gives advanced seminars at Fort Sill, Fort Knox, and Fort Lee; and runs the U.S. Army Force Management School at Fort Leavenworth. With the army's permission, MPRI employees appear in uniform in front of cadets. The next generation of U.S. officers will have acquired their knowledge and skills exclusively from PMCs.

In the late 1990s, as the Pentagon began to replace career officers stationed abroad with private training staff and consultants, MPRI received foreign contracts as well. In Taiwan and Sweden, the company held seminars about the technical lessons learned from the first Gulf War. In Nigeria, it trained troops for deployment in peacekeeping missions. And MPRI was not the only company active in this area. More than a dozen PMCs, including Vinnell, Trojan Securities, Pistris, DynCorp, Special Operations Consulting–Security Management (SOC-SMG),

Olive Security, and Meyer and Associates, began doing business all over the globe, bringing the armies of foreign countries up to speed about the latest U.S. techniques for waging war.

The training and consulting duties taken over by PMCs are not restricted to boot-camp drills and theoretical and organizational seminars. The firms also show allied military troops how to use surface-to-air missiles and antitank artillery. They reorganize and recalibrate foreign military forces, teach them new strategies, and set up practice sessions in combat simulators at computer centers. They also promote the latest in U.S. weaponry, which usually leads to a corresponding increase in orders placed with U.S. arms manufacturers. Commerce was one consideration that led the military-industrial complex to push for privatization. Indeed, experts like Elke Krahmann are of the opinion that the opportunity for the arms industry to market their products via PMCs was *the* most important reason for outsourcing.[2]

Although the industry enjoyed near-total employment thanks to the "war on terror," it still wanted to expand. The companies themselves began looking for new threats to U.S. interests. With the help of lobby groups, backed by oil companies, other firms exploiting natural resources, and pro-Western rebel movements, they pressured the U.S. government to implement military training and consulting programs in the countries in question. In most cases—for example the Plan Colombia or the military assistance programs Africa Crisis Response Initiative (ACRI) and African Contingency Operations Training and Assistance (ACOTA), the PMCs were successful. The U.S. government adopted the firms' recommendations and initiated special programs and other budget measures to ensure financing for such operations.

According to Juan C. Zarate, deputy assistant secretary

of the Executive Office for Terrorist Financing, MPRI is an example of the fact that military instructors and advisors have at least as much if not more influence on the conduct of war than combat troops themselves.[3] Before the Pentagon entrusted the company with training U.S. reserve officers, MPRI had established its reputation in the Balkan wars, in which declarations of independence by former Yugoslav states led to military conflicts between the Serbian government in Belgrade and Slovenia, Croatia and Bosnia-Herzegovina. In 1991 in the wake of worsening atrocities on all sides, the UN instituted a freeze on military activities and an arms embargo that covered all of former Yugoslavia's territory. That measure covered not only arms shipments but also military training and advice. Croatia and Bosnia turned to the West, and particularly the United States, for help. Although both countries were official "partners of peace" for NATO, it was not possible to get directly involved without violating the UN resolution. MPRI, which was awarded a contract worth $75 million, was the alternative. The unofficial "Croatian army" had been routed by Serbian forces, but within a few months, MPRI succeeded in forming members of the Croatian mafia, paramilitary groups, irregular militias, police officers, and some regular army soldiers into combat-ready troops. A military leadership was established and acquainted with the latest forms and techniques of warfare. In July 1995, MPRI and the Croatian Army leadership met ten times on the Brioni Islands to run through the details of a planned offensive against Serbian troops in Serbian-majority Krajina. On August 3, five days after the last such meeting and while a Croatian government delegation was still negotiating with Krajina Serbs in Geneva, Operation Storm was launched. Lightning strikes eliminated

Serbian control systems and disabled their command center, and in a few days concentrated Croatian forces took power in Krajina. While the fighting was under way, U.S. secretary of defense William Perry said his country understood Croatia's action, and German foreign minister Klaus Kinkel referred to Krajina as part of Croatia. The consequences of Croatia's speedy victory were devastating. For the first time in the conflict there was large-scale "ethnic cleansing," whole villages were bombed and burned to the ground, hundreds of civilians were brutally murdered, and more than one hundred thousand people had to flee their homes.

MPRI disputed ever being directly involved in Operation Storm, but virtually all the military experts agreed that such a highly professional operation, one which looked as though it could have come from a "NATO textbook," would not have been possible without the participation and support of the private military company.[4] Three months later, the remnants of Serbian Yugoslavia decided to accept the facts and signed the Dayton Peace Accords with Croatia and Bosnia-Herzegovina. Bosnian president Alija Izetbegović refused to put pen to paper unless assured that MPRI would assume responsibility for building up his country's armed forces, and the company, which had proved so successful in Croatia, received contracts valuing $400 million. The money was raised, with the help of U.S. mediation, from fellow Muslim states Saudi Arabia, Kuwait, Brunei, the United Arab Emirates, and Malaysia and deposited with the U.S. Department of State, where the private military company could then easily access it.[5] After Bosnia, MPRI got another lucrative engagement in Macedonia. The firm's increasing involvement in the Balkans was halted in 1999, after it became known that the company was supporting separatist rebels in Kosovo. MPRI does, however, continue to train and advise the militaries of Croatia and Bosnia.

With the dawn of the new millennium, MPRI refocused on Africa. Applying lessons learned in the Balkans, the company militarily engaged in a number of countries rich in natural resources and oil, with which the United States had limited or no official contact. Equatorial Guinea—the "Kuwait of Africa"—and Angola were two examples. MPRI developed new defense plans, established a coast guard, built up combat-ready troops and governmental guards, and took over the education and training of police forces for both of those countries. In April 2000, the company also received $7 million to bring Nigeria's army up to a "professional standard."[6] In the meantime, one could almost say that the entire continent of Africa has become an MPRI boot camp. They have developed security plans and conducted training programs for 120 African presidents, heads of state, and party leaders. Within the framework of the ACOTA program, they have trained the armies of Benin, Ethiopia, Ghana, Kenya, Mali, Malawi, and Senegal.

Meanwhile in South America, MPRI worked in close conjunction with the Defense Department. The company has been heavily involved in the Plan Colombia, carrying out the primary analysis of structural needs and developing the security and military aspects of the plan. In Taiwan MPRI has trained soldiers. In South Korea it has supported U.S. troops. In Indonesia it has trained the local navy and come up with "maritime security strategies" with the help of computer simulation programs.[7]

The U.S.-led wars in Afghanistan and Iraq led the company to transfer the majority of its activities to those two regions. In Afghanistan, MPRI developed the Karzai government's national security plan and made recommendations about the future form of the country's defense system. In Kuwait, it trained U.S. soldiers in how to secure convoys along major supply routes in Iraq and protect themselves against ambushes, land mines, roadside bombs, explosive attacks, and vehicular attacks by insurgents. It also provided technical and personnel assistance to the Iraqi provisional government. In addition, it has been involved with the formation and training of the new Iraqi army and police forces. The contracts MPRI received for these services were worth several billion dollars.

The directors of other PMCs and critical observers from U.S. nongovernmental organizations agree that MPRI's coup de grace was Field Manual 3-100.21. In 2000, the U.S. Army Training and Doctrine Command (TRADOC) in Fort Monroe, Virginia, hired the firm to draw up guidelines for contracts between the U.S. government and PMCs.[8] The result was, as the company's website put it, a catalogue establishing "a doctrinal basis directed toward acquiring and managing contractors as an additional resource in support of the full range of military operations." The manual was approved by the Pentagon, and it was published as a government document on January 3, 2003, shortly before the United States invaded Iraq. Since then, military service providers receive contracts and are paid according to rules written not by the Pentagon itself, but by MPRI.

KELLOGG, BROWN AND ROOT (KBR)

Along with equipment and personnel, logistics, supplies, and maintenance represent the largest expenditures for a standing armed force. The running costs total billions, and the outsourcing of these areas has meant hundreds of millions in profits for private military companies.

One of the market leaders in this sector is Kellogg, Brown and Root (KBR), a subsidiary of Halliburton, which, according to its own figures, employed sixty thousand employees in forty-three countries in 2005. In recent years, the company has received contracts worth billions from the Pentagon. For example, in the fiscal year 2003, the firm recorded income of $3.9 billion for services rendered in Afghanistan and during the Iraq War. In 2005 it recorded a contract for supplies, equipment, and maintenance in Iraq worth $13 billion. That sum, when adjusted for inflation, represents approximately 2.5 times what the first Gulf War cost and is equivalent to what the United States spent on all its wars from the American Revolutionary War to World War I. In addition, the government of the United Kingdom outsourced its entire logistics in Iraq to KBR.

As was the case with MPRI, the rise of KBR as a private military logistics specialist came with the Balkan wars. In 1994 the company received its first contract, worth $6.3 million, for the unspecified "supplying" of the U.S. air base in Aviano, Italy, where reconnaissance flights over Yugoslavia took off and landed.[9] A year later twenty thousand U.S. troops were stationed as peacekeepers in the Balkans as part of the NATO-led Implementation Force (IFOR) mission. KBR received more than $546 million to take care of logistics—at that point the largest contract ever awarded in the history of the industry. They also received supplementary contracts for services in Croatia and Bosnia until 1999.

With the outbreak of the war over Kosovo in March 1999, the firm made another leap. Neither humanitarian organizations like the Red Cross nor NATO were prepared for the massive flight of ethnic Albanian refugees to Macedonia and Albania. The United States outsourced the logistical side of this problem to KBR. The company was given a five-year contract worth $180 million a year (almost $1 billion total), which, however, was used up after just one year due to what were called "unforeseen events." The money was increased as it became clear that the entire Kosovo War, including its humanitarian missions and U.S. peacekeeping duties, was dependent on the PMC. Without assistance from KBR, the allies could not launch attacks on military and civilian targets, KFOR troops could not be stationed in crisis areas, and humanitarian groups could not erect tent cities for or feed the many refugees. KBR delivered more than a billion warm meals, two hundred billion liters of water, and a billion liters of gasoline to U.S. troops alone. During the same time, the firm disposed of ninety thousand cubic meters of waste. KBR services included construction; transport and engineering; building and equipment maintenance; roadwork; electrical, water, gasoline, and food supplies; and the cleaning of uniforms and delivery of mail. In almost all of these areas, the U.S. military was completely dependent on the company from Texas.[10] Without KBR, U.S. soldiers would not have been able to eat or sleep; they would have had neither motor vehicles nor fuel to run them; and they would have been forced to forgo weapons and ammunition. It is therefore no exaggeration to say that the entire U.S. mission in Kosovo owed its success to the skills and capacities of a single private military company. The distribution of humanitarian resources was likewise dependent on KBR. But the firm dealt with the needs of refugees according to who was paying the bill. Some of those fleeing the conflict were quartered in five-star tent cities since the money to pay for them came from oil-rich Arab sheiks. Others had to make do with far more modest accommodation, since the humanitarian contributions were coming from poorer countries.[11]

In the eyes of many observers, KBR's "masterpiece" during the Kosovo War was the building of Camp Bondsteel. The facility was less a traditional military camp than a small city, surrounded by mountains near the town of Ferizaj in southeastern Kosovo. With an area of three hundred sixty thousand square meters, the facility with its nine wooden guard towers has a circumference of just under eleven kilometers. It is divided into a "North Town" and a "South Town," with the Albania-Macedonia-Bulgaria oil pipeline running through the middle. Today the pipeline is run by a U.S. consortium, which pressured the U.S. government beginning in 1994 to realize the project (it was officially inaugurated on December 27, 2004, in Sophia). The city contains 250 wood-paneled houses—so-called Southeast Asian huts with wraparound balconies, six large rooms, and a shower—and is crisscrossed by wide paved roads. Soldiers stationed there can visit two luxury restaurants with large menus as well as Burger King, Anthony's Pizza, and a cappuccino bar. There is a twenty-four-hour delivery service for cold cuts and drinks. Two PX centers sell everything from groceries, DVDs, and clothing to souvenirs. In their free time, GIs can visit a volleyball and basketball facility or go to the fitness center. They can shoot pool, go bowling, have a round of Ping-Pong, or play any one of countless video games. There are computer rooms with Internet connections, television lounges with film libraries, and a large space for video- and teleconferences. There is usually two of everything, including churches, in Bondsteel—one for North Town and one for South Town. There is, however, only one stockade, one hospital, and one Laura Bush Education

Center, where soldiers have the opportunity to learn Albanian, Serbian, or German. Spirits are not allowed in Camp Bondsteel, but alcohol-free beer is permitted.[12]

Yet a series of negative headlines has clouded the KBR success story. The company has been accused of manipulating its books, overcharging the Pentagon, accepting money for services never performed, and using nontransparent means to acquire contracts—vice president Dick Cheney, it has been alleged, has made millions by ensuring his former company gets secret, no-bid contracts that skirt the normal public awarding procedures. William D. Hartung, Director of the World Policy Institute and author of a book titled *How Much are You Making on the War, Daddy? A Quick and Dirty Guide to War Profiteering in the Bush Administration*, has characterized the government's relationship with KBR and Halliburton since 2001 as an unprecedented instance of cronyism. A number of media experts have concluded that KBR is a corrupt company with a bizarre idea of what clients have a right to expect for their money. Such accusations are supported by testimony from high-ranking members of the army itself, including Bunnatine "Bunny" Greenhouse, the former chief contracting officer for the Army Corps of Engineers, who was responsible for checking the contracts between the Pentagon and PMCs. Greenhouse testified to Congress that KBR's relationship with the Pentagon was "the most blatant and improper contract abuse I have witnessed during the course of my professional career"—and was subsequently demoted.

Another insider witness who backed up the allegations of impropriety was former KBR employee Marie de Young. The logistics specialist was sent by KBR to Kuwait, where the headquarters of the company's operation in Iraq were located, to undertake an internal check of its books and contracts. Her investigations uncovered not only grotesquely inflated bills to the Pentagon but also cases in which KBR managers pocketed millions in bribes, which were then deposited in Swiss bank accounts, from subcontractors. The company, she found, billed $73 million a year for accommodations in Kuwait's most expensive hotels and imported dozens of luxury limousines for "inspection trips"—while failing to procure $7 air filters needed by transport vehicles, which were then stranded, nonoperational, in the Iraqi desert. De Young's testimony, as well as that of other insiders, became a matter of public record in conjunction with the hearings led by Democratic congressman Henry Waxman about abuses by Halliburton and other private military contractors.[13]

EXECUTIVE OUTCOMES (EO)

In many respects, the now-defunct Executive Outcomes was a pioneer and trendsetter in the military service industry. Founded in 1989 in South Africa and officially registered in London and Johannesburg three years later, EO was one of the first enterprises of its kind. It was also a novelty insofar as a whole empire of companies was created around it. Executive Outcomes possessed a small but completely autonomous private army, encompassing combat units, military and strategic planners, logistics, and the entire chain of military service providers. This army had its own weapons, intelligence system, spy agency, supply bases, and transportation. The core comprised two thousand highly specialized infantry, artillery, and air force troops, who earned on average $3,000 a month (pilots made $7,500). Its arsenal included BMP-2 armored tanks and BTR60 amphibious transport vehicles. The company's air force consisted of helicopter gunships as well as MiG-23s, MiG-27s, and Su-25s, mostly acquired from the armed forces of the Soviet Union. Within the Executive Outcomes empire, its subsidiary AES was responsible for spying, Saracen for arms dealing, El Vikingo for information systems, and ASC for radio and satellite communications. The consortium also included two airlines, Ibis Air and Air Capricorn, responsible for troop transport and air surveillance.[14]

Executive Outcomes' clients rented the services of an extremely experienced and modern small army, which was both cheap and efficient. Immediately following their first military operations in Namibia and Angola, they earned a reputation as a state-of-the-art, high-tech fighting force against which no national army in the third world stood a chance. Further successful interventions in Mozambique, Malawi, and Zambia reinforced the message that EO was anything but a ragtag assembly of old-fashioned mercenaries. In the course of its official ten-year existence, the firm was involved in nearly every armed conflict in Africa—from Botswana in the south to Madagascar, Zaire, Kenya, Uganda, Congo, and Sierra Leone in central Africa to Algeria in the north.

For a long time, analysts ascribed the success of the South African–English company solely to its military efficiency and effectiveness. But equally if not more crucial were the economic interests grouped around EO. The company's owners—South Africans Eeben Barlow and Nick van den Bergh and Britons Anthony Buckingham and Simon Mann—were particularly keen on servicing the needs of the mineral and oil industries, organizing the Byzantine construction of companies in their empire around diamonds and petroleum. The various stages of the production process—from mining and drilling to trading in raw materials—

were split among small, individual companies, which were in turn subordinated under two larger entities: Branch Group for minerals and Heritage Group for energy.

Branch Group had its legal headquarters in the Bahamas, as did the Strategic Resources Corporation, a holding company uniting the military and security areas that was centered around Executive Outcomes. The entire complex of companies, economic as well as military, was administratively managed and directed by Plaza 107, a company named after the building where it was located (535 Kings Road in London's Chelsea district).

Taken as a whole, it's difficult to say today whether Executive Outcomes' interventions in African conflicts were more economically or more militarily motivated. Some critics see greed for diamonds, gold, and oil as the guiding force behind the company's activities; other say EO was informed by a traditional mercenary mentality and was merely paid in natural resources. It is difficult to settle the issue given the lack of documentation, for instance, about whether the Branch-Heritage group received licenses to drill for oil or mine diamonds before conflicts broke out or reached a certain intensity—or whether such licenses were granted in return for EO's intervention. Former owners Barlow and Buckingham have never made any statements on this issue. But what was cause and what was effect hardly matters. For those who suffered or profited from EO's interventions, it made little difference whether they were undertaken to protect existing business interests or in hope of procuring valuable licenses. In individual cases the reality on the ground was even more complex. A number of Executive Outcomes' clients paid the company, directly or indirectly, in natural resources[15]—but only after they themselves had exploited a portion of those resources by securing shares in Strategic Resources Corporation or Branch Group. Former Kenyan president Daniel

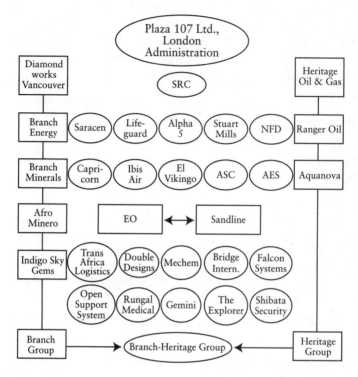

Diamond Works Vancouver—diamond trade

Branch Energy—diamond mining

Branch Minerals—mineral mining

Afro Mineral—diamond mining in Angola

Indigo Sky Gems—diamond trade

SRC (Strategic Resouces Corporation)—holding company

Saracen—arms dealing

Lifeguard—object security

Alpha 5—security services

Stuart Mills—security services/mine clearance

NFD—object security

Capricorn—air transport

Ibis Air—airline

El Vikingo—information systems, communication services, cryptography

ASC (Advanced System Communication)—telephone, radio, and satellite systems

AES (Applied Electronic Services)—countersurveillance technology

Trans Africa Logistics—customs organization, import, and export

Double Designs—engineering

Mechem—mine clearance

Bridge International—infrastructure, logistics

Falcon Systems—support services for NGOs

Open Support System—investment and capital consulting

Rungal Medical—medical assistance/field hospitals

Gemini—advertising agency/advertising film company

The Explorer—tourism

Shibata Security—security for UN services

Heritage Oil & Gas—oil and gas exploration/production

Ranger Oil—oil exploration

Aquanova—geophysical and hydrogeological evaluations/underwater drilling arap Moi, for example, was a partner in Ibis Air. In Uganda, general Salim Saleh, the half brother of the country's former president, owned 45 percent of Saracen Uganda and 25 percent of Branch Energy Uganda. Thus he directly profited from the exploitation of Uganda's gold resources, since Branch Energy was responsible for gold mining, and Saracen for security at the mines.

The end of Executive Outcomes was announced on January 1, 1999, after South Africa enacted the Regulation of Foreign Military Assistance Act, which drastically limited the activities of mercenaries and affected a number of the company's core activities. The company was officially disbanded a short time later amid fears of prosecution. Tim Spicer's Sandline took over some of EO's activities, while other services were offered by companies with new names. In recent years, the entire enterprise, concern, and holding structure—following the trend in the military services industry and in reaction to growing public criticism of the merging of economic and military power—has been organizationally and financially transformed. But the underlying interests of the diffuse group of owners have not changed dramatically. According to research done by the International Consortium of Investigative Journalists, those owners are London bankers, stock-market traders, intelligence operatives, military elites, publishers, and insurance managers.[16] The most prominent among them is Frederick Forsyth, the best-selling author whose works include *The Dogs of War* (about a British mining executive hiring a group of mercenaries to overthrow an African government) and *The Day of the Jackal*.

BLACKWATER WORLDWIDE

The armed protection of people, material, and facilities is one of the realms that the United States has almost completely outsourced to private military companies. In Afghanistan and Iraq, after the end of formal hostilities, such so-called security services have proven to be a gold mine for the private military industry. Blackwater is one of the world's best-known service providers in this area—not least because the company has been the subject of so many negative headlines.[17]

The outsourcing of security tasks initially seemed to be unproblematic since private companies had abundant experience providing bodyguards in the civilian realm, as well as security guards for protecting property. But it soon became clear that experience gained in stable, industrialized countries could not simply be transferred to crisis-ridden, unstable, and embattled postwar societies. And indeed the image of private security forces quickly became tarnished as they began harassing civilians, intimidating local populaces, ignoring regulations, violating state laws, exceeding their authority, and making unauthorized use of their weapons.

Companies like Blackwater commit most of these offenses on a near-daily basis, and incidents involving the use of weapons happen on average at least once a week. There are no reliable statistics on how many civilians have been killed by private soldiers, but the Iraqi Interior Ministry has documented more than two hundred such cases. The actual number is likely far greater. Relatives of those killed seldom receive compensation. Those who do are usually given sums between $5,000 and $15,000.

Blackwater received its first government contract, worth $21 million, in Iraq in 2003. The job was to protect the head of the provisional government, Paul Bremer, and involved the deployment of thirty-eight close-combat specialists, two units of K-9 dogs, and three combat helicopters. Since then, Blackwater has earned more than $340 million for security services provided in Iraq—worldwide, the company had earned over $1 billion by the end of 2006. The main client is the U.S. State Department, which has hired Blackwater to protect the U.S. embassy in Baghdad and provide "diplomatic security" in and around Baghdad and Al Hillah. DynCorp handles security in the northern Iraqi regions around Kirkuk and Erbil, while Triple Canopy is responsible for the south, including the cities of Tallil and Basra.

Blackwater was founded in 1997 by former Navy Seal Erik Prince, then a twenty-eight-year-old son of an industrialist. A fundamentalist Christian, Prince used an inheritance to purchase seven thousand acres of swampland (hence the company name) near Moyock, North Carolina, along the Virginia border. This quickly became the largest military training center in the United States.

According to the company's own information, Blackwater is currently at work in nine different countries, and it defines its four core areas as: "training centers," "mobility & logistics," "technology innovation," and "human & material resources."[18] Its training facilities include state-of-the-art firing ranges, an artificial lake (for practicing measures against captured sea vessels), a building for rehearsing house-to-house antiterrorism operations, exercise grounds for some twenty K-9 units, and a testing track for trying out self-developed military vehicles. More than forty thousand people receive training there every year. Most of them are state employees from police forces, the military, customs departments, and penitentiary systems. Transport of personnel and material resources to distant theaters of operation is provided by the Blackwater subsidiary Aviation Worldwide Services (AWS), which itself consists of the subsidiaries STI Aviation, Air Quest, and Presidential Airways. Most of their facilities are located in Florida. Along with various attack helicopters, these companies own a Boeing 767, a Super Tucano fighter jet, and even a blimp.

Blackwater employs some twenty-five hundred people spread across the nine countries in which it operates, but it also has a database containing the details of around twenty-four thousand available fighters, so as to be able to choose personnel specifically suited to individual missions. According to Blackwater president Gary Jackson, also a former Navy Seal, a significant portion of these private soldiers come from third world countries and include Chilean specialists who previously worked for the Pinochet regime. The firm runs a recruitment office in the Philippines, and the press there has reported that increasing numbers of Filipinos have been hired by PMCs to fight as mercenaries in wars to benefit the United States. Around 30 percent of the nine hundred specialists Blackwater employed in Iraq in 2007 came from the third world.

Along with Prince and Jackson, the key players in Blackwater include CEO Joseph E. Schmitz (former general inspector at the Pentagon, leading antiterror specialist in the George W. Bush administration, and, from 1999 to 2002, a CIA division director), Cofer Black (for many years the head of the CIA's Middle East division and a close associate of Jordan's King Abdullah II), Robert Richer, and Rick Prado, who was active for the CIA in Latin America. Prado was responsible for Blackwater's special programs, while Black and Richer controlled the firm's own intelligence division. In fall 2007 that division was split off into a separate company, Total Intelligence Solutions (TIS) in order to better acquire contracts. TIS is a joint venture of Prince's Terrorism Research Center, Black's the Black Group, and a company called Technical Defense. The new firm is Blackwater's attempt to gain more of a foothold in the booming intelligence sector. Blackwater does between 80 and 90 percent of its business with government contracts and works for Japan and Azerbaijan as well as the United States. The remainder of its business comes from the private sector. In 2006, for example, the company was hired by both the Department of Homeland Security and private industry and insurance companies to provide 164 civilian personnel and around 50 armed personnel to maintain security in New Orleans after Hurricane Katrina. Blackwater's deployment there was controversial, especially as it was never confirmed that the company had indeed delivered all the police services it had been contracted to provide.

Blackwater is, of course, most widely known for its activities in Iraq—and in particular for its heavy-handed dealings with the Iraqi civilian population. Continual clashes between the company and civilians, with numerous Iraqi casualties, led to a crisis between the Iraqi government, which wanted to expel Blackwater in the fall of 2007, and the U.S. State Department. U.S. secretary of state Condoleezza Rice had to intervene personally to settle the conflict, which was triggered on September 16, 2007, when Blackwater employees killed seventeen Iraqi civilians in Baghdad's Nisour Square. Eyewitnesses said the private soldiers started firing without reason, while the latter said they were responding to an attack. This incident, together with others, led the U.S. House of Representatives to hold a hearing on the activities of Blackwater and other PMCs in Iraq and Afghanistan the following month.

Statistics about the "accidental" incidents in which Blackwater was involved between January 1, 2005, and September 12, 2007, speak volumes. Although bound by both law and contracts to use armed force only to defend diplomatic personnel, Blackwater employees opened fire first in the vast majority of cases. The following State Department figures do not even include the Nisour Square casualties of September 16, 2007.

	2005	2006	1/1–9/12/2007	Total
Incidents of Gunfire Involving Blackwater Employees	77	61	57	195
Incidents in which Blackwater Employees Opened Fire	71	53	39	163
Confirmed Iraqi Casualties	7	3	6	16
Incidents Causing Material Damage	71	52	39	162[19]

Documents reveal that the State Department did not take any sanctions against Blackwater because of these incidents; indeed even those cases involving fatalities were deemed to be consistent with the contract between the two parties. Blackwater itself has attempted to mitigate the fallout from the incidents by doing damage control. In the worst cases, relatives of the victims were offered compensation via the U.S. embassy—although the embassy, fearing a precedent could be set, usually reduced the sums offered so that "death wouldn't become profitable for Iraqis."[20] In addition, Blackwater has often fired employees involved in the "accidents" and removed them from Iraq—around one-seventh of Blackwater personnel in Baghdad and Al Hillah were dismissed in this fashion. The statistics about the reasons for dismissal given by the firm were as follows:

Incidents with weapons	28
Cases of Drug and Alcohol Abuse	25
Improper/Indecent Behavior	16
Insubordination	11
Poor Performance	10
Aggressive/Violent Behavior	10
Rules Violations	8
Failure to Report Incidents/Lying	6
Public Conduct Detrimental to Blackwater	4
Problems with Security Checks/Clearance	3
Posttraumatic Disorder	1
Total	**122**

Blackwater charges the U.S. government around $1,222 per day for every employee, meaning that a single Blackwater worker costs U.S. taxpayers $445,891 per year. By way of comparison, a sergeant in the U.S. military, depending on rank and length of service, costs between $140 and $190 per day, or between $51,100 and $69,350 per year, maintenance costs included.[21] Thus Blackwater services cost Americans as much as nine times more than regular army soldiers, who are subject to military hierarchy, discipline, and rules.

5

Globalization and "New Wars"
A Short History of the Private War Economy

*Man is incapable of recognizing truths where he has been
programmed to the contrary.*
—KONRAD LORENZ

Mercenaries are as old as civilization itself, and a comprehensive
history of them would fill whole libraries. Ever since the rise
of permanent, agrarian settlements some six to eight thousand
years ago, societies have sought to protect their interests by
hiring foreigners to fight for or alongside them against enemies.
Every epoch of history has known mercenaries in some form,
and rulers of every stripe have utilized their services.

In the course of the centuries, there have been major changes
in mercenaries' appearance and equipment as well as in their
character and function. The corresponding general changes
in status can be clearly apprehended from the images of mercenaries in any particular era. At some points in history—for

instance, the present day—mercenaries have been frowned upon. In other eras, however, they have been considered more efficient, brave, reliable, and cost effective than a society's own soldiers. Although today's new mercenaries, the employees of private military companies, are only somewhat comparable to their historical predecessors, examples from history can be useful in sharpening our view of how mercenaries evolved and bettering our understanding of the positive and negative consequences that result from the privatization of internal and external security. What follows is a swift overview of how mercenaries were viewed by various societies from biblical times to the twentieth century.

BIBLICAL BANDITS AND GREEK HOPLITES

Long before Hebrew and Greek historians began recording details about mercenaries, foot soldiers, archers, and wagon drivers were already working for foreign rulers in Euphrates and Tigris valley, in China, and in ancient Egypt. The story of David from the book of Samuel in the Old Testament (circa 1000 BC) is probably the first example of such a record. In the Bible, David, having killed Goliath, falls out with King Saul, flees, and forms a "mercenary troop" with which he travels around the Holy Land, robbing and plundering. His military reputation beyond question, he defects to the enemy, the Philistines, whose king, Achish, uses him and his men as bodyguards. Eventually, of course, David himself seizes power and becomes king of Israel by eradicating the remnants of the Hebrew royal family. David's biography was not so unusual for the time.

Most mercenaries of this period, as well as later ones, were not motivated by a lust for adventure and the promise of vast riches, but by concerns of simple survival. "And every one that was in distress," the book of Samuel reads, "and every one that was in debt, and every one that was discontented, gathered themselves unto [David]; and he became a captain over them: and there were with him about four hundred men."[1] Mercenaries were paid in goods, occasionally silver or gold, but more often a share of the booty seized from the enemy: "And David smote the land, and left neither man nor woman alive, and took away the sheep, and the oxen, and the asses, and the camels, and the apparel, and returned . . ."[2] Conflicts often arose about who should get what share.

It was in ancient Greece that mercenaries began to be compensated regularly in money, rather than acquired goods. The Greek historian Herodotus claimed that money had been invented around 560 BC by a people called the Lydians in what is today Turkey in order to pay for their temple whores. Other accounts say the Lydian king Croesus started minting coins to pay for foreign soldiers. The issue cannot be resolved—both the world's oldest professions can claim to have provided the impetus. What is undeniable is that half a millennium before the start of our current calendar, rulers used money to pay for hired soldiers. This was necessary because mercenaries from various parts of the civilized world had begun to agitate for compensation in "liquid" form. Croesus had no booty to distribute. He engaged his foreign warriors to protect his own riches from attacks by envious neighboring realms.

Around 150 years after Croesus, Xenophon—the writer, historian, and student of Socrates—wrote the *Anabasis*, an epic tale of Greek mercenaries hired by Cyrus the Younger in his attempt to seize the Persian throne from his brother Artaxerxes II. The decisive battle took place at Kunaxa in Babylon, where

Cyrus was killed. Xenophon, himself a mercenary, took command of the ten thousand "men of bronze" and led them though battle, starvation, and cold on a more-than-one-thousand-kilometer-long march to Trapezunt on the Black Sea. The "March of the Ten Thousand" has gone down in the annals of history. Xenophon also took part in other army campaigns, for example the Spartan king Agesilaos's war against Thebes, an ally of Athens. He was subsequently banned from his homeland on having fought on the wrong side of that conflict, and he settled in Olympia.

There are two reasons for the massive presence of Greek mercenaries in all armies of the period and frequently on both sides of a given conflict. One was the specific social structure that had crystallized in ancient Greece; the other was a new battle technique the Greeks had developed. Attica and the Peloponnesus had seen the rise of city-states that had fought hard to conquer their territory and maintained a rough balance of power with one another. Internally, there was an affluent class of farmers, craftspeople, and merchants, powerful enough to fight for their own interests and rich enough to procure costly armaments. At the same time, the populace could not sustain itself on the relatively infertile soil without additional external resources. As a result they offered the capabilities they had learned in their internal wars for temporary hire to rulers outside of ancient Greece.

This new type of mercenary was called a hoplite—the name referring to the Greek word for their characteristic round, iron shields. Hoplites wore helmets and chest- and leg-armor and carried two-meter-long lances. Battles were typically fought in phalanxes of eight to twenty-five soldiers. This sort of "heavy infantry" was not purely defensive but also capable of going

on the attack. The hoplites would sing battle songs, called pae-
ans, while moving forward, gradually picking up speed, until
finally storming the enemy at full sprint in the last one hundred meters. (Many classical Olympic disciplines are based
on the skills required for this sort of warfare.) The moment of
impact must have been dreadful. The first rows of enemies were
gored, trampled, and crushed, and even the vanguard hoplites
themselves were steamrolled by the accelerating phalanxes to
their rear. There was little defense against the lance-carrying,
armored attackers, and it was not uncommon for an army being
confronted for the first time with the massive power of the hoplites to simply turn and run.

Greek infantrymen soon became the most sought-after mercenaries between India and Carthage, the Nubian desert and
Italy. They were deluged by large-scale offers from Persia and
Egypt—insofar as they were needed in their home countries,
hoplites could even afford to turn down lucrative missions.
They became a kind of brand name, to the extent that minor
rulers often had their own troops dress up as hoplites in an
effort to convince their enemies that they were facing the origi-
nals on the battlefield.

This innovation in warfare technique was made possible
by ancient Greece's relative overpopulation, which created a
surplus of battle-ready soldiers, and it revolutionized the way
armed conflicts were conducted.

ROME'S POPULAR ARMY VERSUS CARTHAGE'S MERCENARY FORCES

A new development commenced with Rome, whose empire was
to become the largest in the world for half a millennium. The
city on the Tiber achieved greatness thanks to a frugality that
bordered on miserliness, a pronounced sense of pragmatism,

efficiency in agriculture, and a popular army drawn from its own citizens. In contrast to the Greeks several centuries before, the Romans succeeded in enlisting their neighbors as allies, which allowed them to expand their sphere of influence gradually and protect their prosperous state from attack. It was thanks to these characteristic strengths and their popular army that Romans were able to defeat a bold and intelligent general like Hannibal, with his enormous mercenary forces, in the Punic Wars, and establish themselves as the leading power in the Mediterranean.[3]

But as Rome rapidly progressed from a state to an empire, the original idea and organization of Roman society could not keep step. The republic disintegrated, and the popular army became one of career soldiers and later had to rely heavily on foreign legionnaires. Rome's history can be seen as a five-hundred-year transition from relative democracy to autocracy and dictatorship. The word *soldier* comes from the Latin *soldare* meaning "to pay," and as long as the provinces produced sufficient riches, and enough booty was procured in foreign military campaigns, professional soldiers and mercenaries could be kept content enough to secure their loyalty. The early years under the rule of the Caesars were prosperous. At the same time, the middle classes that had borne the republic were dwindling, the lower classes swelled, and the upper classes were becoming more excessive in their economic demands. There was a Roman saying: "The roof of a temple cannot rest on its foundation"—there can be no solid structure without supporting pillars. With the demise of the productive middle classes and the disappearance of the taxes they paid, which were crucial to Rome's fiscal household, the supporting pillars of the empire became ever fewer. In the year 476 AD, Germanic mercenaries elected Odoaker to be the new king of Italy, and the Western Roman Empire ceased to exist.

MERCENARY BANDS IN THE MIDDLE AGES

The new imperial power came not from Germania, but from the eastern border regions of the old Roman Empire. Starting from the Arabian Peninsula, the new dominant cultures spread across the entire non-Byzantine Mediterranean. With a new form of monotheism, which had been adapted from nomadic tribal culture and which was, in some predominantly social areas, more highly developed than Judaism and Christianity, the Arab tribes at the core of the ruling warrior classes presented a novel and increasingly popular religious ideology: Islam. Yet as early as the seventh century, only a few decades after the death of Muhammad, the Arabs were forced to call in foreigners, including mercenaries, to secure their area of influence.

The external security of the Arab Empire was almost completely dependent on mercenary bands, recruited primarily from the disintegrating nomadic tribes of central Asia, and their loyalty could only be won with generous financial concessions and power-sharing agreements. Increasing social unrest, repeatedly leading to upheavals, also made it necessary to employ mercenaries to keep internal order. Equipped with a growing amount of military power and political influence, the soldiers-for-hire occasionally turned upon the ruling elites—as was the case with the Seljuks in Iran and Iraq and the Mamluks in Egypt and Syria. Ultimately, the Osmanlis—a band of mercenaries that united a colorful assortment of tribes from the Black Sea, the Caucasus, and the Asian steppe country—dealt a simultaneous fatal blow to the Arab and Byzantine Empires and created the new Ottoman Empire.

In terms of military security after the fall of the Western Roman Empire, the picture in Western Europe was much the same as it was in the East. Charlemagne founded the Holy Roman Empire of the German Nation with the support of mercenaries, who helped drive the Arabs from France, participated in the Crusades, supported Frederick Barbarossa in his battles against rebels, pursued heretics for the pope, and were instrumental in the German Knights of Order conquering Prussia and the Baltic region. The main reason for the dependency of kings, emperors, popes, princes, and knights on mercenaries throughout the Middle Ages was the extreme inefficiency of the feudal military system. First, a relatively limited number of soldiers, mostly conscripted peasants, were available for short intervals only. Second, they were hardly trained and completely unable to use specialized equipment like lances, crossbows, and bows and arrows. Third, rulers had to recruit their personnel from the same lieges and vassals against whom their military actions for preserving internal and external order were often directed. Bands of mercenaries were thus the more reliable instrument for successfully waging war.

COMPANIES, "FREE LANCES," AND CONDOTTIERI

Mercenaries gained significance during the twelfth century as vagabond soldiers, with no fixed address or profession, gradually organized into "free companies"—the word *company* being derived via French from the Latin *com panis* or "with bread." These organizations were conceived to locate employment for all of their members, secure a common livelihood and offer mutual protection and support. In search of new jobs, company members would travel around with their retinues, including their wives and children, through various European countries. They were usually quartered at the cost of the populace of the cities and towns while they offered their services as "free lances" to sufficiently solvent nobles. The meistersinger Michael Beheim from Württemberg described them in the following (originally rhyming) couplets: "For whomever paid the most / they were willing to serve. / Had our Lord in Heaven / waged war with the devil, / and the devil had offered them more, / they would have gone over to him."[4]

The early Renaissance of the fourteenth century saw a transition in the military realm and an increased need for better security provisions. The double change in supply and demand was especially apparent in the resurgent cities of Italy. Venice, Florence, Genoa, and Milan had developed enormously productive middle classes: handicraft, trade, farming, banking, and health services became central pillars of urban society. The ruling classes could avail themselves of the resulting wealth to consolidate and expand their power—but only if they could guarantee secure conditions for private economic activities. The inefficient security system of knights protecting the nobility was beginning to fall apart and even becoming something of a joke, as Cervantes showed to great comic effect in *Don Quixote*, and enterprising guilds pressured the nobility to hire professional military associations. The guilds thought it was only fair that the upper classes should be responsible for modernizing the area of security, upon which their own existence depended. It was also in the interest of the economy to avoid a total military mobilization of society and protect tradesmen from the unprofitable burdens of defense and war. In their eyes, the perfect solution to their demands was the professional alternative provided by the condottieri—literally, "contractors."

Mercenaries had been quick to adapt to the need for new security services in Renaissance Italy. Members of the minor nobility, who were without jobs and fell through the holes in the feudal network of privileges, joined up with free companies, recasting them as private fighting units under their own command. The basis for their cooperation was no longer the prospect of booty, but a fixed salary guaranteed by contract or *condotta*. These contracts specified both wages and the services expected to be rendered. Over the course of time, provisions were even laid out in writing for sanctions in case of violation or breakage of contract. (The word *condottieri* originally referred to the negotiators of these contracts.) Soon agreements were so complicated that specialists were needed to draw them up. This, together with the growing need for trade and sales contracts, created a new profession—lawyers. The earliest condottieri included the Germans Konrad von Landau and Werner von Urslingen (alias Duke Guarnieri); the Englishman John Hawkwood, who under the name Giovanni Acuto led Florence to military victories over Milan, Pisa, and Bologna and whose portrait can still be admired today in the city's main cathedral; and the Italians Erasmo da Narni, Jacopone da Todi, Braccio da Montone, and Federico da Montefeltro, who earned a fortune, was named a duke, and became a world-famous patron of the arts. Another Italian mercenary, Muzio Attendolo, acquired so much influence in the cities where he plied his trade that his son Francesco eventually became the most powerful man in Milan.

SWISS GUARDS AND GERMAN LANSQUENETS

The condottieri soon faced competition from the North—first the Swiss guards and then German lansquenets. For the small Alpine nation, the handicraft of war proved a very popular export, and in most cantons the only rule limiting their activities was that

Swiss were not allowed to fight against other Swiss. If Swiss mercenaries looked set to square off, the one with the older contract was given precedence, while the other had to dissolve his contract with his employer, leave the field of battle, and forfeit his pay. The Swiss guards were a very tightly knit and efficient military organization. Its individual groups consisted of young men all from the same village or valley, and they developed a heavy-infantry technique with lances that greatly resembled that of the Greek phalanx. They were both cheap to employ and capable of winning battles against cavalry. Their victories on European battlefields turned them into something of a brand name, akin to Swiss watches. A wide range of kings and princes used their services, and in 1506 Pope Julius II stocked up his own troops with Swiss guards—a tradition that continues today.

Initially the lansquenets were an inferior copy of the guards and were often defeated by them in combat. It was only with the Battle of Bicocca in 1522 that the lansquenets bested their role model, having expanded their capabilities to include special units for specific battle situations, procured new types of weaponry, and begun using artillery. In the years that followed they could be found everywhere in Europe—from the high north to the Bosporus and Tagus in the south.

With the discoveries of America and the ocean route to India and Asia, the radius of action for German mercenaries gradually became global. In his conquest of Mexico, Hernán Cortés was accompanied by a German armor-maker named Johann as well as four other German soldiers. Germans Jost Hammer and Barthel Blümlein followed Francisco Pizarro as he destroyed the Inca civilization. A man named Kasimir Nürnberger led a troop of mercenaries in Venezuela. Several units of lansquenets were involved in the search for the legendary city of El Dorado.

They were everywhere in the Caribbean islands, and the lansquenet Ulrich Schmidel, the son of a well-to-do family from the German town of Straubing, marched to the Río de la Plata and helped found, together with other mercenaries, the city of Buenos Aires. Other lansquenets went to Amsterdam and Lisbon or sought adventure in eastern India.

THE ASCENDANCY OF THE NATIONAL STANDING ARMY

The coalescence of modern cities and the money that flowed from the conquered regions of the Americas and Asia made it economically desirable and possible to create large armies, paid and directed by a sovereign. Using a special tax on merchants in 1445, King Charles VII of France was the first to achieve this. Over the years, the freelance mercenary associations were gradually absorbed into standing armies. German lansquenets, Swiss guards, Italian cavalry, English infantrymen, and Spanish artillery were employed by various countries for fixed wages plus room and board. The national forces of countries like England, Sweden, and France became gigantic foreign legions. Yet only in the Habsburg Empire did freelance mercenaries persist into the seventeenth century. One of the last such fighters was Albrecht von Wallenstein, who established the largest force ever seen up to that point in Bohemia, including both fighting units and weapons production. Thanks to lucrative contracts from Emperor Ferdinand II, he eventually became the richest man in Europe. Freelance enterprises in the area of military services completely ended after the Thirty Years' War, from which Wallstein, before being murdered, had also greatly profited. The Treaty of Westphalia in 1648 officially sanctioned the state's monopoly on the legitimate use of force. From that point on, and as is still the case today, private individuals were officially forbidden from offering military services or weapons to foreign countries without express permission of the state.

THE EAST INDIA COMPANY

One of the few exceptions to that rule developed in the colonies in America, Africa, Asia, and Oceania. The colonial powers tried to concentrate military might in their own hands, but the influence of colonial merchants was sufficient to protect their own interests, when the need arose, with armed force. The importation of cheap labor in the form of slaves also contributed to the practical undermining of the state's de jure monopoly on the legitimate use of force.

The large Indian trading societies from Holland and England represent a particular case study. The English East India Company was founded in 1599 and survived until 1857, while the Dutch VOC (East India Company) was formed as the world's first joint-stock company in 1602 and closed its doors, shortly before declaring bankruptcy, in 1799. For a long time, such enterprises were the largest customers for mercenaries. In 1780, for instance, the private army of the English trading company was significantly larger than the troops in service of the Queen throughout the British Empire.

Traces of Holland's VOC can still be found all over the Netherlands, and it owed its status as the largest and strongest trade and military power of its age both to its monopoly on the spice trade and to its brutal campaigns of repression. One of the company's most successful chairmen, Jan Pieterszoon Coen, who founded the colony of Batavia (today's Jakarta) on Java, subjugated almost all of the Southeast Asian islands to VOC domination and extended the firm's influence as far north as Japan. Trading centers were protected by forts and military bases. If there were uprisings, a mobile military force could be deployed at all times and all locations. The majority of the forces consisted of German mercenaries, who signed on for five-year tours of duty in Amsterdam and were then brought by merchant vessels sailing from Texel to what they believed would be the fairy-tale lands of Southeast Asia.

On the Molucca islands, Coen set up the first monopoly on nutmeg, which was greatly coveted in Europe, after breaking the resistance of local rulers. Coen had all males over the age of fifteen killed and impaled their severed heads on poles as a warning to potential rebels. Likewise, on the Banda Sea islands, the VOC reduced the native population by 95 percent within the space of fifteen years. Labor—chiefly in the form of slaves—was brought in to replace the dwindling supply of local workers. The VOC confiscated land, built plantations, and forbade natives throughout their area of control from planting and harvesting spice plants. Violations were punished by torture and death. By 1670, thanks to such brutality, the VOC had become the world's richest business enterprise. The firm paid shareholders a dividend of 41 percent. It had fifty thousand employees and an equal number of mercenaries, and two hundred armed ships sailed under its flag. The economic secret behind the VOC's success was simple: Demand at home was matched with a supply that was militarily protected and controlled by force. The company used its troops to secure its thirty branch offices and its personnel, wares, and plantations in the territories it occupied and to enforce its repressive policies against the colonized native populations.

But military expenditures rose as resistance by natives against the unscrupulous and extremely bloody regime increased. The results were sinking dividends—by the mid-eighteenth century, the company was only paying out around 12 percent. As security costs began to eat up 70 percent of revenues, the end was nigh. Moreover, the French broke the VOC's monopoly on cloves by importing stolen plants from east Asia to their plantations on Zanzibar and the Seychelles. The VOC declared bankruptcy in 1799, but continuity was ensured since the Dutch state assumed responsibility for the East Indian trading company.[4]

Yet the historical upshot is that with the VOC and the English East India Company, private capital equipped with enormous military power controlled war and peace far away from their home countries for around two hundred years. The companies ruled over the lives and deaths of individuals, issuing laws and regulations. Within their areas of influence, the trading companies were an absolute authority, to which all other powers, even the state, were subordinated.

THE FRENCH REVOLUTION AND THE DECLINE OF THE MERCENARIES

The Treaty of Westphalia brought an end to the mercenary bands in Europe, but not to mercenaries themselves. With its monopoly on the legitimate use of armed force, the state could always decide whether it wanted mercenaries or its own subjects in its armies. The needs of standing armies for increased numbers of soldiers meant a boom for mercenaries. Like all the other large European powers, the Prussian kings regularly augmented their forces with legionnaires, although Frederick the Great was of the opinion that mercenaries did not possess courage, communal spirit, confidence, willingness for sacrifice, or loyalty. Between the mid-seventeenth and late eighteenth centuries, war became one of the biggest industries on the continent. It was controlled by the state, which built up military facilities and profited from them. Some countries bought in mercenaries, while other smaller ones—for example the German state of Hesse—made a flourishing business renting out its citizens. England was one of the largest consumers, employing thirty thousand Hessian mercenaries in an attempt to suppress the American Revolutionaries in 1776. The tiny principality of Schaumburg-Lippe, which suffered from a shortage of saleable personnel, set up a respected international military academy, where officers-in-waiting from a variety of nations could learn their handicraft from acknowledged experts.

Absolutist states greatly profited from military industries and from war. But while their large standing armies were more or less capable of guaranteeing external security, internal order in some of these states was another matter. The middle and to some extent the lower classes found that the upper echelons consumed too much of their countries' wealth in maintaining profitable conditions for their own activities and privileges, tying up desperately needed capital to no good purpose. Together with the hardly idyllic living conditions of the lower classes, the permanent uncertainty as to whether contracts and agreements, which could be rescinded at any time from above, would be kept, stoked dissatisfaction and exacerbated conflicts.

The French Revolution of 1789 ushered in the end not only of the age of absolutism but also of the mercenary. On February 20, 1790, the Constitutional Assembly decided to ban the employment of mercenaries on French soil. That may not have prevented Napoleon from employing Tartars and Mamluks in his Imperial Guard and using massive battalions of mercenaries in his campaign across Europe—at the Battle of Waterloo, some three hundred fifty thousand mercenaries fought under Napoleon, compared with forty thousand under Wellington. But Napoleon was to prove an exception. Within a few decades, the other major

European nations followed France's example, introducing the universal draft and converting their national forces into popular armies. Popular armies were cheaper, and various wars of liberation had shown that citizen-soldiers were more prepared to sacrifice their lives than mercenaries on mediocre wages. Mercenaries, once held in high regard, began to be considered vagabonds of dubious character. Most countries also forbade their citizens from being employed by and fighting for foreign nations. Numerous national laws and international conventions were passed restricting mercenary activities. Until the late twentieth century, mercenaries would play only a marginal role in military history.

International condemnation forced those who still did ply the trade to distant regions. In the Wilhelmine Empire in Germany, for instance, German legionnaires fought in China, for and against the Turks, and in South Africa. After World War I, some found themselves unwillingly caught between the White and Red Fronts in Russia. Some were even engaged as pirates in the Yellow Sea. After World War II, several hundred veterans of the Waffen-SS joined the foreign legion and fought in Indochina. Remnants of the Afrika Korps stayed in Arab countries, serving as weapons makers and military advisors. Others hired themselves out in the United States and dealt in arms under the protection of the CIA. Like many of his former comrades, the former head of the Gestapo in Lyon, Klaus Barbie, went to South America, where he organized groups of European neofascists into death squads and helped coordinate military coups d'etat. Others, like Siegfried Müller (an Iron Cross recipient nicknamed "Congo Müller") and the right-wing terrorist Horst Klenz ("The Mecernary Boss of Pretoria"), settled in sub-Saharan Africa. In the 1990s, hundreds of such men fought in the wars in ex-Yugoslavia.

This short historical summary has been necessarily fragmentary, but it does illustrate that there has been no straight, linear development—either in a quantitative or qualitative sense—in private military service providers from their inception to the present day. This is especially true in terms of mercenaries' relationship to the "state war economy." External security or military might did not always depend on whether a country deployed citizen-soldiers or mercenaries. What was more important was the strength of the authority that deployed and controlled military personnel. There were "strong states" with mercenary armies and "weak states" with popular ones, and vice versa. What we can say, however, is that mercenaries, especially when they banded together in organized units or companies, required greater control than militaries formed from a country's own citizenry. The supervisory authority was much more extensive and therefore expensive. And when supervision—whether in the form of a prince with a noble entourage or a state institution—was lax, mercenary leaders often usurped power, and society descended into military dictatorship. What is also characteristic is the rise in the supply of mercenaries, usually accompanied by a certain increase in demand, at times when living conditions sink under a certain level (for example in times of famine), or conversely when there are prospects for immense wealth (such as the search for El Dorado).

The historical consequences that followed from recruiting mercenaries depended on how systems for external and internal security were established, constructed, and conducted. The questions were: Did they work within the constraints and on behalf of the given form of society? Did they stand in reasonable relation to the wealth being produced? That is, were they neither too expensive nor too minimal to deter the desire of neighboring states for easy bounty? Were they effective or, as in the case of the feudal military system, inefficient? Were they adequately monitored and controlled, or did they take on a logic of their own and become a state with a state? With an eye toward history, there is no one conclusion to be drawn about the effects of mercenaries on society in general—other than that the presence of mercenaries always represents a potentially extraordinary danger to social well-being.

6

The End of the Cold War
Different Conditions for Military Services

The new world order: peace in the West, war everywhere else.
—UNKNOWN

In the post–World War II era, mercenaries mostly fought as individuals or in small groups, seeking adventure and fortune in former colonies, especially in Africa. But with the end of the cold war, they began to come together in privately run, civilian business enterprises. After two hundred years of stigmatization and marginalization, mercenaries experienced a sudden renaissance.

Leaving aside a handful of military-supply companies in the United States, South Africans and Englishmen were the first to offer private military services. Both—the South Africans on their own continent and the English on the Arabian Peninsula and in Asia—were experienced soldiers who had become unemployed with the end of apartheid and the conflict between East and West. Some of them foresaw the security vacuum that would open up with the withdrawal of Communist troops from their former spheres of influence. And they were convinced that this hole could be profitably exploited.

Men like South Africans Eeben Barlow and Nick van den Bergh and Britons Tony Buckingham and Simon Mann, the founders and owners of Executive Outcomes, decided to treat the provision of military services as a serious business, covered by civilian law and requiring the requisite legal permits. Tim Spicer got involved at a somewhat later point on the encouragement of Mann, his friend and comrade in arms. He, together with a London marketing expert, created the phrase "private military company" to describe this new sort of enterprise. It soon became a watchword for the industry, creating a distinction between PMCs and both the traditional image of the mercenary and old-style security firms, whose main tasks were to guard property and protect money transports.

Economic and political developments played into the hands of these new entrepreneurs. Demand was huge, contracts came pouring in, and their initial successes were impressive. The military service sectors expanded with breathtaking speed. Assisted by clever managers and market experts, the companies soon went on the stock exchange. Investors loved the stocks of these fast-growing companies, whose dividends significantly exceeded these Dow Jones or FTSE average.

The era in which mercenaries or other armed-conflict specialists could only operate in secrecy was over. Henceforth, PMCs concluded regular contracts with states, governments, aid and peace organizations, and even with the UN. What once had been troops of soldiers of fortune became—at least externally—serious, hard-calculating economic enterprises. In little more than a decade, unnoticed by the majority of the public, hundreds of such firms were established.

The conclusions to be drawn about this development depend on one's perspective. Political observers in the third world, whose countries are directly subject to the activities of PMCs, naturally view them differently from those in industrialized countries, who see military privatization as a cost-cutting instrument, freeing up resources in domestic budgets for education and social programs, or as a means of increasing their own national armed forces' capabilities. In general, one can make out several tightly interwoven constellations of factors and specify the conditions that have encouraged the rise of PMCs. Four conditions made the rise of the PMCs possible. The first was the end of the cold war; the second, the globalization of the world economy; the third was the new national energy policy among the United States and its allies as of 2001; and the fourth, the technological-electronic revolution. All four of these conditions were factors in the worldwide reduction in national defense budgets; the expansion of national security policies beyond mere national defense; the sudden increase in international, national, and local areas of conflict; and the increasing reluctance, especially among industrialized nations, to take part in peacekeeping missions.

THE END OF THE COLD WAR AND GLOBALIZATION

At the end of the cold war, the United States was the world's one remaining superpower, creating an asymmetry in global politics. Whereas previously the interests of the world's nations were oriented around one of two poles, after 1989 certain centrifugal forces began to take hold and accelerate. The result was a fragmentation of spheres of interests. Former Warsaw Pact countries and those in the third world that had counted on support and assistance from the Soviet Union had to seek new partners and alliances.

The sudden "absence of the enemy" and the feeling among many populaces of being freed from a looming menace put intense pressure on governments to reduce military expenditures. Almost every country—not just those of the former Warsaw Pact and NATO—drastically cut its defense budget. As a result, national standing armies shrank drastically, together with their weapons arsenals, and military facilities and bases took on smaller dimensions. Military reductions put some seven million soldiers worldwide out of jobs, and they began looking for work in swarms beyond their national borders. The jobless included not just common soldiers. Military redundancies also affected pilots and mechanics, members of special units, and communications and espionage experts. The surplus of personnel meant that nongovernmental practitioners of violence—from warlords (as in Sudan), organized criminal networks (including the various mafias in the former Soviet Union), and terrorist groups (most prominently Al-Qaeda)—were able to afford specialized military services and procure them on open global markets. Almost at the same time that armies in the East and West were reducing troop strengths, they also thinned out their arsenals. Surplus weapons that could not be sold to allied countries were auctioned off to the highest bidder on the free market. For example, almost all of the equipment formerly owned by the National People's Army of Communist East Germany was put up for sale, as were Russian artillery, machine guns from China and Belgium, French tanks, and American helicopter gunships.

Even complete weapons systems were on offer. The global markets of the 1990s were flooded with weapons.

In addition, the industrialized nations of the West began to develop new security policies anchored in national as well as international institutions like NATO, the European Union (EU), and the UN. The focus was on an expansion of the idea of national security based on a different understanding of state sovereignty, humanitarian and ecological responsibility, and more activist strategies of intervention. The expanded catalogue of security-related tasks could be best covered, in times of troop-size reduction, by transferring some of the tasks previously carried out by national armies and other state security organs to private service providers. These new tasks, together with older ones such as national defense and border security, would be dealt with by restructuring and reorganizing national armies and security organs.

The fall of the Iron Curtain created a global world with ever more permeable borders, and globalization became the hot-button topic of the 1990s. For most nations, the unleashing of the subjugating force of the world market and the partial disempowerment of the nation-state it entailed was "a compulsory process from which they could not withdraw."[1] The opening of markets, the free flow of commodities, and borderless financial transactions—the liberalization and deregulation of all areas of economic life—did not just bring advantages. It also unleashed merciless competition in which the weaker participants perished. Those negatively affected lost their jobs and were reduced to paupers, and many populaces were driven to the brink of nonexistence. The third world was hit especially hard.

The end of the bipolar system meant the abrupt end of the protection, financial assistance, and transfer of resources provided by the military blocs. This hurt not only people in "weak states" but also Western firms. Especially vulnerable were those sectors that were dependent on raw materials or half-finished products outside their own national borders. Their forests, mines, and production facilities were often located in conflict-ridden third world countries. Increasing poverty and violence and reduced protection rapidly led to higher security risks. Consequently, such businesses were among the first to replace the protection previously afforded by the state with the services provided by PMCs.

NEW CONFLICTS IN THE THIRD WORLD

The new uncertainty occasioned by the disappearance of the security umbrella provided by the superpowers and the globalization of the world economy produced—primarily in Africa, but also in Asia and Latin America—internal conflicts over the distribution of wealth as well as ethnic and religious disputes. Neither the East nor the West had previously attached much importance to the development of democratic states with a solid legal foundation in their respective spheres of influence. The "proper attitude"—loyalty to their own power bloc—had been what was important. Left to their own devices in terms of security and with less money in their state budgets, many third world countries slid gradually toward catastrophe.

In addition, first and second world nations rarely summoned up the political will to intervene and alleviate conflicts with peacekeeping missions or other peace-building methods.[2] Even in the context of the United States' unsuccessful mission "Restore Hope" in Sudan in 1994, President Clinton declared that Washington would only support UN peace initiatives if they were crucial to international security or in the U.S. national interest. South African military expert Phillip van Niekerk has said in an interview with the Inter Press Service: "During the 1990s Western governments increasingly shied away from sending national troops into conflicts in the Third World that were not popular at home. The common refrain was that these countries were not worth shedding the blood of Americans, Britons, or Frenchmen. In order to get the job done, governments increasingly relied on contractors to perform tasks that national armies would have performed in earlier decades."[3] These policies were encouraged by lack of enthusiasm for foreign missions among voters in wealthy nations, dwindling material and personnel resources at the United Nations, and differences of opinion among the world's larger powers about new spheres of influence.[4]

The vacuum of inadequate international and national security for large populations in the third world was filled by self-appointed guarantors of social order—rebel organizations, insurgent groups, and even terrorist networks. Their influence was the greatest in areas that had been the hardest hit, economically and socially, by the effects of globalization. The results were internal social conflicts, which with increasing frequency escalated into armed battles and even bloodbaths. In many cases a vicious cycle developed: As the civilian population was drafted into military conflicts and financial resources tied up by arms purchases, economic production was hindered, and the state of war promoted. War then added further misery with the destruction of land and property, and the killing and wounding of civilians. Poverty and declining standards of living in turn further stoked armed conflicts. Many countries experienced the rise of a veritable war economy, in which local troop leaders expanded their activities into a lucrative business. Sources of income were various: the illegal cultivation and sale of drugs; robbery, plunder, and blackmail; the collecting of protection money from transports of international aid to conflict regions; kidnappings of people who worked for humanitarian organizations and transnational companies; and international people trafficking. The revenues were spent on acquiring weapons and military equipment of all sorts.

Globalization made it possible for states and other entities to encourage and finance conflicts with unprecedented ease. Among those who adopted the slogan "think globally, act locally" were terrorist groups—which maintained lobbying groups, support committees, and external reservoirs of helpers and fighters throughout the world—as well as interest groups of every economic and political slant imaginable. The new international financial system, working round the clock around the entire globe, enabled money to be collected in one country, deposited in another, and spent in a third—for example, to buy weapons in a fourth and fifth country, have them transported to a sixth, and then used in the original conflict region itself. This sort of structure with its countless far-reaching strands in different directions is why we refer today to "network warfare."[5]

THE NEW NATIONAL ENERGY POLICY

One of the most important factors behind the rapid rise of PMCs was the new National Energy Policy (NEP) adopted in the United States and other Western countries. In January 2001, the National Energy Policy Development Group under U.S. vice president Dick Cheney drew up a complex prognosis of the global developments in the energy sector expected from that time to 2020–2025—and their consequences for the United States and its allies. With little amendment, the recommendations of this working paper were adopted as the National Energy Policy announced by George W. Bush on May

17, 2001.[6] The paper predicted that, due to increasing needs for energy, in particular oil, demand would exceed supply for the first time in history—even, the paper contended, if new oil and natural gas resources were discovered. The "peak point of oil," the document maintained, would likely come in 2008,[7] leading to a worldwide battle for petroleum since China and India, with their rapidly expanding economies, would drive competition on the market. The 170-page document assumed that both absolute and relative energy production in the United States would decline, so that the country would soon have to import more than 50 percent of its energy needs. Those demands could not be covered by primary suppliers in the United States' own hemisphere: Canada, Mexico, Venezuela, and Colombia. That made Caspian and African oil reserves, as well as those on the Arabian Peninsula, strategically more important than ever. Another assumption was that the regions of production, supply, and resources would generally be located in "weak states" and insecure areas.

The most critical points in the supply lines, according to the 2001 report, were Afghanistan and Iraq. Afghanistan was crucial to the transport of eastern Caspian oil to the Indian Ocean, and Iraq was important because it could use its enormous oil reserves to pressure the West and its military might to destabilize Saudi Arabia. The horror scenario for the United States and many of its allies in 2001 was that Iraq under Saddam Hussein would rise to become a hegemonic power in the Arab world.

The NEP drew a direct link between the security of oil fields, supply lines, and future energy resources and the national security of the United States. Supply shortages in energy would have drastic consequences for the U.S. economy and the standard of living enjoyed by all Americans. This being the case, the United

States had to be prepared in an emergency to secure its energy by military means.[8]

In early summer 2001, the Bush administration was already taking steps to turn the security recommendations contained within its National Energy Policy into reality. U.S. military presence in oil-producing regions was increased, and training of national armies in the countries concerned was stepped up. PMCs took over the lion's share of these activities. Even at the time, NEP critics prophesied that the U.S. Army would gradually be transformed into little more than an oil-protection service. Such criticism increased, if in a different sense, with the Afghanistan War and the Iraq War. Intentionally or not, the oil-security aspect of the NEP was melded into the "global war on terror." Even without the latter, the NEP would have filled the coffers of private military companies, but the war on terror, as previously mentioned, has been called a full-employment program for PMCs.

In the years since 2001, the United States has succeeded in getting most allied nations and organizations to make oil security a primary goal. Even Germany and France have acceded. Although the German and French governments set different priorities and refused to participate directly in the Iraq War, the German Navy, for instance, still helps secure energy-supply routes around the Horn of Africa as part of "Operation Enduring Freedom." Likewise, in NATO's overall strategic concept, the disruption of supplies of essential resources is treated as a threat to the security of the alliance. At least since the beginning of Operation Enduring Freedom, if not earlier, concerns about oil and energy security have been seen as clear justification for military action.

At an internal meeting in Prague in October 2005, NATO

debated expanding this strategy. The Supreme Allied Commander Europe James Jones insisted that with the end of the cold war, the alliance had to be transformed from a purely military force in order to keep up with new tasks such as peacekeeping as well as preventive and humanitarian operations. Future security challenges, Jones argued, could only be met with assistance from the private sector. Among these tasks, Jones emphasized three in particular: the securing of oil and gas pipelines from Russia to Western Europe against terrorist attack; the securing of ports and shipping traffic within member states of the alliance; and the security of the oil-rich Gulf of Guinea off Africa's western coast. There, Jones noted, piracy, theft, political unrest, and tensions between Islam and Christianity combined to present "a serious security problem."[9] Views like these were, of course, music to the ears of private military service providers.

THE TECHNOLOGY AND ELECTRONIC REVOLUTION

Another very different type of phenomenon that hastened the rise of private military companies was the transformation of the leadership envisioned under rubrics like Revolution in Military Affairs and Network-Centric Warfare.[10] At the core of these ideas were radical modifications in weapons technology and the techniques of waging war brought about by the employment of electronics and information technologies. The arms industry had pushed these developments to the point where no weapons other than light arms could be used without electronic systems and IT networks.

The use, operation, and maintenance of these new weapons systems, including the computer-networked "precision weapons systems" that cause a minimum of collateral damage, require highly specialized personnel. But as yet, U.S. armed forces have never had sufficient numbers of technicians, engineers, and computer experts at their disposal. Earlier, the U.S. Army trained soldiers for those tasks, but it soon gave up such training, citing reasons of cost. Instead, the Pentagon began buying in operating specialists, together with weapons systems, from arms companies. Firms like Northrop Grumman and Lockheed Martin reorganized the military service sector, acquiring PMCs like Vinnel and MPRI and distributing operating personnel among their new subsidiaries.

Two phrases—"information warfare" and "command and control warfare"—characterize the technological changes in the waging of war. Information warfare refers to the offensive and defensive use of information and information systems in order to eavesdrop on, exploit, divert, disable, or destroy an enemy's computer-based networks, electronic data processing systems, and informational basis. Control warfare is about coordinating electronic, physical, psychological, and espionage resources to influence, mislead, and weaken an enemy's control organs and mechanisms so that command centers can be paralyzed and then physically destroyed. MPRI, for example, successfully used these tactics in Operation Storm in Croatia, discussed in a preceding chapter, and control warfare was used far more extensively in the Afghanistan and Iraq War. The speed with which enemy forces were neutralized in both those conflicts was not necessarily solely due to this new idea of waging war, but it was only possible, in both cases, with the massive deployment of PMCs and private-sector specialists. High-tech weapons like Predator drones, unmanned Global Hawks, as well as the B-2 Spirit stealth bomber and the U.S. Navy's Aegis Ballistic Missile Defense System, were operated and maintained by employees of private companies.[11] The U.S. Army's information systems were likewise controlled largely by people outside the armed services.

As U.S. military expert Thomas Adams has pointed out, the U.S. Army also seems to have decided to deploy contracted personnel directly in battle. It can be assumed that in the future, information warfare will be increasingly dominated by new mercenaries.[12] The dependence of armies on high-tech weaponry means they are no longer operational without the assistance of private-sector personnel. Indeed, sometimes, multiple outside contractors are needed to make a military unit ready for battle. The result is a steep rise in the number of private-sector employees—technicians, programmers, systems analysts, and simulation specialists—on the virtual "battlefield." These individuals become integral parts of military operations themselves. The thousands of "civilians" working at operation headquarters to make "digitalized warfare" a reality are de facto soldiers. International law may still consider them noncombatants and civilians. But the enemy sees them for what they are—parts of the war machine. The employment of private soldiers has opened up a dangerous gray area, populated by people without a clear legal status.

RADICAL CHANGES IN INTELLIGENCE SERVICES

Parallel to the changes in the military-industrial complex, a similar development has occurred in intelligence, information-gathering, and espionage agencies. Indeed, the electronic revolution has made itself even more strongly felt in this ultra-sensitive area. On the one hand, the dominance of computers in the means of and techniques for collecting information has effected a radical change in the way intelligence service providers go about their jobs. On the other hand, espionage agencies have become ever more dependent on the technologies and know-how of private industry. The result has been a merging of state and private entities that is perhaps even more fundamental than in the strictly military sector.

A number of factors have contributed to this change. The increasing flood of information, due especially to the expansion of the Internet, has primarily concerned the civilian sector, including the realms of economics and the media. The rationalization of institutions like banks, insurance companies, and energy concerns using data-processing systems has increased the dependency on information technologies. Developments have been extremely rapid both in hardware, with ever-faster generations of computers, and software, with increasingly intelligent programs for every sort of task imaginable. As a result a cyberspace intelligentsia has arisen in the civilian private sector and assumed a nearly unassailable position of power. The computer specialists in organizations like the police, the military, and intelligence services were no match for their civilian peers. This fact largely escaped the notice of the general public—people's eyebrows were only raised when there were media reports about hackers who succeeded in breaching the U.S. president's security systems or releasing computer viruses that paralyzed electrical plants, transport connections, or the like. State security organs tried to close the holes in the system by improving their equipment and better training their employees, but the results were mixed. The most cost-efficient and elegant solution was to buy in or temporarily hire outside experts, enlisting them for security agencies' own work. The need for private help was bolstered by the fact that private individuals and groups posing a threat to public security—such as organized criminals or terrorists—enjoyed unlimited access to high-tech equipment and specialists, while state security organs lagged behind in technological development. To close these holes as quickly as possible, access to state security structures was opened up to the computer industry, private systems analysts and technicians, programming experts, and digital troubleshooters.[13]

In the course of the past few decades, activities like data procurement, information encoding and decoding, and information analysis have become possible only with the most up-to-date information technologies. Data collection usually proceeds in three sectors: human (HUMINT), signals (SIGINT),[14] and imagery intelligence (IMINT). The first sector works with informers from diplomatic, economic, or media circles as well as with spies and agents. The second gets its material by intercepting, recording, and listening in on data sent via electromagnetic signals—for instance, by telephone, radio, the Internet, laser, radar, or satellite. The third sector collects visual information procured by photographic, electronic, infrared, ultraviolet, and other sorts of satellite imaging; drones like the Predator and the Global Hawk; and other aircraft, ships, or ground stations.

While HUMINT has also undergone developments, the true quantum leaps have taken place in the other two sectors, which are fundamentally dependent on the capabilities and personnel of private industry. The massive investment by the transport and transportation industries in satellite-guided navigation systems has created new standards such as GPS. Moreover, transport companies possess more data about the cross-border movement of goods than public institutions do. This is data that could be of eminent significance to customs offices in cases of potential smuggling of weapons or drugs. Satellite images of every corner of the globe are generally accessible and private individuals can exploit them for their own purposes. Organized crime, for instance, can use the images for human trafficking and drug smuggling, extraction industries for finding natural resources, and private industrial espionage agencies for speculating on the stock market. Aerial surveillance over stationary or moving objects on the ground has become a private-sector domain. Telecommunications companies, for example, have much more powerful and cost-effective data-transmission channels than the military. This has led the Pentagon to outsource its entire telecommunications network to a private provider, even though that is necessarily less secure.

The second stage in the work of intelligence agencies—the comparing and decoding of data—has also undergone a fundamental transformation. Automated, computer-based data-sorting and comparison procedures are far more advanced in the private than in the state-intelligence sector. The decoding of data, as well as its encoding, has for a long time been no longer the exclusive province of military intelligence services. The private sector has been refining its fortress of information for a number of years now. Despite the huge resources at its disposal, even the NSA—the world's largest and most powerful intelligence service in the areas of SIGINT, IMINT, and cryptology—could not keep pace in research and development with specialized commercial companies. As a result, the NSA has outsourced a number of its responsibilities to private contractors and has hired private computer firms like CSC (DynCorp) and SAIC to do some of its research and development.

And private companies have even gotten a foothold in the third work stage, the analysis of data into usable information. Ever since the private economy recognized knowledge as one of the most valuable resources in the production process, knowledge management has been undergoing radical changes that have been reflected in innumerable, highly creative, and elaborate software programs. "Intelligent tools" for solving complex problems, for multicriteria evaluations of situations, and for the development of dynamic strategies have been virtual standards at transnational concerns like Shell or Mercedes and globally operating consulting companies like McKinsey. Because of the immense capital private industry has at its disposal, the private sector is generally several steps ahead of intelligence agencies when it comes to knowledge-producing instruments and methods. As is the case with the NSA, these agencies try to compensate by buying in expertise and outsourcing—a situation the military service industry has been eager to exploit. The sector has invested heavily in intelligence areas and has constantly expanded its products on offer there. Today, the majority of PMCs have their own intelligence department. Some have made this branch one of their specialities. Approximately a dozen firms exist upon their intelligence activities alone, more or less. The most important private military firms in this area include CACI, Control Risks Group, Logicon, ManTech, CSC (DynCorp), Diligence, SAIC, AirScan, and Kroll Security International.

7

Clientele Systems and Shadow Economies

The Development of New Security Needs

*In the bush, you follow the elephant
so you don't get wet from the dew.*
— AFRICAN SAYING

The conditions giving rise to new security policies, discussed in the last chapter, have not only wrought permanent change in Western industrialized countries. The effects on the so-called weak states have been far more extreme. Many former colonies that achieved independence in the 1950s and early 1960s were only able to paper over the gaps in their security by relying, like Nigeria or Ivory Coast, on help from their former colonial masters or by allying themselves, like Somalia or Kenya, with one of the cold war superpowers. In the last fifteen years, with the end of the East-West conflict, such countries have been left to their own devices, and the fragility of their security systems has become apparent—together with their lack of self-sufficiency and inability to solve economic, social, political, cultural, ethnic, and religious problems with civilian, nonviolent means. The increase in armed conflicts is only the most apparent sign of this weakness.

Today the vast majority of the world's states are completely or partially unable to guarantee internal and external security. After 1989, traditionally "weak" states like Colombia, Haiti, Liberia, Sudan, Afghanistan, and Sri Lanka were joined by others, including many former members of the Soviet Union. Other nations, including Indonesia, the Philippines, Brazil, Peru, and most states in sub-Saharan Africa, have been hard-hit by globalization.

For various reasons, many countries find themselves incapable of maintaining a health-care system that at least guarantees that their soldiers will be combat-fit. The percentage of army members infected with AIDS, for example, is around 50 percent in Angola and Congo, 66 in Uganda, 75 in Malawi, and up to 80 in Zimbabwe.[1] Many nations don't have institutions for controlling banks or the flow of money into and out of the country—others have no instruments to monitor trade and the traffic of goods. Several have so few personnel that their borders remain unguarded. In sub-Saharan states like Mali, Niger, and Burkina Faso it is rare to encounter a government official or soldier when crossing the border. And other states like Afghanistan and Sudan have never known any legitimate state controls of this kind.

THE RISE OF MARKETS FOR VIOLENCE

The accelerating decay of the nation-state, the erosion of the government's monopoly on the legitimate use of force, disappearing sovereignty, the gradual disintegration of society, and the formation of social factions are just some of the developments that have crystallized in the third world in the past decade. The logical—if not completely unavoidable—consequence has been the increase of markets for violence. Where state institutions are no longer able to deliver security, where justice and order have been subjugated to special interests, where the distribution of national wealth no longer follows predetermined principles, and apportioning of gross national product is subject to arbitrary rules, individuals usually take over functions of the government. Looking at the conflict regions of Southeast Asia, Latin America, or Africa, it is difficult, indeed virtually impossible, to determine what are causes and what are effects.

Nonetheless, to explain the phenomenon of markets for violence, it takes more than the two economic and two social variables cited by the former director of the Development Research Group at the World Bank, Paul Collier, in his highly regarded position paper of 2001. [2] Those variables are the proportion of primary goods within total exports, drastic economic decline, low standard of education, and disproportionately high number of young men in the total population. Because these four characteristics often appear in countries with markets of violence, Collier argues that most rebellions are motivated more by economic "greed" than by political "grievance."

The reality is, however, far more complex. The real question is not whether the grievance over the weakness of state institutions itself or the weakening of those institutions through the mafia is responsible for organized crime—with its surrounding political and financial network—developing in several formerly communist countries. Instead of postulating chains of causality, it's more important to recognize that the two phenomena feed off one another and are complexly interconnected. Sometimes greed will be in the forefront; other times it's grievance. From this vantage point, we can see that the dividing lines between various violent individuals on the world stage—warlords, rebels or insurgents, mafiosi, and terrorists—are becoming increasingly blurred, as the various groups interweave. The civil wars of Sierra Leone and Liberia saw the rise of a category of "soldier by day, rebel by night." Likewise, the lines are blurring between violent individuals and their legal partners—including state institutions, private firms, financial institutes, and commercial enterprises. Gray zones of cooperation have developed in which it is next to impossible to distinguish between what is legal and what is not.[3]

PROBLEMS WITH THE CLIENTELE SYSTEM

One structural characteristic of many third world countries, particularly in sub-Saharan Africa, was the patrimonial clientele system, a kind of hierarchically ordered cronyism financed with developmental aid and proceeds from the sale of raw materials. With the reductions in aid money and political support from wealthy nations after 1989, this system fell into crisis. That greatly contributed to the fragmentation of political leadership and denationalization of violence.

The clientele system rewarded obedience and loyalty to government authority, which was often concentrated in a state president. Formally, clientele-system nations had a state apparatus with institutions, checks and balances, and rules adapted from Western democracies. Factually, though, this apparatus either did not function or existed only on paper. It was more like a cinematic backdrop for political leaders and the media than a true state entity. Ex-presidents Mobutu of Zaire and or Houphouët-Boigny of Ivory Coast virtually perfected the exploitation of such systems.[4]

Similar to the situation in feudal and absolutist Europe, the system's guiding principle was the dependence of all realms of society on the will and whims of a charismatic leader or leadership clique. This created an uncertainty that was reflected in economic and cultural life as well as in social and political reality. It was never clear from one day to the next which agreements and rules mattered, whether the size of a bribe paid to an official today would be sufficient tomorrow, whether contracts concluded with the state would still be valid in a month's time, whether media censorship would remain constant or be changed, and whether political opposition would be tolerated or suppressed. The legal status of the individual and the rights to which he could lay claim were permanently up in the air. Even the political mediators of the head of state or ruling clique could not feel secure about their positions. The better they functioned, the more they became a potential danger for those with real power and risked replacement. In this way, the persons of reference for the middle and lower social strata constantly rotated. Medium- and long-term planning was out of the question—in the economic realm as well as in every other social area.

Once the financial means for maintaining the clientele system began to run out, the system collapsed, leaving a vacuum that every political, economic, cultural, or social group tried to fill in its own way. With the disappearance of the arbitrary but ordering hand, no institution possessed the legitimacy or strength to compensate for the diverging interests that went head-to-head. On the contrary, everyone tried to survive the chaos with the least harm and the greatest advantage. These conditions applied not just to Africa, just as their development was not restricted to that continent. Similar phenomena occurred in central and Southeast Asia, in Latin America, and in the Middle East.

The oil-producing countries—which, thanks to the enormous revenues at their disposal, have better succeeded in maintaining most of the state-financed clientele system—were not hit as badly. Yet even there, disputes arose as the populace refused to just sit back and accept political elites and military leaders pocketing the lion's share of the gigantic profits. Countries like Indonesia, Nigeria, Colombia, and Saudi Arabia still have the financial means at their disposal to control or, if need be, violently repress any opposition that cannot be bribed outright.[5] The effort necessary to restrain opposition and secure oil reserves, however, increasingly exceeds existing capabilities and raises demands for additional security services, including overtly military ones. Other "weak states," which bought off or otherwise tamed their clientele with income from natural resources, were left out in the cold with the drop in raw-material prices on the globalized market and the corresponding decline in state revenues.

THE RISE OF PARTICULAR COMMUNITIES

The demise of the clientele system not only rendered social conflicts more visible but also heightened and caused them, with increasing frequency, to turn violent. In the social-cultural realm, two connected developments arose. There were communities based on traditional values and ethnic or religious identities that sought some salvation in successfully mastering conflicts over the distribution of resources. They were offset, however, by groups—ideological or not—who agitated for the destruction of the "materialistic" social system and the Western model of modernization, or tried to achieve their material ends by using all means, including military ones, at their disposal.[6]

The worsening social impoverishment, the uncertainty of the future, and the threat to identity led the former category of people to focus their efforts on their own ethnic groups or religious communities. The existing order and established models for solving conflict in such particular communities, together with their sense of commonality and group solidarity, offered a soothing sense of safety to replace the one that had been lost. In taking upon themselves the responsibility for aspects of society like education, health, and welfare, they took over from a weak, corrupt, or no-longer-existent state. Their appeal was reflected in an increasing number of adherents and a number of these particular communities—for instance, in Algeria, Somalia, Sumatra, Sri Lanka, and Afghanistan—developed into efficient large-scale organizations with political aspirations. Success strengthened their internal cohesion, but also heightened tensions with other particular communities and the state apparatus. With the Taliban in Afghanistan, one ethnic-religious group usurped power and laid exclusive claim to the legitimate use of force—that power was then destroyed by outside intervention, and Afghanistan reverted to its former clan structure. In Sri Lanka the situation spiraled into an ongoing civil war. In Somalia, the central state was dissolved to the benefit of particular communities. In Algeria, state repression silenced the Islamic political party FIS (Front Islamique du Salut). In Aceh, Sumatra, a temporary compromise would seem to have been reached. But in all these cases, social change was accompanied by the bloodiest sorts of violence, with the civilian populace bearing the brunt of more than 80 percent of the casualties.

Movements that try directly to secure their material existence through force basically fall into three types. The first are political or religious rebel and insurgent movements such as the various "liberation fronts" in Colombia, Sierra Leone, and the Philippines. The second are warlords who, in contrast to late-medieval condottieri or the warrior-aristocrats of the Thirty Years' War, do not hire out autonomous military units to others, but rather themselves occupy territory and exercise local power. Some warlords have seized territory from failed states, where they then ruled as military sovereigns. Others took over whole nations and became autocrats. Examples of such warlords can be found throughout the history of most western and central African countries, the Caucasian republics, Islamic nations like Yemen and Pakistan, and Burma in Asia. Similar to their predecessors, the "free companies," soldiers loyal to warlords feel a sense of commonality, group solidarity, and, to some extent, security. Moreover, warlords compensate for the lack of an ideological or ethnic purpose behind their movements by satisfying their followers' material and existential needs. Some of the means they use for generating funds are "taxing" companies that exploit the natural resources of their territory, setting up "highway tolls," for instance on the transport of humanitarian aid, and extracting protection money from the producers and dealers in contraband wares.

The third type of movement, one which has swelled to previously unimaginable proportions, is organized crime. Often it is structured along ethnic boundaries, which no doubt encourage the requisite reliability within the groups. Organized crime gangs are, to a much greater extent than soldiers loyal to warlords, literally as thick as thieves, protecting and supporting one another so as to be better safeguarded against state prosecution. But members of a mafia are guided even less than warlords' followers by shared values—organized crime represents a marriage of convenience in its purest form. Revenue is generated by trading in illegal wares and services such as drug or human trafficking and money laundering, by dealing in legal goods like weapons or diamonds, and by illegal forms of otherwise legal activities such as financial or technological transactions or pirating trademarked products. In 2005, various nonprofit institutions estimated that the total volume of more or less illegal economic activities amounted to 2 trillion—or 20 percent of the world's total commerce. The turnover from organized crime per se was far smaller. The United Nations estimates that the percentage of gross national product directly linked to organized crime in individual countries is around 2 percent.

Terrorists represent a further type of private, nonstate group that pursues its ends by means of violence. But terrorists do not make up a particular community. The Islamist terrorism that predominates today is a loose association of individuals, mostly raised in relative affluence, who join or can be joined together in functional groups, but who usually then immediately go their separate ways again. Formally speaking, the ideology of most of today's terrorist networks is inflected by religion. The actual content, however, is a hostility toward modernity much like the terrorist groups in the West in the 1970s and 1980s. The primary difference between the terror cells of then and now, apart from the language and formulations of their messages, is how they use violence. While earlier terrorism was also directed against civilians, the principle of maximizing casualties and destruction is becoming ever more prominent and dominates the battle logic of Islamist terror. The attacks of September 11, 2001, were, of course, a prime example of this.

THE ILLEGAL GLOBAL NETWORK

In recent years, the various private parties that use violence have established intense, mutually advantageous relationships with one another. What began as intermittent contacts between insurgents and religiously inspired particular societies, terrorists and mafiosi, or warlord and rebels, have developed into standing cooperation arrangements. Today, it is hardly inaccurate to speak of a single worldwide illegal network that spans the globe with operations designed to benefit all its members. Terrorists, guerrillas, and warlords, for example, satisfy their need for weapons by selling drugs and diamonds to the mafia.[7] Terrorists use safe havens provided by warlords and religiously motivated particular communities. Rebels control diamond mines, while the mafia supervises the commercial exploitation of such raw materials.[8] Mafiosi, in return, require extraterritorial bases to conclude weapons transactions and receive cargos of contraband.

The illegal network of nonstate, violent entities is also dependent on legally operating partners: financial institutions, raw-materials industries, customs and government offices, and trading companies. The illegal arms trade, for example, would be impossible without the support of various legal entities. Moreover, the lucrative business of money laundering does not just take place on remote islands. It requires the active support of legal financial institutions and, when done on a large scale, the cover of political allies. Countries like Hungary, Egypt, Ukraine, Israel, Russia, and Indonesia—together with the so-called money-laundering factories in the Caribbean—are all firmly established in this business.

The infiltration of the legal parts of society by organized crime has spread to every country in the world, although the extent varies to extremes. Organized crime plays a relatively minor role, for example, in Scandinavia. Its influence is moderate in other industrialized countries, peaking in Japan and Italy, whereas it is dramatically on the rise in less developed nations like Turkey, the Baltic states, Brazil, and India. In some countries, it has become a permanent component of the state and the economy. In Albania or Zambia, for instance, the merging of legal and illegal enterprises is such that it's virtually impossible to distinguish whether parts of the government are constituent elements of the mafia, or vice versa. It's also hard to say whether large segments of the economy are part of the organized criminal network, or whether the mafia engages in a number of legal economic activities.

The fact that the proportion of criminal to legal economic activities varies so dramatically from country to country has to do with a whole complex of variables. But a good rule of thumb is that the nations in which state, community, and social checks as well as monitoring mechanisms and instruments are most advanced and transparent will be the ones in which the proportion of organized crime is the lowest. Organized criminal activity increases in reverse proportion to the strength of government monitoring and overall economic transparency.

SHADOW ECONOMIES: THE LINK BETWEEN LEGAL AND ILLEGAL MONEYMAKING

The fact that rebels, warlords, terrorists, and organized criminals have seeped into the legal realms of nation-states is directly related to another post–cold war development: the rapid spread of informal or shadow economies. This phenomenon, which has increased the demand for private security services, affects all countries, but is most prevalent in the weakest states. There have always been shadow economies, even in highly industrialized nations, but in weak states, their proportional relationship to legitimate business has grown enormously in the wake of globalization. Today more than half of the world's population depends on shadow economies for their existence, suffering from constant legal and physical uncertainty. The United Nations Development Programme has calculated that per-capita income in sub-Saharan Africa sank by 0.4 percent annually between 1990 and 2002, while the number of people living below the poverty line increased by seventy-four million per year. At the same time, public investments in education, health, and social programs were drastically reduced.[9]

The opening of borders, the broad-based elimination of export and import licenses, the eradication of currency controls, the privatization of state enterprises, the free flow of capital, and the comprehensive liberalization of all economic sectors led to many third world governments losing grip on their economies and to state revenues drastically declining. Moreover, the forcible opening of markets due to globalization bankrupted many parts of the legitimate economy, with national businesses being unable to stand up to competition from much more productive transnational firms.

The consequences were an explosion in the number of the unemployed, the destruction of the already fragile social network, and the gradual slide of many parts of the economy into a legal twilight zone. Many businesspeople could only survive by operating at the edge of the law—for example, by avoiding taxes, violating labor and welfare statutes, or by carrying out refinancing and other monetary transactions in the unofficial realm. Myriads of small enterprises replaced state industries and national businesses that had been driven out of profitable markets by foreign, chiefly Western competition. Because of their semilegal status, such small firms rarely enjoy state protection in either a legal or physical sense. Thus, breach of contract, broken financial promises, blackmail, and threats have become part of daily reality. The "informal economy" has also become a second-class-security zone.

The vacuum left by the withdrawal of state protection was gradually filled by criminal gangs and mafia or corrupt security entities that successively undermined the values of public law and order. Protection money was paid to mafias; corrupt police officers were rewarded with supplementary salaries. Since such businesses were dependent on other state authorities such as chambers of commerce or construction and transportation offices, an unofficial contact network developed between dubious businessmen and civil servants, who were paid extra for performing tasks outside their official duties. As a result, a self-contained system of economic give-and-take arose and was tightly interwoven with both the illegal business activities of organized crime and the legal sphere of the official economy and the state. For reasons of cost, illegally acquired raw materials and half-finished products were processed and passed on by enterprises from the shadow economy. The legal economy then took them over and marketed them. The upshot is that in many parts of the world informal economies have become a permanent link between legal and illegal business activities.

The far-ranging consequences are particularly visible in a number of Latin American countries. Declining state revenues as a result of the shadow economy force the government to reduce internal security expenditures. Zones with different security standards arise. There are realms of relative security and relative uncertainty, which largely correspond with the distribution of wealth. Affluent segments of society enjoy adequate state protection, while poorer demographic groups get little to none. The state monopoly on the legitimate use of force is never formally questioned, but it is eroded in a de facto sense. In many areas of urban sprawl, for example the favelas in Brazil, state forces of law and order no longer have any influence whatsoever. The application of force is now the province of nongovernmental entities. In the form of youth unemployment, the apartheid between rich and poor permanently generates people who know no means of survival other than violence, assuring a continual supply of fresh recruits for organized crime, as well as insurgent movements, warlord clans, and terrorists. Conversely, the rich increasingly fear violent segments of society that can no longer be held in check by state authorities. This does not necessarily lead to conflicts between particular communities, but inevitably, affluent and integrated members of society try to bolster security by enlisting the private sector. Thus the state is disempowered, too, by those at the top of the income pyramid—and its monopoly on the legitimate use of force further pecked away. More and more security gaps develop, and the entire security structure of the state is undermined.

The loss of state authority, the increasing segmentation of society, and the rising potential for violence among individual have-nots destabilize the state and its institutions. Today, the majority of weak states are characterized by a mixture of illegal business activities, shadow economies and legitimate enterprise, poverty bordering on pauperism, cultural alienation and loss of identity, and authoritarian power structures and autocratic repression. Statistics from the United Nations Development Programme and the World Bank show that the quality of these characteristics and how they are combined differ from country to country. Until the end of the 1980s, third world countries typically spent twice as much on health and education as on arms. Between 1990 and 2002, that situation was reversed. Military expenditures now exceed money spent on education and health initiatives by 30 percent.[10]

If characteristics like organized crime, shadow economies, social impoverishment, and loss of identity develop in a country, it becomes highly likely that violent conflicts will break out, leading to the formation of economies of violence and war. Weak states exist in a permanent state of security limbo that encourages a constant need for ever more security services.

This is not just a problem for the state as an institution. Instability in the security realm also causes uncertainty in the legitimate economy. Fear of organized crime notwithstanding, such instability also encourages the desire for more protection. If the state is unable to provide additional security, the need will be met via private firms. The need for security is especially true of transnational corporations operating in weak states. Often viewed by local populaces as foreign, dominant masters, such firms see themselves as being particularly at risk.

8

Dangerous Consequences
Militant Cooperation—Business and Private Military Firms

What God is permitted, the ox is not allowed
—ROMAN SAYING

PMCs have been active throughout the world for more than a decade, although early on their existence was scarcely noticed and even more rarely discussed. It took a number of scandals and the Iraq War for the general public to begin registering this new phenomenon. Nonetheless, the issue of private military companies usually disappeared soon after it appeared on the political and media agenda. This is all the more puzzling since virtually all observers agree that the rise of PMCs has created a grave problem with wide-ranging consequences, which urgently require legal redress and regulation.

In Germany, the problem was briefly subject to political debate in autumn 2004 following media reports about the activities of new mercenaries. The conservative faction in Parliament submitted a proposal that stated: "In the long term, privatization can lead to a fundamental shift in the relationship between the military and the nation-state. The state's monopoly on the legitimate use of force could be called into question or possibly even eradicated . . . The rules of warfare that have coalesced after centuries of development could now be undermined by private security enterprises . . . Clear legal guidelines are needed at the international and national level."[1] A cross-party consensus saw PMCs as a potential danger to the state. But nothing much was done other than issuing a statement of principle calling for the government to take urgent action, and the conservative proposal was buried in parliamentary committee. With the exception of France, which passed antimercenary legislation in April 2003, most Western nations have done little or nothing to tackle this issue, preferring to ride out scandals and wait for the public to forget.

The complexity of this topic is just one reason why legislative solutions have been so long in coming. Western nations have maneuvered themselves into a dilemma from which there is no easy escape. The Stockholm International Peace Research Institute, together with other academic organizations, has identified a fundamental "conflict of goals." On the one hand, governments want to reduce security budgets and the number of troops; on the other, state armed forces are being charged with more and more tasks, and the number of foreign interventions is increasing. These two contradictory aims have necessarily led to shortages of material and personnel. The United States, for example, reduced its standing army by a third to some 1.5 million soldiers, but now employs around a million private forces, so that overall troop strength is greater than before the reductions. Privatization has set in motion changes of which we at present have no overview. Nonetheless, many problems can be identified and discussed on the basis of the ten-plus-year history of private military companies. This chapter and following chapters will analyze the consequences that arise from the activities of PMCs in cooperation with other businesses, in particular with transnational companies. The situation will be examined in the context of "strong" and "weak" states as well as aid organizations and peacekeeping missions.

Private industrial enterprises have thus far had the fewest problems working with military service providers. In general, they prefer to get the protection they need in custom-tailored form from private firms, rather than having to accept the conditions and regulations that accompany state-provided security. Difficulties seldom arise since both PMCs and the large firms that employ them are private, profit-oriented enterprises accustomed to thinking in terms of business contracts. In many cases, increases in profits for one also mean higher revenues for the other. Nevertheless, economic power and military might can only cooperate to their mutual advantage if their activities do not elicit resistance from other interest groups in a given society—for instance, when profits from private industry increase the living standards of the populace or when they do not create inhumane conditions for the working classes. Standards as to what constitutes a living wage or humane working conditions vary from country to country, and culture to culture. Yet serious conflicts are inevitable when private enterprises achieve such power that they alone decide, without compromise with institutions like labor unions, how people should work and how income should be distributed. This resulting tension is heightened even further in third world countries, when political parties, the military, the police, or paramilitary forces are co-opted to pursue commercial interests.

INTERVENTION IN THE ANDES

Colombia is a good example of how divergent interests can collide, and how private industry approaches conflicts in conjunction with military companies and other interested parties. Colombia lives in part upon income from cocaine, which accounts for 6 percent of the economy, and high-quality coffee production. But the South American country's wealth also derives from its enormous oil, coal, gold, and platinum reserves. Some 90 percent of the world's emeralds come from there, and the country also has a flourishing agricultural industry, whose exports include bananas and wool. Companies from around the world have Colombian affiliates: Four hundred of the top five hundred firms in the United States have invested heavily there. Yet Colombia is by no means among the world's more developed or wealthier nations, ranking only seventy-third behind Cuba and the Seychelles on the list drawn up by the United Nations Development Programme. The reason for the discrepancy between natural riches and lack of development is the decades-old civil war between the political and economic oligarchy, assisted by state apparatus of power including the military and the police, and the rebel armies of the FARC (Revolutionary Armed Forces of Colombia) and the ELN (National Liberation Army), left-wing parties, unions, intellectuals, farmers, and indigenous populations.

The conflict has heated up in the past decade as foreign firms have increased their Colombian activities. Attempts at mediation have proven virtually impossible since 1999, after the U.S. government's Plan Colombia assured U.S. companies and the Colombian government of Washington's political and financial assistance. In the French newspaper *Le Monde diplomatique*, Hernando Calvo described this initiative in drastic terms: "Washington decided upon the billion-dollar Colombia Plan because native terrorism by paramilitary groups wasn't sufficient to check the increasingly powerful guerillas."[2] Today, the UN estimates that around 2.5 million of Colombia's forty million inhabitants are internal refugees, and that some forty-five hundred political murders are committed every year, with the majority of victims being union activists and workers. Most of those who carry out the killings come from the ranks of paramilitary groups with close ties to the army and the police. "The euphemistic use of the term 'paramilitaries' is primarily aimed at concealing from the public eye the true masterminds behind the politics of extermination—the army and politicians with vested interests," wrote Ospina. "The 'paramilitaries' take care of the dirty work, allowing the army and the politicians to keep their image clean and stake a claim to US aid despite massive human rights violations."[3] Lobbyists for U.S. firms active in Colombia—above all oil, arms, and military companies—made $6 million in campaign contributions to convince the U.S. Congress to approve the Plan Colombia, which was sold to the public as a humanitarian assistance program for the crisis-ridden Andean nation. Yet of the $1.3 billion initially approved for the program, only 13 percent went to the Colombian government to improve its security infrastructure. The rest flowed into the coffers of U.S. firms.

The majority of this money was spent on security, for which U.S. and British firms, together with some Israeli PMCs, were contracted. In total, around thirty such companies are active in

Colombia. California Microwave Inc. and Vinnell, for example, do highly sensitive surveillance work, using seven advanced radar facilities, coordinated with an airborne reconnaissance system. ManTech, TRW Inc., Matcom, and Alion take photographs of Colombian territory, in particular rebel-controlled areas, with high-definition, satellite-based cameras; intercept electronic communications; and evaluate the data received and pass it on to the Southern Command of the U.S. Army and the Pentagon. Sikorsky Aircraft Corporation and Lockheed Martin supply helicopters and military aircraft. Their subsidiary MPRI is responsible for educating and training the Colombian military and police. Arine builds runway refueling stations for airplanes; ACS Defense provides logistical support; the British companies Control Risks Group and Global Risk are primarily active in risk consultancy, kidnapping negotiations, hostage liberation training, and the armed guarding of production facilities for the defense of transnational concerns.[4]

Meanwhile, DynCorp is predominantly involved in the "war on drugs." According to the contract issued by the U.S. government, the firm provides pilots and mechanics and carries out training, surveillance flights, and material and troop transports aimed at destroying coca fields and cocaine laboratories. In practice, they fly T-65 aircraft spraying coca fields with the notorious, Monsanto-produced herbicide Roundup and support the Colombian police with teams of Special Forces in helicopters. This, as Colombian journalists have noted, leads to constant armed confrontations with FARC rebels who sell cocaine in order to purchase weapons. "With the spraying of herbicides on coca fields, the borders with military activities become blurred," wrote Sandra Bibiana Flórez in 2001. "To secure the area, machine guns are fired from helicopters, which afterward accompany missions with planted artillery gunners."[5] The *New York Times* and other American newspapers have reported that the herbicides have caused serious, sometimes fatal harm to farmers and make their land infertile. Other PMCs are involved in antiguerrilla and antiterrorism training not only on behalf of police and the Colombian military but also—according to UN Special Rapporteur Enrique Ballesteros—on behalf of paramilitaries.[6] The Israeli firms Spearhead and GIR S.A., too, have been accused of training paramilitaries and providing them with arms and munitions.[7]

THE SECURITY STRATEGY OF TRANSNATIONAL CONCERNS

This is the situation in which foreign companies operate in Colombia. From the business perspective, opposition workers as well as the FARC and the ELN threaten the smooth running of the economy. Since the Colombian police and military are unable to provide the desired protection, the United States sends consultants and trainers (mostly employees of PMCs) to improve security work. In addition, companies have hired private firms to cover the remaining security gaps. The various service enterprises and other private forces are usually hired for specific tasks, but they cooperate closely with one another. PMCs, for example, collect via satellite or reconnaissance flights information about guerrilla troop movements that they then pass on to the military. They plant informants within the workers' movement or village populations and share what they learn with the police and the paramilitary groups. PMCs responsible for protecting companies also closely consult with police officers and paramilitaries about their strategies for combating striking workers.

In the 1990s, Colombian labor unions accused Nestlé of using paramilitary forces to murder union representatives during contract negotiations. Around the same time, multinational companies involved in the banana trade succeeded in killing four hundred labor representatives and busting the banana workers' union in the Urabá region. The U.S.-based firm Drummond Company has been accused of providing safe havens—as well as money, food, fuel, and equipment—for operations aimed at suppressing unions. Within a decade, security forces working for Coca-Cola Columbia have successfully reduced average wages from $700 to $150 a month and the number of workers on regular contracts from ten thousand to five hundred. Seventy-five hundred jobs have been outsourced, and the percentage of union employees on the payrolls has declined from more than 25 to below 5. Coca-Cola has also been accused of conspiring to liquidate labor leaders, and similar accusations have been leveled against the U.S.-based gold corporation Corona Goldfields and other transnational concerns.[8] In the meantime, with the help of legally specialized nongovernmental organizations, Colombian unions have been able to file suits against some of these companies in their home countries, but no verdicts have been rendered.[9]

The crimes and human-rights violations committed by security firms against workers and union leaders with the support or approval of foreign companies are greatly outnumbered by those aimed at destroying the FARC and the ELN. The FARC has around twenty thousand armed troops at its disposal, the ELN approximately twelve thousand. Their attacks against businesses are largely directed at transnational oil companies and are, they say, aimed at ensuring that some of the profits from Colombia's petroleum reserves go to the country in general, instead of being siphoned off by oligarchs, members of the government, and high-ranking military leaders. The Colombian military, private security firms hired by companies, and PMCs sent to Colombia by the U.S. government cooperate closely in battling the guerrillas—just as PMCs, police, and paramilitary coordinate their activities against workers. Two examples suffice to illustrate the situation.

UNSCRUPULOUS MULTINATIONAL OIL COMPANIES

One of Colombia's main oil fields is located in the country's northeastern plains near the city of Arauca. Some 20 percent of Colombia's oil is pumped from here via a nearly one-thousand-kilometer pipeline to the Caribbean port of Coveñas. Roughly half is shipped to the United States. Together with Colombian company Ecopetrol, the U.S.-based multinational corporation Occidental Petroleum (Oxy) runs the production facilities and pipeline. Every year, the pipeline is the target of several dozen attacks and acts of sabotage from FARC and ELN. To protect it, the U.S. government has allocated several hundred millions of dollars in the past five years—the equivalent of a $3-per-barrel subsidy on Oxy oil. The private military company AirScan is responsible for the security of the production facilities and the pipeline. A landing strip has been set up at the main facility where AirScan flies reconnaissance flights with Skymaster aircraft equipped with video and infrared cameras. They hand out data collected about rebel bases and troop movements to the Colombian army. AirScan uses military helicopter gunships for their missions, and units of the Colombian military operate from the company airstrip. Oxy supports the antiguerrilla operations of PMCs and the regular army with planning assistance, troop transport, and fuel. American newspapers such as the *San Francisco Chronicle* and the *Los Angeles Times* report that AirScan personnel have repeatedly located targets for attack by the Colombian military and celebrated the liquidation of rebels when a pilot successfully bombed a guerrilla unit. On December 18, 1998, AirScan helicopter warships and the Colombian air force attacked presumed FARC units in the village of Santo Domingo, around fifty kilometers from the pipeline. Eighteen villagers, including seven children, died in the machine-gun fire and bombing.[10] Legal investigations into the incident failed to reach any definitive conclusion—partly because evidence had disappeared. None of the pilots involved were ever convicted.

The Cusiana oil field, which is operated by British Petroleum (BP), is also in eastern Colombia, and the facility, too, is connected by a pipeline, jointly run by BP and a consortium called Ocensa, to the port of Coveñas. BP has hired a private military company, Defence Systems Colombia (DSC), a subsidiary of ArmorGroup, to protect production facilities and the pipeline. Under the direction of the former British MI5 officer Roger Brown, DSC developed an extensive security strategy. It included, along with surveillance and spying activities, the training of police and army units in antiguerrilla and antirebel tactics and psychological warfare. When Brown had to step down because of an illegal deal for attack helicopters and specialized antiguerrilla weaponry with the Israeli PMC Silver Shadow Advance Security System, Colombian general Hernan Rodriguez took over the position. Human-rights organizations accuse him of being involved in 149 murders.[11] Similar to AirScan, DSC collected data about rebel organizations and passed it on to the Colombian military, which is, as the UN High Commissioner for Human Rights has repeatedly stressed, suspected of a long list of human-rights violations.

DSC has been heavily criticized by Amnesty International. "What is disturbing is that OCENSA/DSC's security strategy reportedly relies heavily on paid informants whose purpose is to covertly gather 'intelligence information' on the activities of the local population in the communities through which the pipeline passes and to identify possible 'subversives' within those communities," Amnesty wrote in a report. "What is even more disturbing is that this intelligence information is then reportedly passed by OCENSA to the Colombian military who, together with their paramilitary allies, have frequently targeted those considered subversive for extrajudicial execution and 'disappearance.'"[12] Because these activities occurred with the approval and support of BP, the European Parliament passed a resolution in October 1998 sharply condemning the financing of what amounted to death squads.[13] Groups like Human Rights Watch, Amnesty International, and the Colombian Labor Union Association (CUT) say little has changed on the ground. On January 7, 2004, in Arauca, the president of the teachers' union, Francisco Rojas, received a text message on his cell phone in which the sender threatened to kill Rojas's father and brother and gave him eight hours to leave the city. Rojas had every reason to take the threat seriously. His predecessor Jaime Carillo had received a message threatening his children about a year before. Afterward, Carrillo disappeared without a trace. Dozens of "subversive" labor and farmers' leaders, as well as human-rights activists, have come into the crosshairs of security firms. In 2003 alone, seventy Colombian union members were murdered, and in 2004, fourteen hundred civilians died at the hands of PMC employees.[14] In the first eleven months of 2005, the nongovernmental organization LabourNet recorded at least one murder of a union member per week. On the evening of September 10, 2005, for instance, Luciano Enrique Romero Molina—a leading member of the food-producers' union Sinaltrainal, who was living under the protection of the Inter-American Commission on Human Rights—was seen alive for the last time. The next morning his body was found. He had been bound, tortured, and killed. His body bore forty knife wounds.[15]

Repeated human-rights abuses led humanitarian organizations to appeal to the UN, the government of firms involved in Colombia, and the oil companies themselves. The recommendations made by Human Rights Watch clearly show what the relationship between private industry and forces of violence is—and what it should be, if all parties concerned could be persuaded to remain within legal limits.

Colombia is hardly a unique case. The intervention of "strong states" to protect their own interests and those of transnational companies is not drastically different in many African or Asian nations—especially regarding their collaboration with PMCs. Complaints about the Shell corporation's activities in Nigeria have been appearing regularly for years in the annual reports of the UN High Commissioner for Human Rights—so, too, have accusations about BP policies in Azerbaijan and Indonesia.[16] Exxon's activities in Aceh[17] and in conjunction with the Chad-Cameroon pipeline were investigated after accusations of land theft, unpaid labor, forced removal of farmers, and denied access to supplies of freshwater.[18] In Ghana the Wassa Association of Communities Affected by Mining has accused transnational gold-mining companies like Ashanti Gold of inhumane business practices that extend to torture and murder.[19] Various investigative commissions have pointed their fingers at the world's largest paper company, Asia Pulp and Paper, for human-rights abuses including physical mistreatment, intimidation, and blackmail, above all in Riau

Province in Sumatra. PMCs have been involved in all these abuses.[20]

What varies are the specific conditions and the type of cooperation with local leaders. What is never pursued is a policy toward "weak states" aimed at creating structural stability and long-term peace, and putting the emphasis on local populations.

Human Rights Watch issued the following recommendations to oil companies operating in Colombia to reduce human-rights violations:

- The companies should insert a clause into any security agreement signed with the government or any state entity that requires, as a condition of contract, that state security forces operating in the area of company installations conform to the human rights obligations the government has assumed under the International Covenant on Civil and Political Rights, the American Convention on Human Rights, as well as other international human rights and humanitarian norms.
- The companies' security agreements with state entities should be made public with the sole exception of operative details that could jeopardize individuals' lives.
- The companies should insist on screening the military and police who are assigned for their protection. In consultation with the Defense Ministry and civilian government agencies in charge of investigating human rights violations (the Fiscalía General de la Nación, the Defensoría del Pueblo, and the Procuraduría General de la República) as well as nongovernmental human rights organizations, the companies should seek to ensure that no soldier or

police agent credibly implicated in human-rights abuse be engaged in their protection.

- Careful background checks should also be undertaken to ensure that former police or army officers who work as private contractors or part of company security staff have no history of human rights abuse or paramilitary involvement.

- The companies must make absolutely clear to the police and military defending them—as well as to company staff and subcontracted personnel—that human rights violations will not be tolerated, and that the companies will be the first to press for investigation and prosecution if any abuses occur.

- Whenever credible allegations of human rights abuses surface, the companies should insist that the soldiers and officers implicated be immediately suspended and the appropriate internal and criminal investigations launched.

- The companies should actively monitor the status of the investigations and press for resolution of the cases. If the investigations or prosecutions are stalled, the companies should publicly condemn the failure to conduct or complete the investigations.

- The companies' assistance should be audited to ensure that the aid is, in fact, nonlethal. Those audits should be made public.

9

Out of Control

The Questionable Legality of the Privatization of Force in the West

> *People don't pause to consider before beginning something*
> *that offers a temporary advantage and blinds them*
> *to the dangers it entails.*
> —MACHIAVELLI

A series of as yet unresolved problems has arisen in "strong states" as a result of transferring military tasks to private service providers. They range from the questionable sanctity of contracts to the problem of democratic monitoring and accountability. The political powers in the United States and Britain have no studies analyzing the results of the work of the PMCs they've hired. The only information one can use to identify, debate, and evaluate the consequences of the actions of military service providers is material collected by journalists, academics, critical military leaders, NGOs, and political observers like the UN Special Rapporteur on Mercenaries.

Events from the Iraq War are particularly well suited to

illustrating various aspects of private military companies since it is in Iraq that PMCs have been most heavily used and that, consequently, the most material is available.

PRIVATE SOLDIERS IN IRAQ

On March 31, 2004, four Blackwater employees were killed in a grenade attack in Falluja, and their bodies strung up demonstratively from a bridge in the city. One of them was Steven "Scott" Helvenston, a thirty-eight-year-old former member of the Navy Seals. Tall, blond, well-tanned, and broad-shouldered, Helvenston fit the idealized Hollywood image of the elite U.S. soldier to a tee—indeed, he had previously appeared in minor roles in a number of movies and television series. When not on the set, Helvenston sold fitness videos. He was employed by Blackwater as a security consultant, and it was never determined what he and his three former special-forces comrades were doing without a military escort in Iraq's most dangerous city. The evidence was completely contradictory. Blackwater, the provisional government in Iraq, and the majority of the U.S. media claimed that the four "civilians" had been ambushed and brutally killed, and their bodies maimed.[1] Iraqi insurgents countered that the four men were by no means civilians, but rather heavily armed special fighters who, under the pretense of looking for terrorists, had carried out nighttime raids, mistreated women and children, and tortured and murdered local men and teenage boys.[2] Earlier that year, South African newspapers such as the *Star*, the *Cape Times*, and the *Pretoria Record* ran reports about a certain François Strydom, who had died in a bombing in Baghdad on January 28, 2004. Strydom worked for the Erinys company and had been a member—along with Albertus "the Sailor" van Schalkwyk—of the Koevoet, one of the most feared special units of the South Africa military under the apartheid regime.[3] On February 2, 2004, a Belfast newspaper reported that Derek W. Adgey, a felon convicted of terrorist activities in Northern Ireland, was working for ArmorGroup in Iraq.[4] Likewise, one could read in newspapers from Chile, Argentina, Colombia, and El Salvador that former members of special forces units, death squads, and paramilitary units were now employed in high-paying positions for U.S. private military companies. Blackwater's president, Gary Jackson, even admitted to recruiting soldiers from the notorious Pinochet regime in Argentina.[5] Legal experts see this as a logical consequence of the lack of accountability, oversight, and transparency concerning employees within the military service industry.

SECRET CONTRACTS, LEGAL CHAOS

These examples are probably but the tip of the iceberg, given that it is very difficult to establish the facts about crimes like torture or murder allegedly committed by PMC employees. No private soldier in Iraq has ever been convicted of such wrongdoings. Owing to the secrecy maintained and guaranteed in conjunction with government contracts with PMCs, there is no way of knowing what Helvenston and his three comrades' orders were in Falluja—and thus no way of determining whether they were acting on their own or at the behest of the U.S. Army. The U.S. military leadership in Iraq has repeatedly denied possessing knowledge about PMCs. The companies are not part of the military chain of command. They receive their orders directly from the Pentagon, and both the Defense Department and the headquarters of companies concerned keep their lips strictly sealed. Inquiries are either directed to the contract partner or dismissed outright as potentially violating secrecy agreements.

Even questions by Democratic senators and representatives about the number of PMCs contracted or the jobs they have been hired to do have not resulted in greater transparency. In 2004, a request by Democrat Jack Reed and eleven other senators for written guidelines for PMCs in Iraq was ignored by then secretary of defense Donald Rumsfeld. According to an article in the *New York Times*, some Pentagon officials admitted, off the record, that they did not know how many military service companies had been hired. Another Pentagon official, speaking anonymously to the *Washington Post*, claimed that the Iraqi provisional government was handing out contracts to just about anyone, without accounting for them to the United States. In fact, the U.S. government is not legally bound to inform Congress about the specific details of contracts. Frustrated by the lack of response from the executive branch, some congressional representatives turned to the U.S. Government Accountability Office, asking the institution to investigate the role of PMCs in Iraq.[6]

The result is a vicious cycle, and in the end, because the situation is not legally regulated, no more is known than in the beginning. It is still not clear just how many PMCs have been active under the Iraqi provisional government or how many still operate in Iraq today. The official numbers, then and now, provided by the Iraqi Ministry of the Interior are far lower than the real figures.[7] Moreover, even less is known about what sort of tasks individual military service providers have been contracted for, how they carried out their jobs, or whether or not they were successful.

The legal chaos begins with the awarding of contracts. Insofar as one can gain access to such documents, the initial contract is seldom detailed enough to grant the government any legal rights. Sanctions for firms that violate or fail to honor the contract are likewise nebulous or nonexistent. In other words, when it comes to the application of military force, the government is omitting simple legal passages that are part of any normal contract of sale. Nor are the general means specified with which the tasks enumerated in the contracts are and are not to be performed. PMC employees in Iraq, speaking anonymously, have said that they have been able to arrest people, cordon off streets, and confiscate identity cards without any sort of special permission. But no one has been able to confirm whether the contracts concluded between such firms and the Pentagon explicitly allow the former to usurp power normally claimed by sovereign states.[8]

DynCorp received a contract for more than a million dollars from the U.S. State Department to organize the Iraqi criminal justice system. In June 2004, four of their employees, heavily armed and in battle gear, led Iraqi police on a raid of the former Iraqi leader in exile, Ahmed Chalabi.[9] It is doubtful whether this action was in keeping with the spirit of the original contract. But the fact that DynCorp did not receive an official warning suggests that the contract is vague enough to allow for such "violations." As this and many other examples show, it is largely up to the PMCs themselves to decide how to go about fulfilling their tasks.

London's Hart Group was awarded a contract to provide unspecified, limited, "passive" security for the Iraqi provisional government. Hart employees were instructed to call in regular coalition troops in case they came under fire by Iraqi insurgents. The company's CEO told BBC Radio, his employees were forced on countless occasions to take up arms themselves since regular soldiers often arrived late, or not all, at the site of the attack. This case is hardly unique—PMCs such as Control Risks and

Triple Canopy have reported similar situations. An Italian journalist says troops from her country in Iraq abandoned their
posts guarding a provisional government office in Nassirya
after coming under insurgent machine-gun and mortar fire.[10]
In Al Kut, too, Ukrainian forces retreated and left members
of the provisional government and Triple Canopy employees
without support in an attack from the Mahdi Army of Shiite
spiritual leader Muqtada al-Sadr. The PMC employees engaged
in a three-day battle with the militia forces, until a shortage of
ammunition required a risky pullback.[11]

The question is: What is the value of contracts that restrict
firms to non-battle-related tasks but allow for the use of firearms in undefined "critical situations"? German soldiers who
have worked for U.S. firms in Iraq report being allowed to
decide for themselves when and how to use machine guns.[12]
Equally unclear is who decides whether a situation is critical,
and whether the response is proportional. Owing to the lack of
legal clarity at present, and not only in Iraq, it is largely down
to contractors to answer these questions themselves.[13]

LACK OF OVERSIGHT AND ACCOUNTABILITY

For the most part, governments have little oversight of the
activities of PMCs. The authorities that issue the contracts
are barely capable of doing much in the way of monitoring,
because, for example, they're tied down in Washington, and
the state military, which would have the capabilities, has little
interest in babysitting private soldiers who aren't part of the
chain of command. Indeed, oversight is usually a moot issue
since it remains unclear precisely what is to be monitored. Over
the centuries, with good reason, state armed forces developed
a myriad of horizontal and hierarchically branched monitoring

instances. In comparison, governments allow PMCs to exist in a state of near anarchy and arbitrariness.

The contract problems are by no means restricted to the lack of oversight of the use of force. In many cases, the situation is that the services contracted simply aren't provided. It's hardly surprising, given the belief among Western nations in the inherent price advantages of private over public services, that contracts are awarded without competition or specific public advertisement, and that monitoring instruments seldom have any effect.[14] Only if soldiers repeatedly complain about services such as uniform cleaning, or the condition of their quarters and the quality of their food, do questions about the exact wording of contracts get raised. In the past decade, it has been more the rule than the exception that private military firms offer relatively low-grade services at relatively high prices—with quality control left to the final consumer. In Iraq, logistics companies like KBR charged more than twice the normal civilian price for gasoline supplied to troops. They constructed overly expensive electricity and water facilities that had much higher capacities than the military actually needed. Private service enterprises charged the armed forces for hundreds of thousands of never-delivered meals. Costs for vehicle services were set on the basis of over-priced leasing contracts. As author Peter Singer concluded in a 2005 article, the "setup, in effect, gives companies more profit if they spend more. When combined with inadequate oversight, it creates a system ripe for inefficiency and abuse."[15] Instead of exploiting the advantages of privatization, the status quo leads to the worst sort of monopolizing.

Normally, it is the responsibility of the customer or the party issuing the contract to check up on the quantity and quality of the services delivered. But the specific type of contract used often hinders monitoring. The U.S. government favors "indefinite delivery/indefinite quantity" and "cost-plus" contracts—both of which virtually invite inefficiency and abuse. The former set no upper limits on the services and/or products to be delivered, whereas the latter peg profits to costs, with the profit margins varying from 2 percent to 5 percent in cases of "overfulfilment." With ID/IQ contracts, the more private companies provide, the more they earn, encouraging them to deliver more than what's strictly necessary. With cost-plus contracts, service providers' profits go up with their costs, leading them to drive their own expenditures as high as possible. Truck drivers working for a number of logistics companies in Iraq have reported spending 95 percent of their time driving around without any payloads so that they can drive up the costs for which they bill.[16]

In 2004 the U.S. Army published the results of a study drawing conclusions from the military's practical experiences with private providers. "The lack of awareness of contractors and their presence in supporting combat operations," wrote the study's two authors, "has resulted in the following:

- significant gaps in operational doctrine on who is responsible for securing lines of communication used by commercial suppliers
- loss of visibility of assets moving in and around the theater of operations
- loss of control of contractor personnel and equipment
- increased service responsibility for supporting contractor personnel in the areas of life support, force protection, and operational and administrative control.
- use of additional manpower, materiel, and funding resources to support contractor personnel.

- concern about the availability of commercial supplies and services in a hostile environment.
- gaps in providing logistics support if commercial supply lines become disrupted."[17]

U.S. advocates of military privatization, who argued the virtues of a lean state, successfully pushed through dramatic personnel cuts in the area of oversight. Between 1997 and 2005, the volume of contracts for PMCs doubled, while the money allocated for project engineering, accounting, and monitoring was being cut by a third.[18] Private industry's resistance to regulation and state control has become a guiding principle in the military sector, and politicians made themselves complicit in this development by not allocating resources for sufficient oversight. The belief in the cost effectiveness of privatization is precisely that—an ideological belief not supported by any empirical facts. The successful-sounding statistics publicized by the military service industry have never been subject to quality evaluation, nor has there ever been a solid cost-benefit analysis of the sort usually carried out in private industry. On the contrary, all available figures suggest that the outsourcing of state security responsibilities to the private sector actually costs taxpayers money.

A fundamentally graver flaw—one which cannot be gotten rid of with more precisely formulated and monitored contracts— has to do with the nature of the contracts themselves. Service providers are profit-driven enterprises that are rarely interested in the fulfillment of specific social and political goals. Entities that conclude contracts with such firms must accept that the companies can get out of any agreements, citing fears for their own existence or their employees' safety, should they deem it opportunistic to do so. A firm that decides the risks are too great in the process of fulfilling a contract, or that receives another, more lucrative offer, can unilaterally nullify the agreement. The only deterrents are written contractual sanctions and the possibility of losing out on future business deals. There is no way of forcing PMCs to perform contracted services. There is no guarantee that they will fulfill contracts in hostile environments.[19] The consequences of breach of contract are very different in the military than in the civilian realm. In the Balkans, as well as in Afghanistan and Iraq, individual PMC employees and whole firms have repeatedly failed to deliver promised goods and services to combat troops. The risk of being killed, to put the matter bluntly, was too great to provide fuel, water, food, and ammunition to the front lines. In December 2003, for example, sixty South Korean mercenaries deserted their posts and refused to provide contracted services, after two of their comrades were killed in intense fighting in Northern Baghdad.[20] It is thus hardly astonishing that regular members of the armed services often feel disgruntled at PMCs contracted to provide vital supplies—the soldiers feel the companies often put them in risky, occasionally life-threatening situations. And there is no way for armies to court-martial employees of private corporate entities for desertion or failure to obey orders, as would be the case with regular soldiers.

LEGAL IMMUNITY AND AMBIGUITY FOR NEW MERCENARIES

The problems of transparency, accountability, monitoring, and responsibility are broadly legal as well as contractual. State security officials and employees—police officers, soldiers, and others—are subject to strict regulations that determine to whom they are ultimately accountable. But that is not the case with PMCs and their personnel. Civil law contracts do not allow the client to influence a company's personnel affairs. The state can demand and expect from military service providers that they abide by internationally binding regulations and national laws, but how private soldiers behave on the ground in crisis situations is the firm's business. PMCs may maintain that they instruct their personnel to respect national laws and international human rights standards, but aside from such declarations of intent, the state has no assurance about or chance to monitor what will happen when new mercenaries are deployed. Even when clear cases arise in which laws have been broken, the state's hands remain largely tied. Normally, state prosecutors are responsible for taking action against crimes, regardless of the nationality of the alleged perpetrator. In Iraq and other countries, however, mercenaries enjoy special protection. In passing Coalition Provisional Authority Order 17 of June 2003, which was renewed on June 27, 2004, the Iraqi provisional government granted exemption from prosecution to all personnel acting on behalf of the coalition—including PMC employees. The order amounts to a virtual guarantee of immunity, applying even to grave offenses such as murder. The Iraqi Interior Ministry has reported some forty to fifty cases in which new mercenaries allegedly shot civilians without just cause. The ministry said, however, that the PMCs concerned refused to provide information and denied all responsibility.[21]

The situation is even more complicated when private soldiers work for foreign military companies. The dilemmas associated with this situation are especially apparent in Iraq, where insurgents have taken hostage new mercenaries from South Africa, Nepal, Italy, Japan, and Belgium. The kidnappers' demands are not made to the PMCs that employ such people, but to the countries they come from—as the example of Fabrizio Quattrocchi and his three comrades from chapter 1 illustrates. Given the current national and international situation, a state cannot prevent its citizens from working for a foreign military company. The state can only warn private soldiers that they risk prosecution if they engage in armed conflicts in which the state itself is not involved, and in practice, the state has little chance within its own legal system to punish offenders. Nonetheless, in the eyes of enemy combatants, the state is responsible for the actions of its citizens. The legal gray area inhabited by private soldiers is often used as an excuse by insurgents for not adhering to international conventions of war. The logical result is a barbarization of warfare. In Iraq, citizens of Arab countries like Egypt or Morocco who worked for U.S. PMCs have been singled out for target killings. Among them have been translators who had been involved in the Abu Ghraib torture scandal.

Articles III and IV of the 1949 Geneva Convention strictly distinguish between combatants and the civilian population. New mercenaries are not combatants insofar as they are not part of combat troops and aren't subject to the military chain of command. Neither, however, are they civilians since they are involved in the machinery of war, are employed by governments, and frequently carry arms. The Geneva Convention defines combatants as people directly and actively involved in hostilities. But this definition is of little use since it does not specify what "directly" and "actively" mean, and it remains largely unclear what activities private soldiers engage in. New types of warfare further muddy the situation since in virtual warfare, time and space are often divorced from one another. To take an illustrative question: Is a private soldier in Florida who presses a button launching a carpet bomb attack in Afghanistan only indirectly involved in war, while a regular soldier delivering supplies there is directly engaged in hostilities? International human rights conventions have no answers to these questions.

Nor do PMC employees or the firms they work for fit the definitions put forth in the United Nations' 1989 International Convention against the Recruitment, Use, Financing and Training of Mercenaries. In order to be considered a mercenary, an individual or company must clearly fit *all* the criteria laid out in the convention.[22] Thus, international human-rights lawyers say that even if the new mercenaries do most of the same things as the old ones, they are not the same in the legal sense. The result of the diverse legal issues, from contracts to human-rights regulations, is a paradox. The legal status of PMCs is what makes it so difficult for them to be legally monitored.

International Convention against the Recruitment, Use, Financing and Training of Mercenaries (1989)

Article 1

For the purposes of the present Convention,

1. A mercenary is any person who:

    (a) Is specially recruited locally or abroad in order to fight in an armed conflict;

    (b) Is motivated to take part in the hostilities essentially by the desire for private gain and, in fact, is promised, by or on behalf of a party to the conflict, material compensation substantially in excess of that promised or paid to combatants of similar rank and functions in the armed forces of that party;

(c) Is neither a national of a party to the conflict nor a resident of territory controlled by a party to the conflict;

(d) Is not a member of the armed forces of a party to the conflict; and

(e) Has not been sent by a State which is not a party to the conflict on official duty as a member of its armed forces.

2. A mercenary is also any person who, in any other situation:

(a) Is specially recruited locally or abroad for the purpose of participating in a concerted act of violence aimed at:

(i) Overthrowing a Government or otherwise undermining the constitutional order of a State; or

(ii) Undermining the territorial integrity of a State;

(b) Is motivated to take part therein essentially by the desire for significant private gain and is prompted by the promise or payment of material compensation;

(c) Is neither a national nor a resident of the State against which such an act is directed;

(d) Has not been sent by a State on official duty; and

(e) Is not a member of the armed forces of the State on whose territory the act is undertaken.

THE CONFLICT BETWEEN DEMOCRACY AND PRIVATIZATION: A STATE WITHIN A STATE

The intense debates about the role of the military in democracies illustrate how difficult it is to socially control an area like the armed forces. For example, when the Bundeswehr was created in postwar West Germany, political leaders tried to learn from the mistakes of the past by developing concepts like "inner leadership" or "citizens in uniform" intended to prevent the military from abusing its power or being misused by civilian groups.

Sophisticated regulations were needed to establish democratic norms and principles and set up obligatory monitoring and decision-making procedures. They were the only means of protecting the primacy of politics over military power and ensure the state's monopoly on the legitimate use of force. But with the outsourcing of many military tasks, the entire painstakingly constructed, if by no means perfect, division of responsibilities begins to look shaky.

Governments' duty to their citizens to maintain security, which includes democratic control over the use of force, cannot be reconciled with private industry's emphasis on profits. The two have different goals, and that's why, in practice, they're so often incompatible. For this reason, privatizing governmental security responsibilities and subjecting them to the commercial desire for earnings is all the more problematic. Unlike feudal or autocratic states, constitutional democracies understand security as the protection of every individual citizen and not just the sovereign ruler or state itself. It should be a given that, in a functioning democracy, the profit interests of parts of the society take a backseat in security questions.

The problems of privatization are particularly evident in the areas of espionage and intelligence. It has always been a gigantic challenge, and remains so today, to fit this sector into a democratic system of checks and controls—and the rise of PMCs has made the task even more difficult, if not impossible. In light of new military developments such as information warfare, the possession of data and knowledge has taken on greater importance than ever. Since PMCs are primarily interested in profits, not security, there is no way of ruling out the possibility that the knowledge they accumulate will be misused. Take the case of the leader of the Angolan anticommunist leader Jonas

Savimbi and his movement UNITA, which enjoyed the support of the West and fought with the help of South African and
other military companies against the Angolan government. The
result was one of the most horrific civil wars in Africa. With the
end of the cold war, the situation changed drastically. Once the
Angolan government had lost the support of the Soviet Union,
the West, eagerly eyeing the immense petroleum reserves under
government control, changed sides and dropped their assistance
for UNITA. PMCs involved in Angola also swapped clients.
Using the information at their disposal, they had an easy time
capturing Savimbi, destroying UNITA, and trumpeting their
actions as having helped end the civil war.

There are numerous examples of this kind. American PMCs
such as DynCorp, which officially serves the U.S. government
in its "war on drugs" in Colombia, have repeatedly passed on
data collected on reconnaissance flights to local armed forces
and paramilitaries, as discussed in more depth in the previous
chapter. As a result, civilian aircraft have been "inadvertently"
shot down, farming villages razed to the ground, and rebel
troops attacked by paramilitaries.[23] In 2005 after Colombian
guerrillas engaged in gunfire with DynCorp employees, an U.S.
Congressman was quoted as saying, sarcastically, that that was
what one called "the outsourcing of war."[24]

The questionable legality of PMCs' use of intelligence
is threatening to the populations of strong states as well as
those of third world countries. There is no way of gauging the
civil rights consequences of the unmonitored use of information that PMCs, using the latest IT technology, collect on a
daily basis about private individuals as part of the war against
terrorism. Several members of Congress, including Vermont
senator Patrick Leahy, see military privatization as posing

an "enormous danger to the private sphere of American citizens."[25] PMCs subtly erode the state's function as a guarantor of various individual constitutional rights.

One characteristic of democratic states is their ability to control and channel military power and limit the influence of the military on politics and civil society. Privatization has already granted commercial companies much greater direct or indirect influence over international strategies of intervention, conflict, and war. Their growing power is particularly great in the area of realization. PMCs now have a major and sometimes decisive say in how individual intervention missions are carried out and by what means. As bizarre as it may sound, private companies can now specify how a military action proceeds and which foreign-policy aspects are accentuated. Moreover, the pressure exerted on politicians increases when the business interests of PMCs coincide with those of the industrial or financial sectors.

For example, a hardly insubstantial portion of U.S. intervention and aid money for Africa can be traced back to the intense lobbying of Washington by oil companies and military service providers. The close connection in the United States between PMCs, the state bureaucracy, the armed forces, the weapons industry, and the government is personified by vice president Dick Cheney and secretary of state Condoleezza Rice, who previously occupied leadership positions at Halliburton and Chevron respectively. But they are only the most prominent examples of a system characterized by a high degree of cronyism. Influential political representatives (former state spokespeople, diplomats, and the like), state bureaucrats, and high-ranking military men sit on the boards of nearly all private military companies. Diligence LLC, for example, was founded by former CIA and MI5 members, and the firm entourage includes William

Webster, the only man in history to head both the CIA and the FBI; ex-U.S.-ambassador to Germany Richard Burt; Ed Rogers, George H. W. Bush's right-hand man; former George W. Bush campaign manager Joe Allbaugh; ex-MI5 member Nicholas Day; former U.S. diplomat and antiterrorism specialist Steven Fox; Jim Roth, a fifteen-year veteran of the CIA; Whitler Butler, previously responsible for CIA covert operations in Iraq during the Saddam Hussein era; Lord Charles Powell, a former foreign policy advisor to Margaret Thatcher; Mac McLarty, who worked for the Clinton administration; ex-U.S.-ambassador to the EU Rockwell Schnabel; and Professor Kurt Luak, formerly a manager with Chrysler, Feba, and Audi. The boards don't look much different at the Steele Foundation, CACI, Custer Battles, Ronco Consulting, Triple Canopy (Vinnell), Halliburton, MPRI, DynCorp, or SACI. Observers have used the phrase "revolving door" to describe the movement of many PMCs' board members between PMCs and other influential government and arms industry positions.[26]

PMCs use an army of lobbyists, at a cost of between $60 and $70 million a year, to acquire government contracts, block unwanted congressional inquiries, and influence budget decisions. In the 2004 U.S. elections, they made around $12 million in political contributions, some five-sixths of which went to the Republicans. And the investments paid off—the industry experienced unprecedented growth under the George W. Bush administration, particularly when backed by a Republican Congress. So many large contracts came in that the military service industry was stretched to capacity and began to recruit members of special forces units such as the Rangers, the Seals, the Delta Forces, and the British SAS. Today more people trained by the SAS work for PMCs than for the British armed forces, and the departures have meant that many British Special Forces units are no longer combat-capable. Some U.S. Special Forces units have started granting members who agree to return to service a year's "vacation" so that they can work for the lucrative private sector.[27]

PMCs have caused dangerous cracks to appear in the democratic foundations of "strong states." There is no telling at present whether they represent a danger to such states' long-term stability. But what is unsettling is that politicians have yet to consider how the gaps can be filled and what sort of repair measures need to be taken. Continuing to operate according to the status quo, however, means endangering democracy.

10

Deceptive Security
National Betrayal in the "Weak States"

If you see a goat in a lion's den, you should be afraid of it.
— African saying

Private military companies are overwhelmingly located in the West, but they do most of their work in the third world. They are paid by the "strong states," which directly or indirectly exploit the natural resources of weaker ones. They act primarily in the foreign-policy interests of Western industrial societies—only secondarily servicing the needs of the countries in which they are active. Experience shows that the deployment of military service enterprises has not been able to establish lasting peace in conflict regions. One telling example of this is Sierra Leone, a country which because of its immense diamond reserves has repeatedly been the site of violent conflicts, and in which foreign interests have played a major role.

In March 1995 Executive Outcomes began a massive intervention in Sierra Leone at the behest of president Valentine Strasser, who like his Western allies was most concerned about the country's natural wealth. The aim was to put down the rebels of Revolutionary United Front (RUF) under Foday Sankoh—a brutal paramilitary opposition movement that used child soldiers and had taken control of Sierra Leone's diamond-mining areas. Executive Outcomes' task was to drive the self-appointed "freedom fighters" from the diamond-rich Kono region. EO accomplished this mission with extreme speed and efficiency, sending the RUF down to disastrous defeat, driving them from Kono and over the border into neighboring Liberia. Shortly thereafter Strasser was deposed in a coup d'etat. A subsequent putsch ensued, and once EO had left the country, the majority of young men and soldiers in Sierra Leone joined the RUF. In a military attack, the RUF pushed back government troops, which could only hold on to the area around Freetown with the help of Nigerian-led ECOMOG (Economic Community of West African States Monitoring Group) forces. The rebels took over the rest of the country. In the next few years, troops from the Organization of African Unity intervened at the behest of the United Nations. PMCs—initially EO and then Sandline—also got involved at the request of various Western oriented governments. But the basic situation changed little—except for the growing chaos and poverty within Sierra Leone itself.

Things settled down briefly when Foday Sankoh was named, with approval from the international community, the country's vice president. But the basic conflicts in Sierra Leone remained unresolved and continually rekindled. The consequences were further cycles of armed conflicts and foreign interventions. While a fragile cease-fire has been in effect since 2002, the situation in Sierra Leone today is as unstable as it was ten years previously, with rebels continuing to control 50 percent of the country's diamond reserves.[1]

Sierra Leone is hardly an exception—the story is similar in many African countries, including Rwanda, Liberia, Angola, and Uganda. In all those countries, interventions by PMCs decided a conflict in the short term for one of the warring parties. But such interventions did not change the basic relations of power by strengthening state institutes or resolving disputes in the long term. In many regions of the world—for example Congo, the Philippines, Chechnya, and Colombia—short-term military interventions have actually prompted an escalation of conflict. This has been the case in countries where guerrillas, drug cartels, and terrorist groups have also enlisted the services of PMCs and increased their military capacity.[2] Conflicts become entrenched and increase brutality in countries like Colombia or Congo, where rebels have been able to seize regions with natural resources (be they cocaine or minerals and oil) that can be exploited to refinance military campaigns. But even in countries such as Liberia or El Salvador, where disputes have been kept from flaring up into armed hostilities and cease-fires have prevented civil wars, society remains split into two hostile camps, rendering any hopes of lasting security illusory. The native populace continues to dance on the edge of a volcano, watching helplessly as economic and social standards stagnate or decline. There have been reports, for example, of more deaths in El Salvador after the peace treaty of 1992 than during the entire course of the civil war.

DYSFUNCTIONAL RELATIONSHIP AMONG MILITARY, STATE, AND CIVIL SOCIETIES

The intervention of private military companies further undermines what is usually already a tense relationship among the military, the political leadership, and the civilian population. When a state invites foreign military service providers into a country, it demonstrates a lack of faith in its own military, and military leaders feel humiliated at having foreign mercenaries forced upon them. The fact that the political leadership grants foreigners full access to the sensitive area of security only heightens the mistrust. The dramatically higher wages paid to private soldiers also causes resentment among ordinary soldiers. If PMCs, as is usually the case, recruit personnel from the native populace, removing them from the national armed forces and, in countries like Rwanda and Congo, favoring people from certain ethnic groups, the potential for conflict becomes nearly infinite.[3] The lack of success in establishing democratic structures in Afghanistan has led to dangerous tendencies in that country's police force, since police officers prefer to work for foreign military companies than to be integrated into the state apparatus.[4]

In the case of Sierra Leone, the immediate result after the cessation of hostilities was a military putsch. PMCs have difficulty seeing themselves as a supplementary force whose job it is to assist the governments of weak states—assuming they would accept such a contract at all.[5] Even when their contract is restricted to education and training, tensions vis-à-vis the executive branch of the client state and the power-mindful native military are preprogrammed. Moreover, national armed forces that have been trained by foreign specialists remain dependent on them for weapons and strategy if they want to maintain their newly won military might.[6] The superiority of "strong states" in this area is so blatant that the militaries of third world nations are constantly playing catch-up. The civilian population often sees the employees of private military firms as occupation troops and treats them with a mistrust that generally extends to the government responsible for bringing them into a country. The people's faith in their political leadership and their own state disappears. Feelings of uncertainty grow and, with them, the perceived need for protection.[7] The tendency toward self-organization into particular communities gains momentum, hastening social disintegration and ratcheting up existing tensions.

Another frequent consequence of the deployment of PMCs is the "localization of security." When called upon to pacify a specific crisis region, PMCs are well equipped to exploit superior military and security technology and quickly establish "islands of peace," in which the economic activities crucial to the survival of a state can proceed unimpaired. But such operations only transfer the potential for conflict to other parts of a country, where fighting often breaks out in even fiercer form. On all continents of the world, foreign military specialists have gradually transformed oil-producing areas into high-security zones, from which insurgents and rebels have been driven. Yet such groups continue to operate, encircling and besieging such areas—for example, the Angolan exclave province of Cabinda, which is pressured from both sides by the neighboring Republic of Congo and the Democratic Republic of Congo. The national state, in any case, loses its sovereignty in both types of territory.[8]

Even minor affairs can have far-reaching consequences due to the intervention of PMCs. In Nigeria, for example, ethnic groups in the oil-rich Niger Delta squabbled for years over the distribution of revenues and the environmental destruction caused by the Shell company. In 2003 when striking oil workers took hostages to lend more weight to their demands, the

British PMC Northridge Services intervened with a mixture of diplomacy and military force. That intervention unleashed a major domestic crisis involving Nigeria's government, military, and opposition parties. The main dispute was over who had hired Northridge to get involved with the country's internal affairs. The issue was never settled because Northridge refused to name its client.[9]

The maquiladora industrial areas, discussed in a previous chapter, are another example of what is meant by "localization of security." Inside these quasi-extraterritorial zones, PMCs maintain order according to the rules of the foreign companies engaged in production there. External security is usually provided by state military or police forces, which are thereby degraded to the status of security guards. Such "glocal" areas—local regions of cheap production for the global market—have arisen throughout the third world, and PMCs are largely responsible for their security. A kind of apartheid between rich and poor is the norm in and around these areas, and the state can rarely control the potential for conflict this sort of inequality engenders.[10]

THE QUICK FIX: BUYING SECURITY

Here we see another problem that undermines security structures in "weak states." Deploying PMCs to deal with ongoing conflicts represents a quick fix for countries' political leadership.[11] Building up or restructuring one's own security forces, would not only take time but also consume significant budgetary resources. Maintaining an army and police force is a running expenditure, whereas leasing the services of a PMC is one-off expense. The state's duty to protect foreign organizations and citizens on its soil can also be outsourced. Countries like Angola even require private companies wanting to do business on its soil to provide their own security strategies and personnel.[12] Aid organizations and firms thus often have no choice but to use PMCs. The result is a gradual loss of state control so that governments can no longer demand transparency and accountability. Security is thereby transformed from a public right to a private commodity available for purchase only by those who can afford it. There is little chance of monitoring how armed forces hired for protection are actually used. Dictators can employ PMCs against opposition parties and companies can use them to secure their facilities against rebel attacks, just as rebels can hire them to launch such operations.[13]

Although on paper weak states maintain their sovereignty and their monopoly over the legitimate use of force, and though they still occupy seats at the United Nations, they largely cease to exist as autonomous entities. Having lost their de facto sovereignty, they largely devolve into a network of particular interests—the state can only exist as long as the stronger forces within it cooperate.[14] The situation is worsened when strong states hire private military companies to implement security components of aid and development programs without binding those firms to specific tasks. The United States, for example, uses companies like SAIC, DFI, MPRI, and Logicon to carry out the practical and theoretical training it provides to various African national forces under the African Contingency Operations Training and Assistance (ACOTA) Program. The British Department for International Development also outsources security development and the protection of its foreign property.[15] In a parliamentary report from October 2002, the Foreign Office said it employed 121 private companies to protect 102 locations in almost an equal number of foreign countries.[16] Human-rights organizations such as Amnesty International have repeatedly pointed out that internationally legal standards are not part of training and education programs. Nor is instruction on how to behave in accordance with human-rights or weapons regulations.[17] Sponsored training programs are enjoyed even by states such as São Tomé, which have often been investigated for abuses of their own people and occupy the bottom of lists concerning countries that respect human rights.[18]

THE LOSS OF THE MONOPOLY ON THE LEGITIMATE USE OF FORCE

The hollowing out of the state—the weakening and dissolution of governmental institutions in the realm of external and domestic security, which is caused or accelerated by the employment of PMCs—creates security zones of divergent quality and density.[19] Affluent citizens live in gated communities such as Alphaville, in São Paolo, Brazil.[20] Alphaville's borders are protected by high walls, security fences and gates, video surveillance, and ID checks. Outsiders are denied access, and the community is patrolled by armed security company employees who are entitled to shoot interlopers. At the other end of the scale are the favelas, shantytowns, and slums in many metropolises, whose borders are equally visible and where outsiders are also frequently shot at. But state security forces rarely, if ever, venture into such areas.

The two extremes seldom come into direct contact. Nonetheless, the state's withdrawal from both creates the conditions for the rapid radicalization of conflict in the rest of society so that, if security structures are generally weak, disputes can no longer be kept under control. Numerous examples from conflict regions show that states which rely on rented security quickly lose the ability to guarantee various segments of society the safety they require. The state becomes unable to monitor the self-protection mechanisms put in place by particular communities. Brewing conflicts meet with a vacuum of state force in the absence of legitimate institutions based on social consensus. The state's political organs no longer have any way of mediating in conflict situations. If the opposing sides of a conflict fail to find a resolution, the situation threatens to escalate and turn violent.[21]

One direct and indirect consequence of PMC activities in weak states is the growth and rapid spread of organized crime. On the one hand, small firearms become the norm in regions cut off by the apartheid of poverty, as residents seek to protect themselves and compete in internal battles. On the other, weapons and drug dealing, prostitution, and human trafficking become profitable, expanding enterprises as unscrupulous mafiosi move into areas over which state institutions have little to no say. Conversely, unofficial networks and semilegal shadow economies help organized crime penetrate the legitimate economy and the state bureaucracy. Corruption and bribery spread. Profits made on the global market flow back into the system, and money laundering becomes an industry in its own right. Revenues earned by trafficking in contraband and illegal services, to say nothing of crime, are reinvested in the legal economy. Construction, tourism, and leisure are legal branches of commerce that often come under mafia control. As is most famously the case in southern Italy, this economic power, aided by support from part of the populace, gains political influence and eventually becomes political power.[22] The result is that the unavoidable social conflicts that arise in every community can no longer be resolved peacefully by democratic and constitutional institutions, and society is increasingly ruled by the law of "might makes right."

PLUNDERING OF NATURAL RESOURCES

The empire of firms maintained by Executive Outcomes showed how tightly connected PMCs and other economic enterprises could be.[23] Today—thanks in part to the international negative publicity generated by EO—PMCs are seldom incorporated into the same holding companies that include firms that exploit natural resources or raw materials. This sector has developed in a different direction.[24] For legal reasons, clear divisions are maintained between security and industrial firms. This is especially apparent with large, transnational corporations, which contract the services of PMCs but do not share any capital interests with them. But for weak states, it makes little difference whether a PMC and a mining company operate as brothers in arms or whether each independently pursues its own profit-oriented goals.[25]

To supply European consumers with affordable parquet flooring, companies using PMCs chop down forests in Asia, Africa, and South America. The military firms are needed to deal with or break the resistance of native populaces against the destruction of their home environments. States that allocate forestry rights—for example, Malaysia, Liberia, and Burma—restrict their own role to the administration of the revenues from this lucrative business and are perfectly willing to allow the private armies of wood companies to do as they see fit.[26] The situation is not all that different from that of the British and Dutch East India Companies three hundred years ago.[27] The American PMC Pacific Architects and Engineers has two subsidiaries active, in Japan and in Malaysia, to safeguard business activities throughout the Asian Pacific.

Among the clients they service in New Zealand, East Timor, Malaysia, Singapore, Thailand, Vietnam, Korea, and Japan are Esso Malaysia, Brunei Shell Petroleum, and Nippon Steel Corporation—as well as Microsoft, Procter & Gamble, and Walt Disney. Other PMCs are active in Burma for Western oil and gas companies and in Sri Lanka, Nepal, Cambodia, Taiwan, Brunei, and the Philippines for various private economic interests.[28]

But transnational corporations and PMCs aren't the only ones involved in exploitation of the third world's natural wealth. In the course of globalization, the governments of powerful countries, too, have intervened to secure national interests and create favorable conditions for "their" companies. With countries such as China, Britain, Russia, France, and the United States, it is difficult to determine where national interest ends and private enterprise begin. Several examples suffice to illustrate this situation.

In March 2004 former Executive Outcomes employees staged a failed coup in Equatorial Guinea. The goal of the putsch was to oust the ruling dictator, Obiang Nguema—who was supportive of Exxon's exploratory drilling in his country's oil-rich waters and who was in turn backed by the United States and MPRI—and replace him with Severo Moto, who was living in Spanish exile. Competing interests of oil companies from various states provided the backdrop to the attempted coup since the former Spanish colony had for a long time been regarded as an El Dorado by the petroleum industry—and financiers from across the globe wanted to get their hands on the astronomical profits expected from the black gold. Most of the mercenaries involved in the operation were given lengthy prison sentences. But Mark Thatcher, one of the financial masterminds of the coup, was allowed to go free, thanks to the influence of his mother, Maggie Thatcher, former prime minister of Britain. Meanwhile, despite recent dramatic rises in oil production, the populace of Equatorial Guinea remains one of the poorest on the African continent.[29]

In the Darfur region of Sudan, where huge oil reserves have been discovered, the U.S. government employs two firms, DynCorp and Program Analysis and Evaluation (PA&E.) According to their contracts, they are tasked with building up nonspecified bases, creating logistical systems, and providing transport and communications capabilities. They are paid on an open-ended contract basis that allows Washington to deploy the two firms indefinitely—not just in Sudan, but through the African continent. The contract is written in the "cost-plus" mode, which allows the firms to recoup all their expenses plus a 5 to 8 percent profit on top of them.[30] The State Department considers their activities to be part of a peacekeeping mission aimed at resolving the undeclared, twenty-five-year-old civil war between the Sudanese government and the Sudan's People's Liberation Army. In the past few years there have been more than a million refugees and more than fifty thousand casualties in the Darfur region alone. Washington's justification for contracting the two private firms is surprisingly frank. In 2004 a senior U.S. government official was quoted, under the condition of anonymity, as saying: "We are not allowed to fund a political party or agenda under United States law, so by using private contractors, we can get around those provisions. Think of this as somewhere between a covert program run by the CIA and an overt program run by the United States Agency for International Development. It is a way to avoid oversight by Congress."[31]

Darfur, of course, is primarily known internationally for its refugee crisis, not for the battle over its oil reserves. There are no contracts regulating who will be granted the rights to drill for that oil or how the resulting revenues will be split. Currently, China and Pakistan are among the leading oil-drilling nations in Sudan. But to judge from the numerous multilateral talks about the problems and conflicts in the region, many conducted at the behest of the United Nations, it is safe to assume that the refugees and displaced will scarcely profit from the natural wealth of their former homeland.

Regardless of whether one is talking about tropical wood or oil, coltan or copper, diamonds or gold, cobalt or silver, manganese, uranium, cadmium, germanium, beryllium, or other natural resources in the third world, the methods and means of exploiting and transporting them to the strong states (if necessary in processed form) remain the same. With the opening of global markets and the eradication of export duties, more and more natural resources have been removed from "weak states." The revenues generated have constantly declined, siphoned off by native elites, who deposit part of the fees paid for drilling or mining rights into bank accounts in tax havens and distribute the dwindling remainder among their own cohorts.[32] The populaces concerned can hardly defend themselves against this sort of exploitation. The "hollowed-out" state has scant means of demanding that its rights be respected. With a significant portion of society in many African countries hovering at or below the existential minimum, people have little choice but to resort to violence to keep from starving.

Generally speaking, crisis-ridden states that have tried to solve their problems by employing PMCs have gotten even weaker as a result. None of the countries concerned have made any progress toward becoming a strong state—on the contrary, everywhere one looks, security structures and conflict resolution mechanisms have become more fallible and weak. As the UN Special Rapporteur Enrique Ballesteros has observed in many years of studies concerning countries around the globe, PMCs provide the illusion of stability while failing to address fundamental problems and causes of strife.[33] They have never shown themselves capable of long-term conflict resolution. In order to ensure peace and create security structures in crisis nations, what is needed is a political approach that is not based on satisfying immediate interests, but rather aims at reconstructing state and social institutions. This requires endurance. Such aims cannot be implemented quickly, but they can be realized in the long term.

11

Aid Organizations
In the Military Slipstream

Do not repress your anger, but do not yield to it either.
—TIBETAN SAYING

During the war in Afghanistan, the U.S. media repeatedly quoted Colin Powell as saying that humanitarian organizations were important "force multipliers."[1] Powell's choice of words made it abundantly clear what role the U.S. government envisions for aid organizations in countries where Washington intervenes militarily. The fears of NGOs that their work could be instrumentalized to support policies of war were confirmed, and they protested against the attack on their status as neutral, autonomous helpers.[2] But that protest attracted little media attention. The conflict of interests was heightened with the beginning of the Iraq War, as U.S. and British forces pursued a strategy of "embedding" potential critics, including aid workers and journalists, among coalition troops. After the end of major hostilities, the Coalition Provisional Authority (CPA)—the U.S.-dominated civilian authority in Iraq—demanded that NGOs sign a declaration subordinating themselves to coalition forces and that they accept a requirement to file quarterly reports.[3] The NGOs refused, whereupon USAID, the U.S. development aid authority, threatened to ban them from receiving public funding. Still, few NGOs gave in. Most withdrew their personnel and ended their activities in Iraq.[4] Even those who stayed behind soon had to close up shop after coalition forces—in defiance of guidelines drawn up under the auspices of the United Nations—gradually restricted their access to protection, which was largely provided by employees of PMCs.[5] UN Secretary-General Kofi Annan protested to the Bush and Blair governments that the CPA was required by international law to ensure protection and security. But that appeal fell on deaf ears.

ENDANGERED NEUTRALITY

The fundamental disagreement about the role of humanitarian assistance manifests itself not only in the relationship between NGOs and governments but also, in more heated form, in relations between aid organizations and military service providers. For PMCs, international interventions are a business with the aim of making profits. For the state, they are ostensibly aimed at establishing political stability. NGOs understand themselves as providers of help to individual people, independent of political, economic, or other interests. In many, perhaps even most concrete cases, the aims of these various entities are incompatible. At the same time, the "new wars," in which the number of active participants has increased and previous clear distinctions between the military and civilian populations have become ever more blurred, have created new security needs for NGOs while reducing the actual protection they are afforded. In recent years, nearly all of the world's humanitarian organizations—including the Office of the United Nations High Commissioner for Refugees, the International Red Cross, CARE, Médecins du Monde, and Doctors Without Borders—have suffered casualties and been the targets of kidnappings and hostage-takings. Between July 2003 and July 2004, more than one hundred civilians working for the UN or NGOs were killed in conflict regions.[6]

In response to the heightened threat faced by aid workers, PMCs have begun offering protection services that states are unwilling or unable to provide. This creates an insoluble dilemma. In Iraq, the PMCs came out as the winners. The military companies are in a relatively strong position since governments often insist that the security of NGOs can only be guaranteed if they accept publicly financed, private protection.

In various international agreements, most notably the Code of Conduct for The International Red Cross and Red Crescent Movement and NGOs in Disaster Relief, drafted and agreed upon in 1994, humanitarian groups have agreed to maintain strict neutrality and independence from governments.[7] NGOs fear—rightly, as experience shows—that it will be difficult, if not impossible, to preserve their basic principles if they work together with PMCs. In Afghanistan, Iraq, and elsewhere, native populations view aid workers with suspicion if they are protected by private soldiers, armed or not. Some, indeed, view coalition troops as occupiers. They take Colin Powell at his word and see aid workers as a supplementary arm of the military machine.

Such views gain credence among the populace at large when

insurgents, resistance groups, or rebel movements can argue that one and the same PMC protects aid organizations and foreign governmental workers and private companies.[8] The mistrust can turn to outright aggression if it is discovered that intelligence agencies have infiltrated aid organizations with the aim of collecting information. Italian aid workers in Iraq report that most NGOs, including the Red Cross and Red Crescent, have been "bugged."[9] Italian hostages recounted, after being freed from captivity, that Iraqi insurgents were well informed about the level of intelligence infiltration.[10] In these ways the ostensible protection provided by PMCs can raise the security risks faced by humanitarian organizations.

MILITARY FIRMS AS SECURITY RISKS

Aid organizations aren't the only ones facing heightened risk. In many cases, the dangers faced by civilian populations are also increased by the involvement of PMCs.[11] This applies particularly to conflicts surrounding the exploitation of natural resources by foreign firms. There is a huge range of examples from a variety of crisis-ridden countries. For some segments of the civilian populace, accepting protection from PMCs is tantamount to taking sides in the conflict, making oneself a legitimate target for attack.[12] In other cases, civilians are used as human shields for rebels who either mingle with ordinary citizens or exploit them as buffer zones between themselves and the other side of the conflict. If humanitarian organizations use PMCs to create safe havens for civilians in these cases, they deny protection to one side of the conflict and raise the risk that those civilians will be seen as legitimate targets for attack. In still other cases, warlords essentially take civilian populations hostage, demanding ransom before allowing humanitarian aid to be brought to its needy recipients. If NGOs try to bypass such payments and get direct access to the needy by employing private military companies, the civilian population may be directly involved in military conflicts, or access cut off entirely. This can result in not only hunger but also direct physical abuse by soldiers. And if it becomes known that a PMC works both for foreign businesses and aid organizations, contact between humanitarian workers and the native population becomes all but impossible.[13]

Even less obvious examples from everyday practice illustrate the fact that when aid organizations employ PMCs, their work can be devalued, and the opposite effect achieved to one intended. Legal NGOs in Latin America like the Instituto Latinamericano de Servicios Legales Alternativos (ILSA), Colombia Human Rights Network (CHRN), and the Comité Permanente por la Defensa de los Derechos Humanos (CPDH) report that union-rights activists and victims of human-rights abuses refuse to talk to them as soon as it emerges they enjoy protection from private soldiers.[14] The situation becomes even more critical in cases where illegal practices in the exploitation of raw materials are being investigated.[15] NGOs can fall into the same disrepute as transnational companies and PMCs. Trust in "independent" legal representatives diminishes, skepticism grows, and cooperation becomes virtually impossible if legal aid organizations are perceived to be in bed with the enemy. Those who worked with attorneys have been targeted for reprisals, and even some legal aid workers themselves have been attacked. Cultural, economic, educational, and medical aid organizations tell of similar experiences.[16]

In areas with little to no security, protection purchased from private military companies represents a privilege that calls the neutrality of the purchaser into question. The general populace sees aid organizations as unfairly favored entities who have the power to buy safety—unlike the aid recipients. The majority of the population in crisis regions are unable to afford such luxury.[17] That creates a security discrepancy between aid providers and aid recipients, causing tension that can escalate in a variety of directions at any time. Ever conscious of the value of being perceived to be neutral and independent of government influence, most NGOs, including the International Red Cross and Red Crescent, Oxfam International, Caritas Internationalis, and Bread for the World, refuse to be protected by PMCs.[18]

They argue that, in the past, a principles-based code of conduct offered them the greatest protection. The widespread and well-founded image of existing only to help people laid the foundation for a broad acceptance of aid organizations' work, both among hostile parties and the populace at large. The politicization of conflicts and the attempted instrumentalization of humanitarian aid workers caused the populace to question their neutrality, which had been the basis for their acceptance and thus personal safety. [19] Even within the condition of new warfare, most NGOs say that the greatest protection consists in the legitimacy of their work, the trustworthiness of their personnel, their integration into the cultural and social environment where they are active, and the accompanying ability to anticipate risks and dangers. Using PMCs, they say, does not increase their security. It "militarizes" their work.[20]

This impression is strengthened because most PMCs simply try to execute whatever mission they are contracted for, wherever they are deployed. Humanitarian operations are conceived as an expression of solidarity with an entirely different content.

The aid organization Medico International puts the situation in the following terms: "The white helicopter pilot who saves a newborn child from a tree surrounded by floodwaters stands for 'humanitarianism,' the symbol of an 'interventionist' assistance that swoops in from the inside that mostly disappears again."[21] The divergent goals of profit and assistance is just one of the factors making it difficult for PMCs and NGOs to work together. Another is the different ways in which the two entities see crisis situations. Just as an ecological problem can also be seen as a legal, health, or economic one, the issue of security can be viewed from a humanitarian or a military perspective. Where the conditions for work are concerned, a satisfactory result from a military perspective differs from success as defined by humanitarian organizations. This is the reason why many NGOs criticize the gradual militarization of conflict resolution. In the words of Christian Aid representative Dominic Nutt, contracting PMCs to provide protection is akin to "robbing Peter to pay Paul."[22]

THE NEED FOR NEW PROTECTION CONCEPTS

Cooperation between the two entities is also difficult because humanitarian organizations have little chance of effectively monitoring the work done by private military companies. When such firms are hired by the state, NGOs don't even enjoy the privilege of helping draw up the contract, which would give them more influence over the behavior of the company's employees. Aid organizations are in no position to demand, to say nothing of ensure, transparency.

Should human rights violations occur within a region where PMCs are responsible for maintaining order, the reputations of humanitarian organizations can be swept into disrepute.[23]

In the worst-case scenario, the native populace may even consider NGOs to be complicit in the abuse. Moreover, even when humanitarian organizations do conclude contracts directly with PMCs, holding the firms accountable for their employees' behavior, the problem of enforcement remains. Experience shows that private military companies are hardly able to live up to the ethical, political, and professional accountability standards of NGOs.[24] Even if they are guaranteed on paper, there is hardly any way of practically implementing them. Especially in so-called sensitive theaters of operations, that is, in regions where powerful economic or political interests play a major role in conflicts, and espionage activities promote those interests—humanitarian organizations can never be entirely sure how PMCs will carry out contracted tasks. For example, NGOs have no way of guaranteeing that private firms won't use the information and knowledge they garner from their operations to earn, perhaps via a subsidiary, additional profits by working for the "other side." Fears that they could are hardly baseless.[25] British companies such as ArmorGroup and Global Risk are known to have exploited insider knowledge gained from government work to write their bids to aid organizations—there is no reason that the inverse shouldn't be the case.[26]

Since 1989, as various international research institutes have determined, humanitarian assistance has been politicized and militarized.[27] Meanwhile, private military companies have gained influence in how governments allocate aid money. As a result, humanitarian organizations face increased risk. There is no question that the dangers in the world's conflict regions have increased in the past decade, and one reason is that the causes of conflict have grown more complex. "Strong states" abrogate responsibility for such disputes by outsourcing them to PMCs, and it is extremely questionable whether private firms can help humanitarian organizations reduce risks. Practical experience thus far suggests precisely the opposite. Rarely do aid organizations encounter ideologically motivated private soldiers like Zlatan M., discussed in the first chapter of this book. [28] The most positive influence is likely firms such as Mine Tech International or Bactac, which specialize in humanitarian tasks such as the removal of mines from former war zones and also take over protection duties in conflict regions. But even such tasks can often be carried out better by civilian organizations—for example, Norwegian People's Aid, an independent association supported by the Norwegian federation of labor unions, which is active in more than thirty countries. In Mozambique, People's Aid took over the major mine-removal work despite the presence of foreign private military service providers.[29]

PMCs provide only a partial solution for gaps in state security structures. The assistance they offer is locally and temporally limited and often achieves the opposite effect to the one intended in the long term. At present, aid organizations and military companies are almost completely incompatible.[30] The only option for NGOs is to do without private military assistance and adapt their security strategies to the new conditions of conflict and warfare. Many groups—including the International Red Cross and Red Crescent, CARE, the International Rescue Committee, Save the Children, and World Vision—have indeed begun developing new approaches based on their own individual needs.[31] They have established internal security departments, drawn up risk analyses, carried out safety training for their personnel, and hired consultants specialized in crisis management. In "critical areas," they enlist native security forces with police training whose qualifications have been checked.

Nonetheless, as many observers have pointed out, humanitarian groups and NGOs in general are having difficulties finding their feet in a changed world. Above all, they do not speak with a single voice.[32]

12

Conflict Resolution without Private Military Companies?
Markets for Violence versus State Monopolies

> *When fish cry, you can't see the tears.*
> —AFRICAN SAYING

The use of PMCs in various regions of the world has given rise to a number of problems that have yet to be satisfactorily addressed. From the standpoint of the military service industries and many of their clients, there are a number of arguments for privatizing public security services. But from the perspective of the citizens of Western countries and the inhabitants of nations affected by military action, there are at least as many arguments against the use of PMCs. The following table provides a summary of the pros and cons.

Area	Pro	Con
Cost	PMCs work more cheaply	• Savings not proven; evidence to the contrary • No quality monitoring; cost-benefit relationship unclear • PMCs are profit oriented • PMCs' business is nontransparent • PMCs are not legally accountable • True costs of military operations remain opaque
Military	• Military can concentrate on core tasks • PMCs operate more flexibly and deploy personnel more quickly • Synergy between PMCs and military	• Military dependency on PMCs • PMCs are unreliable in crisis situations • Short-term warehousing unsuitable for wartime supplying • Unsatisfactory cooperation between military and PMCs • Additional tasks for military, including protecting PMC personnel
Peacekeeping and humanitarian missions	• Rapid reaction of PMCs during crises • Quality and radius of action raised for UN missions • Protection of humanitarian organizations • Deployment of national troop contingents can be reduced	• Security duties of nation-states and UN are delegated and privatized • Nontransparent PMCs are legitimized by UN • NGOs are delegitimized by association with PMCs • Human-rights violations are difficult to uncover and prosecute • Security risks for NGOs heightened

Area	Pro	Con
International Crises	• Stabilization of collapsing states • Involvement of private sector in postconflict societies	• Continuation of fighting is in the interest of PMCs • PMCs may discredit foreign policy of home country • Distinction between civilians and soldiers blurred • PMCs operate as concealed agents of government
Technology	PMCs have better technical know-how	• PMCs unable or unwilling to make know-how available in crises • Know-how can be misused or applied against employer
Politics	Governments can outsource security tasks and make their own armed forces more flexible	• PMCs not subject to democratic monitoring • PMCs difficult to control democratically • Guaranteeing security is the task of the state • Precarious balance between civil society and the military is disrupted
Law	• PMCs are licensed to operate by governments • Codes of conduct could regulate PMC behavior	• Lack of legal rules for PMC deployments; little opportunity to check whether rules are followed • PMCs and their employees are difficult to prosecute • Geneva Convention (distinction between combatants and noncombatants) is superseded

The arguments for and against the deployment of private military companies contain several problematic areas that require further clarification and discussion. The first might be characterized as the "democracy imperative." It concerns the question of how military privatization can be implemented without going against the will of the body politic. The second problem is the state's monopoly on the legitimate use of force, which is undermined by PMC activities. The third refers to a variety of open questions having to do with what we'll call the "peace imperative."

(A note to my American audience: The following section, like the rest of this book, was originally written for a European audience, and the national army with which I am most familiar is the Bundeswehr, so my commentary is based on that.)

VIOLATING THE DEMOCRACY IMPERATIVE

There is little opportunity to legally and publicly monitor how PMCs use military force or carry out policing duties. Their only law is that of the market; their only public is the client. Although the private-industry principle functions relatively decently as far as civilian commodities and services are concerned, the conditions for successful privatization are almost completely absent in the area of security. Citizens can neither test the quality of the product nor determine whether the quantity of services on offer fairly reflects the price. Above all, citizens have no sanctions at their disposal—for instance refusing to accept or pay for services—in order to have a say on issues like quality and price.

Whereas citizens exercise an indirect influence on the quality of public services through the ballot box, they are stripped of any power over the services offered by PMCs. Even private military companies' biggest client, the state, has little chance at present to monitor their activities. In Germany, PMCs are not required to report to the government, which is why the state formed a pub-lic-private partnership to oversee military privatization. There is little transparency. Nor are there any means of checking which contracts have been concluded and for what or whether they have been fulfilled. This opacity dooms any attempt at effective monitoring. Who, for example, can check whether the privately made uniforms German soldiers wear are worth what they cost? Reports published by the GEBB, the aforementioned public-private partnership, don't contain any information on this score. Who can guarantee that DynCorp or its parent company CSC, which get their biggest contracts from the Pentagon and U.S. intel-ligence agencies, won't misuse data from the German military, to which they, with the privatization of nonmilitary computer ser-vices, now have access? Neither the current German government nor the state as a whole can offer any such reassurances.

People have been aware of the dilemma presented by lack of transparency, accountability, and monitoring for some time now. In the Anglo-Saxon world the issue was raised immedi-ately after the first deployments of PMCs. In the meantime, there has been no shortage of publications and seminars in which experts discuss regulatory models aimed at mastering the situation.[1] But an even remotely satisfactory solution has not been found. The standards that govern the military, the police, customs officials, border guards, and state intelligence agencies do not apply at all to contracts given to PMCs.

State-security organs in Germany, for example, are subject to at least five different types of monitoring. There are internal checks (the internal affairs division of the police), legal checks (the prosecutor's office and the courts), government checks (the federal ministries), legislative checks (parliament) and public-sphere checks by citizens and the media. Infractions against rules and regulations can be effectively sanctioned at every level. But where private military companies are concerned, there are no equivalents to these horizontal and vertical instances of "circular monitoring." Moreover, there is little indication that such a system is in the offing. The German parliamentary debates on PMCs of September 2004, which were discussed in a previous chapter, had no effect whatever. No legislation was drawn up, and the government officially proclaimed that it saw "no need for national regulations for private security and military companies beyond existing laws."[2]

Consequently, PMCs exist in a vacuum, free of regulations and hardly limited by law, which allows them to do pretty much as they see fit.[3] The democracy imperative, however, demands circular checks and balances. If consistency were the only issue, governments wouldn't be allowed to issue contracts to private military companies without such guarantees. The problem is that if regulations were in place to ensure transparency and monitoring, the situation wouldn't be economical. The government apparatus needed to apply accountability standards to hundreds of PMCs scattered across the globe would be so huge and expensive that no state in the world could afford it. Monitoring military privatization is thus doomed to fail due to financial constraints alone.

Politicians constantly stress the need to reduce military expenditures, but there are ways of saving money other than outsourcing military tasks. The administration of the German Army's financial dealings, which up until now has been subject to the dictates of the military bureaucracy, is perhaps a relic of the past, and nothing argues against separating the economic and military realms within the Bundeswehr and reorganizing the former along free-market lines. Well-trained managers, who operate within the military realm and use private service providers, would be able to administer a mammoth organization like the German Army more cheaply than midsize enterprises if the Bundeswehr were fragmented into smaller units.

In the past few years, those who previously hailed privatization as the cheapest alternative have lowered their voices. A host of studies has failed to provide any concrete evidence for any such economic advantage.[4] On the contrary, most indicators suggest the outsourcing of military services actually costs taxpayers money. Critical observers of the military suspected right from the beginning that the desire to increase military capacities, rather than the desire for savings, was the real reason behind the trend toward outsourcing. This applies especially to Germany, but also to states like France and Italy, where military privatization is still in its infancy. There are sufficient money-saving alternatives, including the reorganization of forces into quick-response units and battle groups and the formation of European police troops.[5] The mistakes made in the Anglo-Saxon world do not have to be repeated.

JEOPARDIZING THE STATE'S MONOPOLY ON FORCE

The principle of the state's monopoly on the legitimate use of force was laid out in the Treaty of Westphalia from 1648. Today, more than 350 years later, force is once again becoming a free-market commodity. The brief history of mercenaries offered in chapter 5 described the risks the privatization of force has entailed in the past. They range from the intervention of freelance troops in the internal affairs of states that hire them to the assumption of power by coup d'etat. With good reason, as Europe became more democratic, the ability to exercise armed force was taken out of the hands of private actors and given over to the state. The partial undermining of this principle essentially puts military might back in the hands of particular interests. The consequences are wide-ranging and potentially devastating insofar as they can fundamentally destabilize sovereign states. Numerous examples discussed in this book have suggested how PMCs have intervened in the internal affairs of foreign countries. They have helped bring some governments into power and helped overthrow others—and not just in so-called weak states. In strong states like the United States, too, they have directly or indirectly influenced government foreign policy. The growing power of PMCs, fed by their intimate relations with the military-industrial complex, can be felt in ever-larger segments of the state—the military being only the most obvious. In the United States, this development has progressed to the point where the private military industry now exerts direct political influence. Be it in the form of massive campaign contributions or aggressive lobbying, there is hardly a lawmaker who can escape the industry's power.[6]

German history, too, has shown on more than one occasion what can happen when the military begins to function as a state within a state. In such cases, the military not only helps steer the decisions of the government but also influences the cultural life of society and the individual lives of its citizens. The consequences are far graver when military force becomes privatized, as was the case in the early 1930s with the paramilitary Freikorps that marauded the streets of the Weimar Republic. That development was the result of an alliance between purveyors of violence, large parts of Germany's armed forces, and the armaments industry. After the massive destruction of World War II, Germany initially had no military. It was only in the mid-1950s that the Bundeswehr was reconstituted. It was subject to civilian monitoring and control and conceived as an army of "citizens in uniform." A reprivatization with the goal of outsourcing everything not part of the core military tasks might not take Germany back to the situation of Weimar. But it would almost certainly create the same sort of problems as it has in America.

There are also differences, however, between medium-size countries like Germany, Italy, Poland, and Spain and a global superpower like the United States. The employment of PMCs, located mostly in the Anglo-Saxon world, but active around the globe, necessarily leads to a loss of sovereignty for smaller countries, and the fact that all the nations named above are members of NATO does not change this. The example of the Iraq War, which Germany refused to support, shows how vital it is for smaller countries to preserve as much autonomy as they can. As profit-oriented companies, military service providers necessarily focus on the clients that give them the most numerous and biggest contracts. The experience they gather throughout the world is then leased out to the most powerful client and highest bidder, and that—for the foreseeable future—will always be the United States. Consequently, for medium-size countries, using PMCs is an indirect path toward becoming more dependent on America.

Internally, the partial loss of the state monopoly on the legitimate use of force has far-reaching consequences for the maintenance of social harmony. Germany is unlikely to become like Brazil, where society has splintered into three distinct security zones (slums, government-protected middle-class areas, and privately guarded gated communities). But the privatization of protection services does lead to inequitable distribution. The first steps in this direction have been taken in Germany with the outsourcing of security services in shopping malls to public-private partnerships and with the establishment of gated communities.[7] Examples from the Anglo-Saxon world, where this trend is much more advanced, show that unfairness has already become a reality. One of most crass inequities at present results from the privatization of prisons. Construction, furnishing, and personnel standards, as well as the conditions in which prisoners live, vary drastically according to what private companies, with an eye toward the bottom line, deem adequate and what their clients are willing to pay. To reduce costs, companies like Wackenhut—a subsidiary of G4S and one of the world's largest players in the private prison sector—have gone over to relocating their facilities to foreign countries, chiefly Mexico, with lower wages and operating expenditures. The trend toward moving prisons to low-wage countries is particularly popular in the United States.[8]

The inequitable distribution of security leads to social segregation. In countries that fail to guarantee everyone's right to security, regardless of income, citizens lose faith in state institutions. Popular trust in the fairness and sovereignty of the state is undermined when the people are forced to obey the dictates of private security providers. Moreover, if private guarantors of security are not subject to public monitoring, societal order is threatened. Serious conflicts are preprogrammed. Ultimately, there is no guarantee that private actors from military companies and employees of state security organs won't come to see each other as enemies. This is the situation in a number of third world countries and could become reality in strong states as well, if political solutions aren't found to check the growing power of the military service industry.[9]

THE POLITICS OF PEACE IN THE MILITARY SLIPSTREAM

PMCs have become an integral part of the security policies of several strong states, while in others they lead a considerably more modest existence. The discrepancy results from the divergent concepts of conflict resolution that individual states pursue internationally. In order to explain the different status of PMCs in various societies, we need to explore the differences in how those societies tackle crises.

In a globalized, interdependent world, it is both morally untenable and politically myopic to believe that the whole world revolves around the maintenance of the living standards and the security of a handful of highly industrialized nations. "Peace in the Northern Hemisphere and war everywhere else" is an illusion. Like peace itself, security cannot be fragmented. Security in general can only be attained if the goal is to achieve the same standard everywhere, and if that aim guides international politics. Making progress toward this goal would mean that both the international community and every individual nation-state would have to do its part to ensure that conflicts become less violent and less frequently settled by military means. In turn, crisis prevention must be given priority over military stabilization. The latter, however, appears to set the agenda in many wealthy nations, particularly in the Anglo-Saxon world. The result is a kind of "democratic neocolonialism" that cannot guarantee lasting security. Nor is it economically feasible in anything but the short term.[10]

At present, security is unevenly distributed across the world. Conditions in the majority of countries are such that they are unable to settle conflicts by peaceful means. Military interventions are not the proper instruments to remedy the situation since they are fundamentally incapable of creating peace. All they can do, as the examples of Sierra Leone or Congo show, is establish temporary cease-fires. Crises can lead to wars, but they do not originate in armed conflict. Increased effort, therefore, must be applied before divergences within a given society flare into violent conflict.

Most of the nations of the Northern Hemisphere accept this logic, but don't put it into practice. Ironically, the five permanent members of the UN Security Council, who are supposed to keep peace around the globe, produce 90 percent of all the weapons used in the world.[11]

While the wealthy nations of the Northern Hemisphere spent more than $600 billion in recent years for military interventions, they were unwilling to double the amount of international development aid they offered from $60 to $120 billion. The money made by Kellogg, Brown and Root in Iraq alone would probably have sufficed to render military interventions in many parts of the world unnecessary. Moreover, several of the wars in the Southern Hemisphere could have been prevented if the world's rich nations had expanded state institutions for monitoring weapons of mass destruction, internationally prosecuting war crimes, and controlling the flow of revenues resulting from the exploitation of raw materials.[12] As the German Development Ministry noted in a 2004 report, "those who hold back in the expansion of civilian, preventative institutions but are willing to intervene militarily must accept that others have doubts as to their motivations."[13]

The many similarities between the world's wealthy nations notwithstanding, there are major differences. Some like Germany accept the principle that crisis avoidance should take precedence over military intervention.[14] During peacekeeping and nation-building missions, they deploy state soldiers and police forces that work together with civilian organizations. Other countries, such as the United States and Britain, prioritize military intervention and view civilian humanitarian organizations as a vital part of their fighting forces.[15] Today, many people think that the United States and Britain only get involved in places where there's "something to be won," and that both neglect to support civilian institutions where they are needed most. The paradigm shift in U.S. and British aid policies, which began in the late 1990s and was completed with the "war on terror" after 9/11, is seen as a sign that those two countries increasingly view the world through a military lens.[16] Developmental policies are more and more commonly conceived of strategically as means of dealing with the consequences of military interventions and wars. The focus is on examples of "spectacular reconstruction," while U.S. and British aid and development ministries outsource the associated security tasks to private military companies.

CRISIS MANAGEMENT AND PMCS

Private military companies are pushing for ever greater involvement in this strategy of crisis management via military intervention. Not only do they favor short-term military solutions to conflicts over long-term options that aim at just compromises between competing interests; they also offer the means for realizing the former. The solution to countering risk, in their view, is the application of external force, also known as "peace from above." PMCs assume a central role in this strategy, both during intervention themselves, as in the Balkans and Afghanistan, and afterward, as in the case of Iraq, when private companies are largely responsible for providing armed security.

But decades of experience have shown that peace cannot be imposed from above. Instead it must grow up "from below."

Easing tensions and preventing conflicts from flaring into wars is complex work that has to be done simultaneously on a variety of levels. It is not enough to impose security structures on a state apparatus, as PMCs propagate. Diverse means of civilian support must be applied in order to achieve a long-term compromise of interests in a conflicted population. Overarching, legally accountable security organs do play a valuable and sometimes decisive role. But they are a means to a solution and not the solution itself.[17] And PMCs are not adequate instruments for this task because, as private foreign companies, they command neither legitimacy nor the trust of the population.

Compromise is impossible without several preconditions: equal access to medical care and education, a just distribution of wealth that secures everyone's existence, a welfare system that allows all segments of the population to participate in social life, a culture that encourages the easing of resentments and combats stereotypes of the "enemy," and confidence-building measures to bring together the parties in a conflict. The former president of the World Bank, James D. Wolfensohn, put it this way in a German-language position paper: "With sensitivity for issues of social equity, cities will never be safe nor will societies be stable. With a sense of belonging, too many of us will be condemned to leading a marginalized, armed, and terrible life."[18]

PMCs can play no role in this process of compromise. Therefore, it is only consistent for humanitarian and nongovernmental organizations that work in this area to refuse to operate in the slipstream of military interventions. Doing so would be irrational and counterproductive. Military means can only combat the symptoms, but not the actual causes of conflict.[19]

13

Preventing Crisis
and Securing Peace

Only for the sake of the hopeless ones have we been given hope.
—WALTER BENJAMIN

At present, thanks to its dominating role as "global police-
man," the United States is most influential in shaping public
attitudes toward questions of conflict and crisis resolution.
As a result, many people are unaware that there are alternatives to the current U.S. strategy of military interventions
and the massive deployment of PMCs in crisis-ridden third
world countries. But there are alternatives, and not just theoretical ones. They simply receive less media attention than the
spectacular exploits of mercenaries. Moreover, attempts to
mediate the violent conflicts in "weak states" have a different con-
ceptual basis and are seldom seen as an alternative to armed
intervention.

The creation or reestablishment of peace and security is not just a military task. The question of whether to use PMCs in this process is not only a matter of what is most opportune. The question of how to achieve peace is primarily a political issue, depending on the sort of security that is the ultimate goal. There are divergent views on the issue, and they have framed the debates that have taken place on the international level of the UN, the transnational level between NATO and the OAU, and the national levels between various political parties in various states.

"PEACE FROM ABOVE" VERSUS "PEACE FROM BELOW"

The situation can be characterized in somewhat polemic, simplified form as a choice between two fundamentally opposed options. Option one is to make peace by imposing security and stability from above, using legitimated military or police force. PMCs play a significant, indeed integral, role in this idea. Conflict resolution, long-term development, and lasting peace are secondary aims. Option two, by contrast, aims at fostering peace, building up security structures, and stabilizing societies from below. Crisis prevention and conflict resolution are the main means toward those ends, and civil groups play a primary part in them. The use of force is seen as a last resort and the exception to the rule. PMCs play no integral part in this process, and the role envisioned for them, if indeed there is one at all, is restricted to supportive tasks such as the guarding of public buildings.[1]

In reality, option one and option two seldom occur as absolutes. But they can be used to envision a scale representing the political strategies of various countries.

Option 1: Peace from above	Middle	Option 2: Peace from below
Israel, United States, Canada, Poland, Britain	Netherlands, Japan, France	Spain, Sweden, Norway, Germany, Finland

There is a clear connection between a country's position on this scale, on the one hand, and the number of PMCs located there and the frequency with which they are deployed, on the other. More than 80 percent of companies involved in the military service sector come from countries on the left, 10 percent are located in nations to the middle and the right, and the remainder are scattered throughout the third world. States that favor peace from above deploy PMCs both within and beyond their own borders. The other states use them domestically only to take over "nonmilitary" tasks, and as a rule they only officially send state soldiers and police abroad. International organizations like the UN and its various subsidiaries, the Organisation for Economic Co-operation and Development (OECD) and the World Bank—together with the vast majority of NGOs and humanitarian organizations—are all located to the right on the scale or explicitly pursue option two.

In option one, the main emphasis in efforts to create stability and conditions for peace in third world countries is on building up a "strong state" with massive military and police forces and consolidated government institutions. These forces are supposed to guarantee that conflicts within civil society can be regulated. Nations like the United States that prefer this strategy concentrate their foreign aid on measures aimed at training and strengthening armies and police forces. For reasons of political and economical opportunism, a significant portion of those tasks are farmed out to PMCs.[2]

The emphasis in option two is on crisis prevention, conflict resolution, and the creation of peace. It offers an integrative approach that encompasses foreign, financial, developmental, legal, environmental, and cultural policies. In order to be realized practically, option two requires a number of points of intervention at various times. The personnel used is almost exclusively civilian. Although crisis prevention and the creation of peace most often represent a continuum, we can distinguish between two main phases of intervention work. The first is concerned with attempts on many levels to prevent conflicts from escalating. The second comes after the end of an armed conflict. (Interventions also take place during the intermediary phase of war.)

The German Federal Ministry for Economic Cooperation and Development has drawn up a list of conditions to be met during such interventions. They are (1) respect for human rights, (2) participation of the people affected in political decisions, (3) legality and the maintenance of legal protection, (4) the creation of market-oriented and socially just economic systems, and (5) developmental goals as a guideline for state action.[3]

The following illustration depicts three levels of intervention (local, intrastate, and national) with native partners (which I have chosen to call "participants") and provides examples of who gives support on what level and with which instruments provided by donor countries.[4]

Conditions for Interventions

Participants		Intervention
High functionaries and members of:	**Upper Level** state, government, political parties	**Official diplomacy** for example, cease-fire negotiations
Representatives and persons of respect from:	**Middle Level** administration, business media, culture, regional institutions	**Unofficial Diplomacy** for example, roundtable discussions, well-drilling, establishment of judicial system
Local leaders, teachers, doctors from:	**Lower Level** local institutions, health and education, basic necessities	**Practical and technical assistance** Provision of necessities (water, food), hospitals, schools, etc.

The time frames involved are determined by the specific short-, medium-, and long-term goals to be attained, together with the vision of permanent social and governmental stability, continual socioeconomic development, and lasting peace. Short-term measures may include emergency aid for refugees, assistance for famine victims, and medical treatment for the ill and wounded. Medium-term measures are things like providing schools for children, reintegrating soldiers into society, protecting the rights of women, providing water, and improving agrarian infrastructure. Long-term measures encompass structural changes such as the establishment of a universally accessible health-care system, a transparent and accountable state financial apparatus, reliable administrative structures, an equitable judicial realm, and a participatory political system.[5]

THE GERMAN PLAN OF ACTION

As early as 1999, Sweden proposed a plan of action that would take an option-two approach,[6] and in May 2004, the German government presented a version of its own entitled "Civilian Crisis Prevention, Conflict Resolution and Peace Consolidation."[7] The analysis of the world's crisis regions contained therein proceeds from the assumption that armed conflicts are both the result and the cause of broad political, social, economic, and ecological imbalances. On the issue of whether commercial purveyors of force should be involved in armed conflicts, the German plan criticized the fact that nonstate participants currently play a significant role in current conflicts: "The so-called privatization of war can be seen in the complex interrelations of warlords, militias, rebel associations, terrorists and criminal bands, but also in the presence of *mercenary troops* and *private security firms* that hinder the state in the exercise of its monopoly on the legitimate use of force." (Emphasis is the author's.) As far as the economic dimension of the "new warfare" was concerned, the plan identified drug harvesting, smuggling, arms sales, kidnapping, the trafficking of women and children, and slavery to be the pillars of an economy of violence. The trading of legal natural-resource commodities such as oil, diamonds, wood, and coltan, the plan added, "made the application of force economically rational and has led to the creation of difficult-to-eradicate structures of violence." The increasing involvement of organized crime in civil wars and the close connections between illicit and legal economic realms and global economic circulation, said the plan, created "new, central challenges in conflict resolution."

On the basis of this analysis, the plan formulated the following goals. On the one hand, governments should pursue policies of civilian crisis prevention, conflict resolution, and peace consolidation. On the other, in keeping with an expanded concept of security, the plan suggested that it was not enough just to establish and strengthen the state structures necessary for avoiding conflict in regions of actual or potential crisis. Potential motors for peace also had to be created within civil society, the media, and cultural and educational realms, and the opportunities available to the affected population had to be increased with targeted measures in the areas of the economy, society, and the environment.

The plan identified three strategic areas crucial to the achievement of these goals. The first was the creation of reliable state structures; the promotion of legal equity, democracy, and accountable political leadership; and the strengthening of governmental and civilian control over the security sector. The second was the encouragement of potential guarantors of peace, the establishment and development of civil society, of independent and professional media, and of cultural and educational institutions. The third was the equitable organization of economic and social life as well as the protection of the environment and natural resources.

Concerning the security sector specifically, the action plan noted that the vast majority of ongoing armed conflicts took place within individual states.[8] The plan concluded that economic and social development was impossible so long as citizens of such states were not protected from violence and criminality by a functioning governmental monopoly on the legitimate use of force. "Socially disadvantaged groups within the population," the report concluded, "are particularly dependent on minimum standards of physical and legal security." Consequently, the report found that reforms in the security sector were key to the prospects for peace and lasting development. The idea of such a reform was not limited to the state institutions, such as police, the military, or intelligence services, responsible for protecting a government and its citizens against coercion and violence. The plan deemed it equally important to establish functioning civilian checks on these institutions by the parliamentary, executive, and judicial branches of government. Civil society and the media were also given an important role in the monitoring process. The plan did not include PMCs in the proposed projects for reforming the security sector.

But the German Action Plan was not without weaknesses. It was written in an option-two language that stressed crisis prevention, conflict resolution, and the establishment of peace. But it was extremely vague and ambivalent in its visions and suggestions for how those aims should be realized, and remained trapped in the traditional logic of intervention more characteristic of option one. The plan did not detail what the relationship between civilian and military providers of assistance should be. Theoretically, civilian aid was given precedence, but in terms of the budgetary means to be allocated, that relationship was reversed in favor of the military. Today, for example, there are eight thousand German soldiers involved in three world conflict regions, compared to only five thousand German aid workers trying to provide assistance in more than 130 countries. The amount of money set aside for foreign interventions by the German military and the government's antiterrorist measures, €1.5 billion, dwarfs the sums allocated for civilian crisis prevention and peace-building. There is no reason to expect the situation to change. The German Action Plan was thus fated to remain a paper tiger, especially as the document itself states that "due to federal budget constraints it will not be possible to pursue all positive measures in the realm of civilian crisis prevention insofar as they extend beyond the battle against terrorism in the narrow sense."

In principle only two elements remain. First, the German military continues to train soldiers from the third world "with an eye toward a democratic reform of the security sector." Second, the Action Plan sets a favorable political agenda for institutions and organizations involved in crisis prevention and peace building—without, however, placing additional personnel or resources at their disposal.

CRITICISM FROM NGOS

The Association of German development NGOs, VENRO, which includes over one hundred members and is headed by the Catholic and Protestant churches, had the following comments on the plan: "Civilian-military cooperation is addressed in various chapters and actions. But while the Action Plan draws attention to the points of convergence between civilian and military crisis prevention, it does not attempt a clear distinction between these two areas."[9] Furthermore, VENRO added: "We are convinced that militaries and NGOs are guided by divergent goals, interests, and approaches. As a rule, NGOs rule out cooperating with armed forces in the civilian support initiatives they undertake in conjunction with interventions." For NGOs, the question of whether and how to work together with the military depends on the concrete, individual situation. In principle, they reject all forms of cooperation in cases where "political and military goals endanger [NGOs'] own understanding of themselves and call their independence into question."

The association also criticized the fact that, although the

plan contained a declaration of intent encompassing 160 measures, no additional funds were allocated for financing them. That, according VENRO, was the plan's great weakness.

Along with other objections, the association drew attention to two further points, both of which concern the activities of private military companies. VENRO noted positively that the Action Plan had addressed the issue of nongovernmental purveyors of force as an important factor in current conflicts: "In the conflicts currently going on, a role is being played by armed, nongovernmental groups that are supported, equipped, and deployed by states to further their own interests." The association demanded that this development be given more attention in the realization of the Action Plan. On the other hand, VENRO called for more accountability among commercial enterprises and better monitoring of PMCs. The association praised the Action Plan's "emphasis on the responsibility of the private sector in crisis regions" as well as the efforts of the German government to raise levels of transparency and accountability among their allies in the exploitation of natural resources. Such trends should be extended to "the disturbing increase in the privatization of security tasks," VENRO asserted, calling for state instruments for transparency, accountability, and monitoring to be bolstered.

In contrast to a tendency in politics and public opinion to see the world through a military lens, NGOs are remaining true to their primary emphasis on civilian, preventative measures. They fear that, with the increase in the number of military interventions, more and more people will come to accept them as normal political instruments and thereby sanction the idea of peace from above. In contrast, VENRO emphasized: "On their own, military interventions can never establish peace. The best they can do is achieve cease-fires. The difficult tasks of reaching a compromise between competing interests, of reconciliation and creating political and social structures capable of keeping the peace can only be tackled politically and must be done, as a rule, by the society in question itself. Peace must grow 'from below.'"[10]

CONFLICT RESOLUTION AS A CONCRETE CHALLENGE

The German Society for Technical Cooperation, or GTZ, a private enterprise owned by the government, is one institution that has had proven success with crisis prevention and concrete, on-the-ground improvements in the third world. The GTZ gets most of its contracts from the German Federal Ministry for Economic Cooperation and Development. Its mission statement stresses "crisis prevention" and "conflict resolution" with the aim of achieving "structural stability" and the "lasting establishment of peace."[11] Its main areas of activity are law and administration, rural development, organizational and communications consulting, economic and social policy, protection of the environment and natural resources, and education and health.

The GTZ is also involved in reforming the security sector, a project that affects nearly all the other areas of their work, especially if "military, police, the judiciary, intelligence services, and prosecutors' offices are not capable of . . . their original tasks, namely the establishment and maintenance of security, and instead represent a security risk for citizens."[12] In such cases, the GTZ develops concrete programs that aim to "create a democratically monitored security sector of appropriate dimensions and with adequate resources, a precisely defined mandate and a modern culture of professionalism." The GTZ then advocates for its ideas on the political, institutional, economic, and social levels.[13]

Another GTZ focus—one which stands in stark contrast to the ideas of conflict resolution pursued by PMCs—is on coming to terms with the past and reconciliation. NGOs in general stress the importance of such work for the consolidation of peace since "past injustice can easily lead to new outbreaks of violence."[14] In addition to counseling individual trauma victims and establishing sites of cultural exchange and information centers, the GTZ concentrates on five areas:

1. It offers support in solving the problems that typically arise after violent conflicts and the collapse of familiar systems. That includes legal advice on amnesty or reparations legislation, how to resocialize the victims of persecution, and how best to scrutinize the past actions of state employees.

2. The GTZ also helps build institutions capable of resolving conflicts, including truth and reconciliation commissions. They support third world countries in evaluating evidence and help prepare commission members to conduct questioning and consult with other national authorities.

3. Furthermore, the GTZ participates in the criminal investigations of past injustices and promotes alternative institutions for mediating legal disputes. Those tasks encompass things like assisting prosecutors and investigative units, training judges and lawyers, coordinating national and international NGOs to observe trials, and setting up structures to allow all segments of society access to formal investigative, complaint-registering, and legal institutions.

4. The GTZ is also concerned with civilian integration of police forces and uses measures such as the establishment of local police-citizen forums.
5. Finally, the GTZ also helps establish local civilian reconciliation initiatives and create "peace alliances."[15]

The work of organizations like the GTZ shows what form crisis resolution and peace-making can take if approached from a civilian and not a military perspective. Practical experience demonstrates that conflict resolution is too complex a process to be successfully carried through by use of armed force or other solutions from above. Deploying PMCs is a primitive way of addressing such complex problems as the ones that lie at the heart of most armed internal conflicts in the third world. Private military companies are no option for long-term peace consolidation. Instead, as many examples have shown, they tend only to intensify existing conflicts.

CONCLUSION

Resignation is the worst of all virtues.
— GUSTAVE FLAUBERT

In the wake of the horrors and unimaginable atrocities of World War II, the founders of the United Nations decided to condemn all forms of warfare. They revoked the right of nations to wage war as a legitimate form of politics using other than standard nonviolent means, and declared wars of aggression to be criminal under international law. This fundamental idea is anchored in the UN Charter and is binding legal principle in the community of nations.

Simultaneous with the paradigm shift toward the idea that sovereign states only had the right to defend themselves, people came to see that war was much too important and dangerous to be left solely up to the generals. Politicians were mandated to put the brakes on military logic. Today, we might say that

conflict resolution and the establishment of peace are too important to left up to the military-economic logic of private military
companies. If the logic of the military tends to have undesirable
consequences, how much more dangerous is that thinking when
it is paired with the commercial desire for profit?

There is one thing upon which everyone concerned agrees.
PMCs owe their existence to war and make money from conflicts and uncertainty. In contrast, state political action under
the UN Charter is supposed to aim for peace and security. The
military service industry has no interest in such conditions since
they are bad for business. If the world were peaceful and stable,
PMCs would have no reason to exist.

Astonishingly, many politicians continue to argue that the
world cannot do without private military service providers.
PMCs may have fundamentally changed parts of the world
after the end of the cold war, but there is not a single activity
they carry out that couldn't be done more cheaply, effectively,
transparently, and directly. Without PMCs, there would be no
need to fear that the state's monopoly on the legitimate use of
force is being undermined or that private intelligence services
are encroaching on the security and privacy of state citizens. To
put the matter even more drastically: PMCs are both unneces-
sary and dangerous to the democratic coexistence of people
and nations.

If military service providers are superfluous, why are they
deployed? Why has the industry experienced such a boom? The
answer is relatively simple. When speaking off the record, even
those who argue for the economic efficiency of PMCs tend to
admit the real reason for such companies' existence. The executive branches of powerful states or dominant political groups
want—be it on behalf of national, economic, or simple power

interests—to be able to deploy more troops than are available in their countries' official armed forces. They prefer to use military forces that are free of parliamentary oversight. They want to intervene militarily in places where they are forbidden to do so by international law. They want to assist friendly rulers, parties, and other political groups abroad in struggles against their internal political opponents. They want to secure economic resources and energy supplies without visibly deploying their official military force.

The purported necessity of PMCs is nothing other than a cover for political calculation and opportunism. And because this is so, the military service industry creates legal problems, both nationally and internationally, that no citizen of a democracy can afford to ignore.

NOTES

Chapter 1

1   On this set of issues, see Pagliani, *Il mestiere della guerra*, 175–198; Musah,
    "A Country Under Siege: State Decay and Corporate Military Intervention
    in Sierra Leone," *Mercenaries: An African Security Dilemma*, 76–116; Sean
    Creehan, "Soldiers of Fortune: 500 International Mercenaries," *Harvard
    International Review* 23 (Winter 2002): 4.

2   Silverstein, *Private Warriors*, Chapter 2, "Arms and the Man: The Talented
    Mr. Glatt," 47–108.

3   See the International Consortium of Investigative Journalists, *Making a
    Killing*, Chapter 10.

Chapter 2

1   Jim Krane, "Private Firms Do US Military's Work."Associated Press
    (29 Oct. 2003); Sanho Tree, cited by Sheila Mysirekar, "Krieger gegen
    Bezahlung," radio report, Deutschlandfunk(28 May 2004).

2   See the company's website at www.icioregon.com.

3   See Steffen Leidel, "Trainer für den Krieg." 9 April 2003. Deutsche Welle,
    http://www.dw-world.de/dw/article/0,2144,827450,00.html.

4   Diverse examples can be found in Esther Schrader's article, "U.S.
    Companies Hired to Train Foreign Armies," *Los Angeles Times*, April 14,
    2002.

5   See J. Chaffin, "US Turns to Private Sector for Spies," *Financial Times*,
    May 17, 2004.

6   See Corporate Watch, March 7, 2005 (www.corpwatch.org).

7   See Leidel, "Trainer für den Krieg."

8   BASIC collected the material about contracts from diverse sources. The
    majority of this information is based on research done by the International
    Consortium of Investigative Journalists (ICIJ). Neither the American nor
    the British government disputes its accuracy.

9   See "About Us: What We Do." Centurion website,
    http://www.centurionsafetynet/About/What_We_Do.html.

10 See "Appendix 4: PMC Contracts in Iraq." British American Security

Information Council, http://www.basicint.org/pubs/Research/
2004PMCapp4.pdf.

11 See Vignarca, *Mercenari S.p.A.*, 17ff.

12 The sum is based on several calculations. Between 1994 and 2001, contracts worth a total of $300 billion were awarded to private military
firms. For the year 2001, estimates run between $100 and $120 billion.
In the wake of America's so-called war on terror and the U.S.-led wars
in Afghanistan and Iraq, the expenditures for private military firms rose
enormously.

13 Cited in Ken Silverstein's article "Mercenary, Inc.?" *Washington Business
Forward*, April 26, 2001.

14 See Ellen McCarthy, "Pension Funds Press CACI on Iraq Prison Role,"
Washington Post, June 11, 2004.

15 See Doug Brooks. "Write a Cheque, End a War: Using Private Military
Companies to End African Conflicts," *Conflict Trends* 1 (June 2000):
33–35.

16 See *The New Yorker*, May 1, 2004; *The Boston Globe*, August 20, 2005.

17 See Barry Yeoman, "Dirty Warriors," *Mother Jones* (November/December
2004) Also available online at http://www.motherjones.com/commentary/
notebook/2004/11/11_200.html.

18 United States Government Accountability Office: GAO / NSIAD-00-107.
Washington 1997; Ann R. Markusen, "The Case against Privatizing
National Security," *Governance* 16, no. 4 (October 2003): 471–501; and
Wulf, *Internationalisierung und Privatisierung von Krieg und Frieden*, 191.

Chapter 3

1 Cited in: U.S. Department of Defense, Quadrennial Defense Review
Report, September 30, 2001.

2 See Singer, *Corporate Warriors*, 63ff; Eugene Smith, "The New
Condottieri and U.S. Policy," *Parameters* (Winter 2002):116 ff.

3 See NSA press announcement, August 31, 2001. Further details are available at the NSA website (www.nsa.gov). Part of the information technology used by the NSA is provided by the computer and arms company CSC
(DynCorp); on that connection see Greg Guma, "Privatizing War," United
Press International (August 7, 2004). Available online at Commondreams.
org Newscenter, http://www.commondreams.org/views04/0707-14.htm

4 See "Introduction to Business." National Security Agency Central Security
Office, www.nsa.gov/business [3 Nov. 2005].

5 Cited in Tom Ricks and Greg Schneider's article, "Cheney's Firm Profited
from 'Overused' Army," *Washington Post*, Sept. 9, 2000.

6 See Schrader, "U.S. Companies Hired to Train Foreign Armies," *Los
Angeles Times*, April 14, 2002.

7 James Conachy, "Private military companies in Iraq: profiting from colo-

nialism." 3 May 2004. World Socialist Web Site, http://www.wsws.org/
articles/2004/may2004/pmcs-m03.shtml.

8 For an overview of the "oil belt" and its drilling sites, pipelines, and military bases, see Lutz Kleveman's website, http://www.newgreatgame.com/.
See also Lutz Kleveman, *The New Great Game: Blood and Oil in Central Asia*, New York: Atlantic Monthly Press, 2003); and Heather Timmons,
"Kazakhstan: Oil Majors Agree to Develop Field," *The New York Times,*
Feb. 26, 2004, also available online at http://www.corpwatch.org/article.
php?id=10191.

9 Pratap Chatterjee, "Halliburton Makes a Killing on Iraq War." 20
March 2003. CorpWatch, http://www.corpwatch.org/article.php?id=;
See also Senate Democratic Policy Committee, "Contractors Overseeing
Contractors: Conflicts of Interest Undermine Accountability in Iraq," May
18, 2004, http://www.globalsecurity.org/military/library/
report/2004/040518-iraq.htm.

10 On this and the subsequently discussed military training programs,
see Bureau of Political-Military Affairs: Foreign Military Training
and DoD Engagement Activities of interest: Joint Report to Congress,
March 2002, http://www.fas.org/asmp/campaigns/training/FMTR2002/
(b)%20Executive%20Summary.htm.

11 Singer, *Corporate Warriors*, 206.

12 Hernando Calvo Ospina, "Aux frontières du plan Colombie," *Le Monde diplomatique*, (November 2004): 21.

13 Under the second Clinton administration, the program was called ACRI
(African Crisis Response Initiative). Under Bush, it was expanded and
renamed ACOTA (African Contingencies Operations Training and
Assistance program).

14 See www.bundeswehr.de and www.gebb.de, from which the following
quotes have been taken.

15 See Greg Guma, "Outsourcing Defense: The Quiet Rise of National
Security, Inc.," *Toward Freedom* 52, no. 2 (June 2004).

16 See the UN document "Norms on the responsibilities of transnational
corporations and other business enterprises with regard to human rights,"
approved Aug. 13, 2003 (UN Doc. E/CN.4/Sub.2/2003).

17 See the numerous reports by Centre Europe–Tiers Monde (www.cetim.ch),
Global Labour Inspection Network in Denmark (www.labour-inspection.
org), The National Labor Committee in the United States (www.nlcnet.
org), "European Initiatives on Monitoring and Verification," the Centre
for Research on Multinational Corporations (www.somo.nl), and Asia
Monitor Resource Centre in Hong Kong (www.amrc.org.hk).

18 See "What Ever Happened to the UN Norms?" EarthRights International,
http://www.earthrights.org/legalfeature/what_ever_happened_to_the_un_
norms.html.

19 The percentages are based on calculations made in the past six years using

the specially developed computer program EUDOS. See Singer, *Corporate Warriors*, 81, and "Peacekeepers, Inc.: Private military muscle offers its services," *Policy Review*, no. 119 (June 2003). Also available online at http://www.hoover.org/publications/policyreview/3448831.html. See also http://www.earthrights.org/legalfeature/what_ever_happened_to_the_un_norms.html.

20 See the articles in *The Economist* "Risk Returns: Doing Business in Chaotic and Violent Countries" (Nov. 20, 1999) and "Risky Returns" (May 20, 2000).

21 See "Maquiladoras at a Glance." 30 June 1999. CorpWatch, http://www.corpwatch.org/article.php?id=1528 as well as various articles by Maquila Solidarity Network (www.maquilasolidarity.org) and American Center for International Labor Solidarity (www.solidaritycenter.org), an organization affiliated with the AFL-CIO. See also reports by the International Trade Union Corporation (www.ituc-csi.org).

22 See interview with Denis Coutu, general manager of Vogue in Mexico: Linda Diebel, "Lace, sweat and tears: Mexican women who sew Canadian lingerie are pawns in a ruthless game of trade," *The Toronto Star* (March 12, 2000): B1, B3.

23 Comité fronterizo de obreras, Sept. 19, 2005 (www.cfomaquiladorapp.org); International Labor Rights Forum, Sept. 13, 2005 (www.laborrightpp.org).

24 See International Labor Rights Forum, www.laborrights.org.

25 See the International Trade Union Confederation web site, http://www.ituc-csi.org.

26 See "2007 Annual Survey of Violations of Trade Union Rights." International Labor Rights Forum, http://www.laborrights.org/end-violence-against-trade-unions/resources/407.

27 Doug Brooks, "Private Military Service Providers: Africa's Welcome Pariahs." *Nouveaux Mondes*, no. 10 (Spring 2002): 71.

28 See Pagliani, *Il mestiere della guerra*, 121–150; and Khareen Pech, "The Hand of War: Mercenaries in the Former Zaire 1996–97," in *Mercenaries: An African Security Dilemma*, ed. Abdel-Fatau Musah and J. 'Kajode Fayemi (London: Pluto Press, 2000) 117–154.

29 See UN Doc. E/CN.4/1999 – 2003.

30 See Stephen Fidler and Thomas Catan, "Private Military Companies Pursue the Peace Dividend," *Financial Times* (June 24, 2003).

31 Cited in: Joshua Kurlantzick, "Outsourcing the Dirty Work," *The American Prospect* 14, no. 5 (May 1, 2003). Also available online at http://www.sandline.com/hotlinks/Outsourcing_Dirty_Work.htm.

32 Damian Lilly, "The Privatization of Peacekeeping: Prospects and Realities," United Nations Institute for Disarmament Research: Disarmament Forum, No. 3, 2000.

33 Claude Voillat of the International Committee of the Red Cross in an interview with the Deutsche Welle (April 2003).

34 In the 1990s, more Red Cross workers died in combat areas than U.S. soldiers. See Singer, "Peacekeepers, Inc.," *Policy Review*, June 2003.

35 Koenraad van Brabant, "Operational Security Management in Violent Environments," *Good Practice Review* 8 (July 2000); see also Dieter Reinhardt, "Privatisierung der Sicherheit," *Entwicklungspolitik* 16-17 (2003).

36 Interview by Steffen Leidel with Doug Brooks, "Friedenmissionen als Geschäft." 6 August 2003. Deutsche Welle, http://www.dw-world.de/dw/article/0,2144,940789,00.html.

37 See Volker Eick, "Policing for Profit," in *Das Unternehmen Krieg: Paramilitärs, Warlords und Privatarmeen als Akteure der neuen Kriegsordnung*, ed. Dario Azzellini and Boris Kanzleiter (Berlin: Assoziation A: 2003): 201–215.

Chapter 4

1 The experts cited include sociologists and political scientists such as Mary Kaldor, Peter Lock, and Herfried Münkler as well as the professional Chinese military men Qiao Liang and Wang Xiangsui. The "new wars," which have increasingly gained contour with the end of the cold war, are characterized by the gradual undermining of the regulatory functions of states, which no longer possess a monopoly on the right to wage war. Distinctions between civilians and combatants, and between the commercial sector and the public application of force, have likewise been blurred.

2 Krahmann, *The Privatization of Security Governance*.

3 Zarate, "The Emergence of a New Dog of War."

4 Singer, *Corporate Warriors*, 125ff.

5 Ibid, 128.

6 See Jason Sherman, "Arm's Length: The Pentagon Hopes to Foster Good Changes in Difficult Places by Teaming up with Two Nations It Once Ignored," *Armed Forces Journal International*, 138, no. 2 (September 2000); Leslie Wayne, "America's For-Profit Secret Army," *The New York Times* (13 Oct 2002).

7 See the MPRI website, www.mpri.com.

8 For more information, see U.S. Army Training and Doctrine Command, www.tradoc.army.mil.

9 See United States Government Accountability Office: Contingency Operations. Opportunities to Improve the Logistics Civil Augmentation Program, February 1997.

10 For more details, see Donald T. Wynn, "Managing the Logistics-Support contract in the Balkans Theater," *Engineer: The Professional Bulletin for*

Army Engineers, (July 2000); and Karen Gullo, "Peacekeeping Helped Cheney Company," Associated Press, Aug. 28, 2000.

11   See Krahmann, "The Privatization of Security Governance," 10.

12   A virtual tour of the camp is available at: www.tffalcon.hqusareur.army.
     mil/sections/About/camplife.htm. The Human Rights Commissioner of the
     European Council Alvaró Gil-Robles, who visited the camp in 2002, has
     accused the United States of maintaining a Guantanamo-style detention
     center there. A spokesperson for the U.S. Army denied this accusation. See
     Frankfurter Allgemeine Zeitung, Nov. 28, 2005.

13   See various reports by Henry Waxman—sixty in number between March
     26 and October 18, 2005—for example "Halliburton's Questioned and
     Unsupported Costs in Iraq Exceed $1.4 Billion," June 27, 2005, http://
     oversight.house.gov/Documents/20050627140010-82879.pdf See also
     Michael Shnayerson, "The Spoils of War," *Vanity Fair*, March 2005.

14   See Pagliani, *Il mestiere della guerra*, 57–67, 182–189; Herb Howe,
     "Private Security Forces and African Stability: The Case of Executive
     Outcomes," *Journal of Modern African Studies* 36, no. 2 (June 1998):
     307–331.

15   Diamond rights in Sierra Leone have allegedly earned the group of compa-
     nies around $1 billion.

16   International Consortium of Investigative Journalists, *Making a
     Killing*, Chapter 3. See also Mark Hemingway, "Warriors for Hire:
     Blackwater USA and the rise of private military contractors," *The
     Weekly Standard* 12, no. 14, (18 Dec 2006). Available online at:
     http://www.weeklystandard.com/Content/Public/Articles/000/000/013/
     062fxarf.asp?pg=2.

17   See Scahill, *Blackwater*.

18   See the Blackwater Worldwide website, www.blackwaterusa.com.

19   See the House of Representatives Committee on Oversight and
     Government Report Memorandum Re: Additional Information about
     Blackwater USA, October 1, 2007. Available online at: http://oversight.
     house.gov/documents/20071001121609.pdf.

20   Ibid.

21   Ibid.

Chapter 5

1   1 Sam 22:1–2.

2   1 Sam 27:9.

3   Cited in: Augusto Camera, *Elementi di storia antica: Documenti* (Bologna:
    Zanichelli, 1969) 396–397.

4   Cited in: *Kriegsreisende*, Chapter 3: Mittelalter. Die schwarze Legion, 2.
    (www.kriegsreisende.de).

5   In his novel series the Buru Quartet, the renowned Indonesian writer

Pramoedya Ananta Toer vividly describes the quality of life and the relations of power under Dutch rule.

Chapter 6

1 Hans-Peter Martin and Harald Schumann, *Die Globalisierungsfalle: Der Angriff auf Demokratie und Wolhstand* (Reinbek bei Hamburg: Rowohlt, 1996): 296.

2 Whereas some ten thousand UN peacekeepers were deployed in the late 1980s, by the mid-1990s that number had decreased to ten thousand. In 2004, some thirty-four thousand soldiers were deployed for the UN as part of seventeen missions. Less than four thousand are from Europe, and no more than a few dozen from the United States.

3 Cited in: Julio Goday, "Dogs of War Take to Suits," *Inter Press Service*, Nov. 18, 2003. Available online at: http://www.globalpolicy.org/security/peacekpg/training/1118suits.htm; see also Wulf, *Internationalisierung und Privatisierung von Krieg und Frieden*, 33–48, 79–95.

4 See Deborah Avant, "Privatizing Military Training," *Foreign Policy* 7, no. 6 (May 2002).

5 See Duffield, *Global Governance and the New Wars*.

6 The two papers are available at www.whitehouse.gov/energy and www.energy.gov.

7 This analysis was confirmed by a study about "peak oil" from 2005, which was commissioned by the Department of Energy and carried out by the former high-ranking DoE official and later SAIC energy expert Robert Hirsch. See Adam Porter, "US Report Acknowledges Peak-oil Threat," *Aljazeera* (14 March 2005). Available online at: http://www.energy bulletin.net/node/4673; as well as U.S. government information at www.usinfo.state.gov.

8 See Michael T. Klare, *Blood and Oil: The Dangers and Consequences of America's Growing Dependency on Imported Petroleum*. New York: Metropolitan Books, 2005; Michael T. Klare, "The intensifying Global Struggle for Energy." 9 May 2005. TomDispatch.com, http://www.tomdispatch.com/post/2400/mike_klare_on_our_energy_stretched_planet; Michael T. Klare, "Mapping the Oil Motive." 18 March 2005. TomPaine.com, http://www.tompaine.com/articles/mapping_the_oil_motive.php; see also Aziz Choudry, "Blood, Oil, Guns and Bullets." 28 Nov. 2003. *Znet*, http://www.countercurrents.org/us-choudry281103.htm; and F William Engdahl, "The Oil Factor in Bush's War on Tyranny." 3 March 2005. *Asia Times*, "Speaking Freely." http://www.atimes.com/atimes/global_economy/gc03dj02.html.

9 See Martin Walker, "NATO Means Business to Protect Pipelines," United Press International (Oct. 13, 2005).

10 The RMA was originally developed as an official Pentagon doctrine after the end of the cold war. One of its fundamental points was the Network

Centric Warfare (NCW), according to which networking of all units within a given theater of operations would dramatically increase the flow of information and, as a result, military capacities. The idea of Network Centric Warfare was first tried out in the 2003 Iraq War.

11 Singer, *Corporate Warriors*, 64.

12 See Adams, "The New Mercenaries and the Privatization of Conflict," *Parameters* (Summer 1999).

13 See DCAF, *Intelligence. Practice and Democratic Oversight—A Practitioner's View*. Geneva 2003; and Treverton, *Reshaping National intelligence for an Age of Information*.

14 Owing to its enormous importance and the significant technological developments in the past decade, this area has been split up into EMINT (electronics intelligence), COMINT (communications intelligence), and TELINT (telemetric intelligence).

Chapter 7

1 Singer, *Corporate Warriors*, 57.

2 Collier and Hoeffler, *Greed and Grievance in Civil War*.

3 See Uesseler, "Herausforderung Mafia. Strategien gegen Organisierte Kriminalität," Bonn 1993.

4 In his book *A Bend in the River*, the Nobel Prize–winning author V. S. Naipaul described in great detail how the political system in Zaire functioned. In his book *Waiting for the Wild Beasts to Vote*, the Ivorian novelist Ahmadou Kourouma described similar conditions in his home country and neighboring states.

5 The prospect that Saudi Arabia might be destabilized is grounded in its outmoded quasi-feudal system of rule, but perhaps more so in the fact the country's population has exploded—from 3.2 million in 1950 to 20.7 million in 2001, with 75 percent of all Saudis under thirty and 50 percent under eighteen years of age. This development has contributed to a drastic decline in per-capita income from $28,600 USD in 1981 to $6,800 in 2001. Broad dissatisfaction among young Saudi citizens, which Osama bin Laden and Al-Qaeda attempt to misuse, could also lead to destabilization in Iraq.

6 See Stefan Mair, *Die Globalisierung privater Gewalt*; Kurtenbach and Lock (eds.), *Kriege als (Über)Lebenswelten*.

7 See Global Witness, "For a Few Dollar$ More: How al Qaeda Moved into the Diamond Trade." 14 April 2003. Global Witness, http://www.globalwitness.org/media_library_detail. php/290/en/for_a_few_dollar_more_how_al_qaeda_moved_into_the_.

8 See, for example, the account of Leonid Minin from Chapter 1.

9 See the annual reports of the UNDP; above all, "Human Development Report. Millennium Development Goals: A Compact among Nations to

End Human Poverty," New York: UNDP, 2003. Available online at: http://hdr.undp.org/en/reports/global/hdr2003/.

10 See the annual development reports statistics, www.undp.org.

Chapter 8

1 See Deutscher Bundestag, 15. Wahlperiode: Drucksache Sept. 28, 2004.

2 Ospina, "Aux frontières du plan Colombie," *Le Monde diplomatique*, 21.

3 Ibid.

4 See Thomas Catan, "Mercenaries Seek a Change of Image," *Financial Times Special Report: Defence Industry* (1 Dec. 2004); "Private Armies March into Legal Vacuum," *Financial Times* (10 Feb 2005); and "Private Military Companies," SourceWatch, http://www.sourcewatch.org/index.php?title=Private_Military_Corporations.

5 Sandra Bibiana Flórez, "Mercenarios en Colombia: una guerra ajena," *Proceso* (29 July 2001).

6 Enrique B. Ballesteros, "Report of the Use of Mercenaries," New York 2004 (UN Doc. E/CN.4/2004/15), p. 11.

7 See *La Prensa* (Managua), Jan. 22, 2002.

8 See Asad Ismi "Profiting from Repression: Canadian firms in Colombia protected by military death squads," CCPA National Office (1 Dec 2000). Available online on the CCPA website, http://www.policyalternatives.ca/MonitorIssues/2000/12/MonitorIssue1689/.

9 See the publications of the Comité Permanente por la Defensa de los Derechos Humanos on their website, http://cpdh.free.fr and on the website of Human Rights First, www.humanrightsfirst.org/index.asp.

10 See T. Christian Miller, "A Columbian Village Caught in a Cross-Fire," *Los Angeles Times* (17 March 2003). The annual reports of Amnesty International and Human Rights Watch also discussed the massacre in Santo Domingo in detail.

11 See Greg Muttitt and James Mariott, *Some Common Concerns*. London: Platform, 2002, especially Chapter 11: "BP and Human Rights Abuses in Colombia."

12 Amnesty International: AI index: AMR 23/79/98, October 19, 1998.

13 See www.europarl.eu.int/omk/sipade.

14 See www.amnesty.org/countries/colombia.

15 See www.labournet.de/internationalepp.co/lebensgefahr.html.

16 See Office of the United Nations High Commissioner for Human Rights: Annual Report, www.ohchr.org.

17 See Felix Heiduk and Daniel Kramer, "Shell in Nigeria und Exxon in Aceh. Transnationale Konzerne im Bürgerkrieg," *Blätter für deutsche und internationale Politik* 3 (2005), pp. 340–346.

18 See Ewen MacAskill, "Amnesty Accuses Oil Firms of Overriding Human Rights," *Global Policy*, September 7, 2005 (www. globalpolicy.org).

19 See the reports of the WACAM (www.wacam.org); Jim Vallette and Pratap Chatterjee, "Guarding the Oil Underworld in Iraq." 5 Sept. 2003. CorpWatch, http://www.corpwatch.org/article.php?id=8328; "Canadian Mining Companies Destroy Environment and Community Resources in Ghana." 24 July 2003. Mining Watch Canada, http://www.miningwatch. ca/index.php?/AMI_Resources/Cdn_Cos_in_Ghana.

20 See "Indonesia: Paper Industry Threatens Human Rights." 7 Jan 2003. Human Rights Watch, http://www.hrw.org/press/2003/01/indo010703. htm.

Chapter 9

1 See Michael Duffy, "When Private Armies Take to the Front Lines," *Time* (12 April 2004); Isenberg, "A Fistful of Contractors" BASIC, 31.

2 See the reports from April 2004 at Uruknet, www.uruknet.info; the Iraqi Press Monitor www. iwpr.net/; and The Middle East Media Research Institute, www.memri.org. With the increase in the insurgency against the coalition since spring 2004, numerous opposition websites have disappeared from the Internet. Often servers have been shut down because Western intelligence services feared that they were being used to pass along coded Al-Qaeda messages. In some hacker circles, suspicions have been raised that the United States is putting pressure on servers in order to block negative information from reaching the public. In fact, there is hardly any access anymore to authentic Iraqi sources of information on insurgent websites.

3 See, for example, Andy Clarno and Salim Vally, "Privatised War: The South African Connection," ZNet (6 March 2005). Available online at: http://www.zmag.org/znet/viewArticle/6742.

4 See Paul Dykes, "Desert Storm: How Did a Convicted Ulster Terror Squaddie Get Security Job in Iraq?" *Belfast Telegraph* (5 Feb 2004).

5 See Norman Arun, "Outsourcing the War." 2 April 2004. BBC News Online, http://news.bbc.co.uk/2/hi/middle_east/3591701.stm.

6 See David Barstow, "Security Companies: Shadow Soldiers in Iraq," *The New York Times*, (19 April 2004); Dana Priest and Mary Pat Flaherty, "Under Fire: Security Firms Form an Alliance," *Washington Post* (8 April 2004); Lolita C. Baldo, "Senators Seek Investigation into Private Security Firms in Iraq," Associated Press (30 April 2004); Peter W. Singer: "Warriors for Hire in Iraq." April 15–16, 2004. Salon.com, http://dir. salon.com/story/news/feature/2004/04/15/warriors/index.html.

7 Although the official figures about the number of registered private military companies vary, they numbered sixty-eight at the middle of the Coalitional Provisional Authority period, and forty-three afterward. The actual numbers may be around one-third higher.

8   See Clare Murphy, "Iraq's Mercenaries: Riches for Risks." 4 April 2004. BBC News, http://news.bbc.co.uk/2/hi/middle_east/3590887.stm.

9   See Renae Merle, "DynCorp Took Part in Chalabi Raid," *Washington Post* (4 June 2004).

10 This information was provided by Maria Cuffaro, a journalist for the Colombian national broadcaster RAI, in an interview with the author.

11 See Matthew Schofield, "Militants Tighten Grip on Iraq Cities," *Detroit Free Press* (9 April 2004).

12 See Christoph Reuter, "Die Hunde des Krieges," *Stern* (13 Oct. 2005).

13 See Holmquist, *Private Security Companies*, 23ff.

14 See the publications of Deborah Avant and Peter W. Singer cited in the bibliography.

15 Peter W. Singer, "Outsourcing War," *Foreign Affairs* (March-April 2005).

16 See Shnayerson, "The Spoils of War," *Vanity Fair* (March 2005).

17 See Michael McPeak and Sandra N. Ellis, "Managing Contractors in Joint Operations: Filling the Gaps in Doctrine," *Army Logistician* 36, no. 2 (March–April 2004): 6–9.

18 Singer, *Corporate Warriors*, 15.

19 See Holmquist, *Private Security Companies*, 29.

20 See James Surowiecki, "Army Inc.," *New Yorker* (12 Jan. 2004).

21 See Uruknet Nov. 27, 2005, www.uruknet.info.

22 The 1989 UN Convention adopted the definition of mercenaries provided by Article 47 of the Geneva Convention.

23 AirScan, for example, provided data for the Colombian Air Force during the previously described massacre of Santo Domingo and the Air Force of Peru in May 2001, when it shot down a commercial flight with U.S. missionaries on board. See Duncan Campbell, "War on Error: A Spy Inc. No Stranger to Controversy," *The Center for Public Integrity* (12 June 2002). On other similar events, see Leslie Wayne, "America's For-Profit Secret Army," *The New York Times* (13 Oct. 2002); Peter W. Singer, "Have Guns, Will Travel," *The New York Times* (21 July 2003).

24 Cited in: Juan O. Tamayo, "Colombian Guerillas Fire on U.S. Rescuers," *Miami Herald* (22 Feb 2001).

25 See Roman Kupchinsky, "The Wild West of American Intelligence," 2 June 2005. Asia Times Online, http://www.atimes.com/atimes/Middle_East/GF02Ak02.html.

26 See Silverstein, *Private Warriors*, especially Chapter 5, "Still in Control After All These Years: Alexander Haig and the Revolving Door," 189–226.

27 See Ian Bruce, "SAS Veterans among the Bulldogs of War Cashing in on Boom," *The Herald* (29 March 2004); Singer, "Warriors for Hire in Iraq," Salon.com.

Chapter 10

1 See Abdel-Fatau Musah, "A Country under Siege," in *Mercenaries: An African Dilemma*, ed. Abdel-Fatau Musah and J. 'Kajode Fayemi (London: Pluto Press, 2000): 76–117.

2 Numerous examples of cooperation between PMCs and purveyors of violence, including Taliban and Al-Qaeda groups, have been documented. See Mohamad Bazzi, "Training Militants British Say Islamic Group Taught Combat Courses in U.S," *Newsday* (4 Oct 2001); Andre Verloy, "The Merchant of Death," Center for Public Integrity (20 Jan 2002); Peter W. Singer; "War, Profits, and the Vacuum of Law: Privatized Military Firms and International Law," *Columbia Journal of Transnational Law* (Spring 2004): 521–549; Patrick J. Cullen, "Keeping the New Dog of War on a Tight Leash," *Conflict Trends* 1 (June 2000): 36–39; André Linard, "Mercenaries S. A.," *Le Monde diplomatique* (August 1998): 31.

3 Singer, *Corporate Warriors*, 198; see also 191–205.

4 A similar phenomenon can be observed in Iraq. See Ariana Eunjung Cha, "Underclass of Workers Created in Iraq," *Washington Post* (1 July 2004).

5 See Singer, "Peacekeepers, Inc," *Policy Review,* June 2003.

6 See Deborah Avant, *The Market for Force*.

7 See Holmquist, *Private Security Companies*, 14.

8 See Herbert M. Howe, *Ambiguous Order: Military Forces in African States*. Boulder: Lynne Rienner, 2001; Tony Hodges, *Angola from Afro-Stalinism to Petro-Diamond Capitalism*; Jackie Cilliers and Christian Dietrich, eds., *Angola's War Economy: The Role of Oil and Diamonds*. Pretoria: Institute for Security Studies, 2000; Phillip van Niekerk and Laura Peterson, "Greasing the Skids of Corruption," in *Making a Killing: The Business of War*, ed. International Consortium of Investigative Journalists (Washington: The Center for Public Integrity, 2003).

9 See John Vidal, "Oil Rig Hostages Are Freed by Strikers as Mercenaries Fly Out," *The Guardian* (3 May 2003).

10 See Peter Lock, "Privatisierung im Zeitalter der Globalisierung," *Lateinamerika* 38 (1998), pp. 13 – 28; Kristine Kern, *Diffusion nachhaltiger Politikmuster, transnationale Netzwerke und globale Governance*. Berlin 2002.

11 See Holmquist, *Private Security Companies*, 15.

12 See Isenberg, *Soldiers of Fortune Ltd.*; Phillip van Niekerk and Laura Peterson, "Greasing the Skids of Corruption," in *Making a Killing: The Business of War*, ed. International Consortium of Investigative Journalists (Washington: The Center for Public Integrity, 2003).

13 See Naison Ngoma, "Coup and Coup Attempts in Africa: Is there a missing link?," *African Security Review* 13, no. 3 (2004); Jackie Cilliers and Richard Cornwell, "Mercenaries and the Privatization of Security in Africa," *African Security Review* 8, no. 2 (1999).

14 See Doug Brooks, "Write a Cheque, End a War," *Conflict Trends*, June 2000, 33–35.

15 DFID personnel in Iraq are protected by various PMCs. See Deborah Avant, "The Privatization of Security and Change in the Control of Force," *International Studies Perspectives 5*, no. 2 (2004): 154.

16 See UK Government: Private Military Companies. London 2002 (Ninth Report of the Foreign Affairs Committee). The British Defence Ministry has never provided information about how many military companies are active abroad and what their missions are. The only information is domestic data concerning which tasks have been or are scheduled to be outsourced. See the Defence Ministry statements from 2004: "Signed PPP Projects" and "PPP Projects in Procurement" (www.mod.uk/business/ppp/database.htm).

17 See "International Trade in Arms and Military Training," Amnesty International USA, http://www.amnestyusa.org/our-priorities/arms-trade/page.do?id=1011003&n1=3&n2=24.

18 See Alex Belida, "Private US Security Firm Assessing Sao Tomé Military," *Global Security*, June 6, 2004, www.globalsecurity.org.

19 See Leander, *Global Ungovernance*.

20 Gated communities—once a third world phenomenon—can now be found in countries throughout the West.

21 See Stefan Mair, *Die Globalisierung privater Gewalt*, and "Intervention und 'state failure': Sind schwache Staaten noch zu retten?" *IPG* 3 (2004): 82–98.

22 See Rolf Uesseler, *Stichwort Mafia*. Munich: Heyne, 1994; Antonio Roccuzzo, *Gli uomini della giustizia nell'Italia che cambia*. Rome: Laterza, 1993.

23 See chapter 4.

24 See Mungo Soggot, "Conflict Diamonds Forever," Center for Public Integrity, (8 Nov. 2002).

25 See Geoff Harris, "Civilianizing Military Functions in Sub-Saharan Africa," *African Security Review* 12, no. 4 (2003); Mark Taylor, "Law-Abiding or Not: Canadian Firms in Congo Contribute to War," *The Globe and Mail* (31 Oct. 2002); See also the publications of the Norwegian social-research institute FAFO (www.fafo.no).

26 See the documentary film by Patrice Dutertre, *Die neuen Söldner*, broadcast on Arte, June 21, 2005.

27 See Henri Myrttinen, "Alte neue Kriege: Die Privatisierung der Gewalt in Indonesien," in *Das Unternehmen Krieg: Paramilitärs, Warlords und Privatarmeen als Akteure der neuen Kriegsordnung*, ed. Dario Azzellini and Boris Kanzleiter (Berlin: Assoziation A, 2003): 129–142; "Exxon Mobil: Genocide, Murder and Torture in Aceh," in Terry Collingsworth's article "The Key Human Rights Challenge: Developing Enforcement Mechanisms," *Harvard Human Rights Journal* (Spring 2002): 183. Also

available online, International Labor Rights Forum, http://www.laborrights. org/labor-rights/1380.

28 See David Isenberg, "Security for Sale," *Asia Times* (13 Aug 2005).

29 See Aldo Pigoli, "Mercenari, Private Military Companies e Contractors," *Wargames* (17 April 2004); George Monbiot, "Pedigree Dogs of War," *Guardian* (25 Jan 2005).

30 See Daniel C. Lynch, "3200 Peacekeepers Pledged on Mission to Darfur," *Washington Post* (21 Oct 2004).

31 See Pratap Chatterjee, "Darfur Diplomacy: Enter the Contractors." 21 Oct 2004. CorpWatch, http://www.corpwatch.org/article.php?id=11598. The U.S. company AirScan supported the SPFL in a "covert action." See Cullen, "Keeping the New Dogs of War on a Tight Leash," *Conflict Trends* (June 200): 36–39.

32 Phillip van Niekerk and Laura Peterson, "Greasing the Skids of Corruption," in *Making a Killing: The Business of War*, ed. International Consortium of Investigative Journalists (Washington: The Center for Public Integrity, 2003).

33 See the UN reports in UN Doc. E/CN.4/1999–2004.

Chapter 11

1 Cited in: Lothar Brock, "Humanitäre Hilfe: Eine Geisel der Außen und Sicherheitspolitik?" Medico international, *Macht und Ohnmacht der Hilfe*, Frankfurt am Main 2003, 58–63.

2 On the increasing politicization of humanitarian assistance see International Alert, *The Politizisation of Humanitarian Action and Staff Security*, Boston 2001.

3 See Wulf, *Internationalisierung und Privatisierung von Krieg und Frieden*, 145; on the problems of NGOs in conflict regions in general, see 139–156.

4 See "Oxfam Suspends All Direct Operations in Iraq." 19 April 2004. Oxfam America, http://www.oxfamamerica.org/newsandpublications/ press_releases/archive2004/art7093.html. On the similar situation in Afghanistan, see Mark Joyce, "Medécins Sans Frontières Pull out of Afghanistan," *RUSI news* (29 July 2004).

5 See UN Department of Humanitarian Assistance: "Guidelines for Humanitarian Organisations on Interacting with Military and Other Security Actors in Iraq," New York, Oct. 20, 2004.

6 See Robert Muggah and Cate Buchanan, "No Relief: Surveying the Effects of Gun Violence on Aid Workers," *Humanitarian Exchange* (June 2005). Available online at: http://www.odihpn.org/report.asp?ID=2720.

7 The ICRC code of conduct is available at www.ifrc.org/publicat/con- duct/code.asp. On the issue of the armed protection of NGOS, see ICRC and International Federation, "Report on the Use of Armed Protection for Humanitarian Assistance." Geneva: Council of Delegates, December

1995; Meinrad Studer, "The ICRC and Civil-Military Relations in Armed Conflict," *International Review of the Red Cross* 842 (2001): 367–391.

8   See Holmquist, *Private Security Companies*, 20.

9   See the reports by Gino Strada, the president of Emergency (an organization providing medical and social assistance to civilian war victims), about his trips to Iraq: www.emergency.it.

10 See the report by kidnapped Italian journalist Giuliana Sgrena, in *Il Manifesto*, March 20, 2005.

11 See Karen A. Mingst, "Security Firms, Private Contractors, and NGOs: New Issues about Humanitarian Standard," paper presented at International Studies Association Convention, Honolulu, Hawaii, March 10, 2005.

12 See Alex Vines, "Mercenaries, Human Rights and Legality," in *Mercenaries: An African Security Dilemma*, ed. Abdel-Fatau Musah and J. 'Kajode Fayemi (London: Pluto Press, 2000): 169–197.

13 See Vaux et al., *Humanitarian Action and Private Security Companies*.

14 See the various reports at www.ilsa.org.co, http://colhrnet.igc.org/, and http://cpdh.free.fr. In addition, see the reports of the Latin American organizations Derechos, www. derechos.org and Istituto de Derechos Humanos de la Universidad Centroamerica (IDHUCA), http://www.uca.edu.sv/publica/idhuca/.

15 See Holmquist, *Private Security Companies*, 20.

16 See Peter W. Singer, "Should Humanitarians Use Private Military Services?" *Humanitarian Affairs Review* (Summer 2004); Vaux et al., *Humanitarian Action and Private Security Companies*, 16.

17 See Vaux et al., *Humanitarian Action and Private Security Companies*, 17.

18 See Claude Voillat of the Red Cross (ICRC) in an interview with the Deutsche Welle, April 20, 2004 as well as Claude Voillat, "Private Military Companies: A Word of Caution," *Humanitarian Exchange* (Nov 2004). Also available online at: http://www.odihpn.org/report.asp?id=2675.

19 See International Alert, "The Politizisation of Humanitarian Action and Staff Security," p. 5; Koenraad van Brabant, *Good Practice Review: Operational Security Management in Violent Environments*, London, 2000.

20 See Paul Keilthy, "Private Security Firms in War Zones Worry NGOs." 11 Aug. 2004. AlertNet, http://www.alertnet.org/thefacts/reliefresources/109223838271.htm.

21 See Thomas Gebauer, "Als müsse Rettung erst noch erdacht warden," Medico international (ed.), *Macht und Ohnmacht der Hilfe*, pp. 16.

22 Cited in Italian news agency Adnkronos, April 30, 2004.

23 For example in Kosovo, after the DynCorp sex scandal became public knowledge.

24 See Michael Sirak, "ICRC Calls for Contractor Accountability in War," *Jane's Defense Weekly* (19 May 2004).

25 See Lilly, *The Privatization of Security and Peacebuilding*, 23ff; David Shearer, "Privatization Protection: Military Companies and Human Security," *World Today* (30 July 2001); Zarate, "The Emergence of a New Dog of War."

26 See Vaux et al., *Humanitarian Action and Private Security Companies*, 14.

27 See the Centre for International Studies in Toronto, www.utoronto. ca/cis; the London Overseas Development Institute, www.odi.org.uk; and International Alert, www.international-alert.org. See also Damian Lilly, "The Peacebuilding Dimensions of Civil-Military Relations in Complex Emergencies." London: International Alert, 2002.

28 See the section on Zlatan M. in chapter 1.

29 See Norwegian People's Aid website, www.npaid.org.

30 This conclusion is also supported by the International Alert study *Humanitarian Action and Private Security Companies*, authored by Vaux and others.

31 See Gregg Nakano and Chris Seiple, "American Humanitarian Agencies and Their Use of Private Security Companis," in *Humanitarian Action and Private Security Companies*. London: International Alert, 2002.

32 See Mingst, "Security Firms, Private Contractors, and NGOs," 16.

Chapter 12

1 See UK Government: Private Military Companies: Options for Regulation ("Green Paper"). London, Feb, 12, 2003; Chaloka Beyani and Damian Lilly, "Regulating Private Military Companies." London (International Alert) 2001; Elke Krahmann, *Controlling Private Military Companies: The United Kingdom and Germany*. Portland 2003; Kevin A. O'Brian, *Private Military Companies: Options for Regulation*. Cambridge (RAND Corporation) 2002; Fred Schreier and Marina Caparini: Privatizing Security: *Law, Practice and Governance of Private Military and Security Companies*. Geneva (DCAF) 2005.

2 See the German government's answer to a parliamentary petition by the Free Democrats, Deutscher Bundestag: Drucksache 15/5824, 24. 6. 2005, p. 25. The twenty-five page government statement proceeds from the rather naïve assumption that all parties involved abide by international human-rights laws.

3 Even PMC lobbyists have called for government guidelines. See Singer, "Outsourcing War," *Foreign Affairs* (March–April 2005).

4 See Wulf, *Internationalisierung und Privatisierung von Krieg und Frieden*, 190–197.

5 See Klaus Olshausen, "Das Battle-Group-Konzept der Europäischen Union," www.sipotec.net/X/S_0556.html.

6   See various investigative reports by the Center for Public Integrity, above all, Larry Mackinson: "Outsourcing the Pentagon: Who Benefits from the Politics and Economics of National Security?" (29 Sept 04).

7   See Werner Rügemer, "Gesamtdeutscher Ausverkauf," *Blätter für deutsche und internationale Politik* 11 (2005): 1315–1324; Volker Eick, "Integrative Strategien der Ausgrenzung: Der exklusive Charme des privaten Sicherheitsgewerbepp," *Berliner Debatte initial* 2 (2004): 22–33.

8   See Fox Butterfield, "Privatized 'Prison-for-Profit' Attacked for Abusing Teenage Inmates," *The New York Times* (16 March 2000).

9   See Eppler, *Vom Gewaltmonopol zum Gewaltmarkt*; Wulf, *Internationalisierung und Privatisierung von Krieg und Frieden*, 71–78, 203–218.

10 See the German Ministry for Economic Cooperation and Development (BMZ): "Zum Verhältnis von entwicklungspolitischen und militärischen Antworten auf neue sicherheitspolitische Herausforderungen," Bonn 2004 (BMZ-Diskurs, Nr. 1); Sadako Ogata and Amartya Sen, "Final Report of the Commission on Human Security," New York 2003.

11 See Amnesty International and Oxfam International, *Shattered Lives: The Case for Tough International Arms Control*, London and Oxford: Amnesty International and Oxfam International, 2002.

12 See United Nations, "Human Security Now," New York, May 1, 2003; Amnesty International, *Shattered Lives*.

13 BMZ, "Zum Verhältnis von entwicklungspolitischen und militärischen Antworten," p. 9.

14 The German Action Plan will be discussed in the following chapter.

15 The NATO concept of "force protection" foresees setting up humanitarian programs to accompany military interventions and raise the acceptance of NATO forces among native populaces. See NATO, "Can Soldiers Be Peacekeepers and Warriors?" *NATO Review* 49, no. 2 (Summer 2001).

16 See UK Government: "The White Paper. Eliminating World Poverty: A Challenge or the 21st Century," London, November 1997; UK Government: "Making Government Work for Poor People," London, June 2000; DFID, "Policy Statement on Safety, Security and Accessible Justice," London, Oct. 12, 2000.

17 See the publications of the Development Assistance Committee (DAC) of the OECD, in particular, DAC: "Security System Reform and Governance: Policy and Good Practice," Paris 2004.

18 Cited in World Bank (German): "Sicherheit, Armutsbekämpfung und nachhaltige Entwicklung," Bonn 1999, p. 8.

19 See VENRO, "Streitkräfte als humanitäre Helfer? Positionspapier." Bonn, Mai 2003; VENRO, "Entwicklungspolitik im Windschatten militärischer Interventionen? " Aachen / Bonn / Stuttgart, July 31, 2003.

Chapter 13

1   See Tobias Debiel, "Souveränität verpflichtet: Spielregeln für den neuen Interventionismus," *IPG* 3 (2004): 61–81; Stefan Mair, "Intervention und 'state failure,'" *IPG* (2004): 82–98; ICISS (International Commission on Intervention and State Souvereignty), "The Responsibility to Protect," Ottawa: International Research Centre for ICISS, December 2001.

2   Examples of the consequences have been provided in previous chapters.

3   BMZ, "Krisenprävention und Konfliktbeilegung," *BMZ Spezial* 17 (2000).

4   Angelika Spelten, *Instrumente zur Erfassung von Konflikt und Krisenpotentialen in Partnerländern der Entwicklungspolitik*. Bonn 1999 (Forschungsberichte des BMZ, Bd. 126).

5   GTZ, *Friedensentwicklung, Krisenprävention und Konfliktbearbeitung*. Eschborn 2002; European Platform for Conflict Prevention and Transformation (ed.), *Prevention and Management of Violent Conflicts: An International Directory*, Utrecht 1998.

6   Sweden, Ministry for Foreign Affairs: "Preventing Violent Conflict. A Swedish Action Plan," Stockholm 1999.

7   See German government: "Aktionsplan. Zivile Krisenprävention, Konfliktlösung und Friedenskonsolidierung," Berlin 2004. All citations from the plan refer to this source.

8   This is confirmed by numerous UN investigative reports. See, for example, United Nations: "Larger Freedom. Towards Development, Security and Human Rights for all." Report of the Secretary-General. New York 2005 (Doc. A/59/2005).

9   See VENRO, "VENRO-Stellungnahme zum Aktionsplan Zivile Krisenprävention, Konfliktlösung und Friedenskonsolidierung der Bundesregierung," Bonn, Sept. 9, 2004.

10 See VENRO, "Entwicklungspolitik im Windschatten militärischer interventionen?" p. 3.

11 On the work of the GTZ see www.gtz.de, in particular "Friedensentwicklung, Krisenprävention und Konfliktbearbeitung."

12 See also Adolf Kloke-Lesch and Marita Steinke, "Den Sicherheitskräften auf die Finger schauen. Der Entwicklungspolitik muss es um eine bessere Kontrolle von Polizei und Militär gehen," *Entwicklung und Zusammenarbeit* 43, no. 2 (2002): 44–47.

13 See GTZ, "Friedensentwicklung, Krisenprävention und Konfliktbearbeitung," 82–85.

14 Ibid., 75–80.

15 See also Andreas Mehler and Claude Ribaux, *Krisenprävention und Konfliktbearbeitung in der Technischen Zusammenarbeit*, Wiesbaden 2000, especially Chapter 4.7.

WORKS CITED

Adamo, Alberto, *I nuovi mercenari*. Milan: Medusa Edizioni, 2003.

Adams, Thomas. "The New Mercenaries and the Privatization of Conflict," *Parameters* (Summer 1999): 103–116.

Avant, Deborah. "From Mercenaries to Citizen Armies: Explaining Change in the Practice of War." In: *International Organization* 54, no. 1 (2002).

Avant, Deborah. *The Market for Force: The Consequences of Privatizing Security.* Cambridge: Cambridge University Press, 2005.

Azzellini, Dario and Boris Kanzleiter, eds. *Das Unternehmen Krieg: Paramilitärs, Warlords und Privatarmeen als Akteure der neuen Kriegsordnung.* Berlin: Assoziation A: 2003.

Ballesteros, Enrique B.: *Report on the Use of Mercenaries.* New York 2004 (UN Doc. E/CN.4/2004/15).

Benegas, Richard. "De la privatisation de la guerre à la privatisation du peacekeeping." *Le boom de mercenariat: defi ou falatilté? Document de Damocles.* Lyon 2001.

Beyani, Chaloka and Damian Lilly. *Regulating Private Military Companies.* London: International Alert, 2001.

BMZ. *Zum Verhältnis von entwicklungspolitischen und militärischen Antworten auf neue sicherheitspolitische Herausforderungen.* Bonn, May 2004 (BMZ-Diskurs, Nr. 1)

Brauer, Jürgen. "An Economic Perspective on Mercenaries, Military Companies and the Privatisation of Force." *Cambridge Review of International Affairs* 13 (1999)

Brooks, Doug. *Creating the Renaissance Peace.* Paper for the Africa Institute of South Africa's 40th Anniversary Conference, Pretoria, 2000.

Bundesregierung: Aktionsplan. *Zivile Krisenprävention, Konfliktlösung und Friedenskonsolidierung.* Berlin, 12 May 2004.

Burrows, Gideon. *Il commercio delle armi.* Rome 2003.

Center for Public Integrity. *Windfalls of War.* Washington 2004.

Chojnacki, Sven. *Wandel der Kriegsformen: Die Dimensionen neuer privatisierter Kriege.* Berlin: WZB-Studie, 2001.

Cilliers, Jakkie and Peggy Mason, eds., *Peace, Profit or Plunder?* Pretoria: Institute for Security Studies, 1999.

Collier, Paul and Anke Hoeffler, *Greed and Grievance in Civil War.* World Bank Policy Research Paper, Nr. 2355. Washington: World Bank Development Research Group, May 2001.

Creveld, Martin von. *The Rise and Decline of the State.* Cambridge: Cambridge University Press, 1999.

DAC. *Security System Reform and Governance: Policy and Good Practice.* Paris 2004.

Daclon, Corrado M. *Aspetti strategici della questione idrica.* Turin: Centro Studi per la Difesa e la Sicurezza, June 2002.

DCAF. *Intelligence, Practice and Democratic Oversight: A Practitioner's View.* Genf 2003 (Occasional Paper, Nr. 3).

Debiel, Tobias. "Souveränität verpflichtet: Spielregeln für den neuen Interventionismus." *IPG* 3 (2004): 61– 81.

Dorn, Walter A. *The Cloak and the Blue Beret: The Limits of Intelligence-Gathering in UN Peacekeeping.* Clementsport 1999 (Pearson Papers, Nr. 4).

Duffield, Mark. *Global Governance and the New Wars: The Merging of Development and Security.* London: Zed Books, 2001.

Eppler, Erhard. *Auslaufmodell Staat?* Frankfurt am Main: Suhrkamp, 2005.

Eppler, Erhard. *Vom Gewaltmonopol zum Gewaltmarkt.* Frankfurt am Main: Suhrkamp, 2002.

European Platform for Conflict Prevention and Transformation, ed., *Prevention and Management of Violent Conflicts: An International Directory.* Utrecht 1998.

Fawcett, Bill. *MERCS: True Stories of Mercenaries in Action.* New York: Avon 1999.

Finardi, Sergio and Carlo Tombola. *Le strade delle armi.* Milan: Jaca Book, 2002.

Global Witness. "For a Few Dollar$ More: How al Qaeda Moved into the Diamond Trade." *Global Witness* (April 2003).

GTZ. *Friedensentwicklung, Krisenprävention und Konfliktbearbeitung*. Eschborn 2002.

Hodges, Tony. *Angola from Afro-Stalinism to Petro-Diamond Capitalism*. Bloomington: Indiana University Press, 2001

Holmquist, Caroline. *Private Security Companies: The Case for Regulation*. (SIPRI Policy Paper, Nr. 9). Stockholm: SIPRI, 2005.

Human Rights Watch. *Colombia: Human Rights Concerns Raised by the Security Arrangements of Transnational Oil Companies*. London, April 1998.

International Consortium of Investigative Journalists. *Making a Killing: The Business of War*. Washington: The Center for Public Integrity, 2003.

Isenberg, David. "A Fistful of Contractors: The Case for a Pragmatic Assessment of Private Military Companies in Iraq." BASIC Research Report 2004.2. (Sept 2004): 31.

Isenberg, David. *Soldiers of Fortune Ltd.: A profile of today's private sector corporate mercenary firms*. Washington: Center for Defense Information, 1997.

Jäger, Thomas and Gerhard Kümmel, eds., *Private Military and Security Companies: Chances, Problems, Pitfalls and Prospects*. Wiesbaden: Vs Verlag, 2007.

Kaldor, Mary. *New and Old Wars, Organized Violence in a Global Era*. Cambridge: Polity Press, 1999.

Klingebiel, Stephan and Katja Roehder. "Entwicklungspolitisch-militärische Schnittstellen. Neue Herausforderungen in Krisen und Post-Konflikt-Situationen," *Deutsches Institut für Entwicklungspolitik*, ed. Berichte und Gutachten, 2004.

Krahmann, Elke. "The Privatization of Security Governance: Developments, Problems, Solutions," *Arbeitspapiere zur Internationale Politik und Aussenpolitik (AIPA)* (Jan 2003).

Ku, Charlotte and Harold K. Jacobsen, eds., *Democratic Accountability and the Use of Force in International Law*. Cambridge: Cambridge University Press, 2003.

Kurtenbach, Sabine and Peter Lock, eds., *Kriege als (Über)Lebenswelten*. Bonn: Dietz Verlag, 2004.

Leander, Anna. *Global Ungovernance: Mercenaries, States and the Control over Violence.* Copenhagen: Copenhagen Peace Research Institute, 2001.

Leonhardt, Manuela. *Konfliktbezogene Wirkungsbeobachtung von Entwicklungsvorhaben. Eine praktische Handreichung.* Eschborn 2001.

Lilly, Damian. *The Privatisation of Security and Peacebuilding.* London: International Alert, 2000.

Lilly, Damian and Michael von Tangen Page, eds., *Security Sector Reform: The Challenges and Opportunities of the Privatisation of Security.* London 2002.

Lock, Peter. *Ökonomien des Krieges.* Hamburg 2001.

Lumpe, Lora. "U.S. Foreign Military Training: Global Reach, Global Power and Oversight Issues," *Foreign Policy in Focus Special Report* (May 2002).

Mair, Stefan. *Die Globalisierung privater Gewalt.* SWP-Studie 2002/ S 10, April 2002, 66 Seiten. Berlin: SWP-Studie, 2002.

Makki, Sami et al. *Private Military Companies and the Proliferation of Small Arms.* London: International Alert, 2002.

Markusen, Ann R. "The Case against Privatizing National Security," *Governance* 16, no. 4 (October 2003): 471–501.

McPeak, Michael and Sandra N. Ellis. "Managing Contractors in Joint Operations: Filling the Gaps in Doctrine," *Army Logistician* 36, no. 2 (2004): 6–9.

Medico International, ed. *Macht und Ohnmacht der Hilfe.* Frankfurt am Main 2003 (Medico report, 25).

Mehler, Andreas and Claude Ribaux. *Krisenprävention und Konfliktbearbeitung in der Technischen Zusammenarbeit.* Wiesbaden 2000.

Metz, Steven. *Armed Conflict in the 21st Century: The Information Revolution and Post-Modern Warfare.* April 2002 (Strategic Studies Institute, U.S. Army War College).

Misser, François. "Les mercenaires: en quete de legitimation." *Le boom de mercenariat: defi ou fatalité?* Document de Damocles. Lyon 2001.

Moller, Björn. *The Political Economy of War: Privatisation and Commercialisation.* Kopenhagen 2002 (COPRI Working paper 16).

Münkler, Herfried. *Neue Kriege*. Reinbek 2002.

Musah, Abdel-Fatau and J. 'Kajode Fayemi, eds., *Mercenaries: An African Security Dilemma*. London: Pluto Press, 2000.

O'Brian, Kevin. "Military-Advisory Groups and African Security: Privatizes Peacekeeping." *International Peacekeeping 5*, no. 3 (1998).

OECD. *Guidelines to Prevent Violent Conflicts*. Paris 2001.

OECD. *Multinational Enterprises in Situations of Violent Conflict and Widespread Human Rights Abuses*. Paris 2002.

Offe, Klaus. "Die Neudefinition der Sicherheit." *Blätter für deutsche und internationale Politik* 12 (2001).

Paes, Wulf-Christian. "Zur Konversion von Gewaltökonomien." *Wissenschaft und Frieden* 3 (2001).

Pagliani, Gabriella. *Il mestiere della guerra*. Milan: Franco Angeli, 2004.

Qiao Liang and Wang Xiangsiu. *Guerra senza limiti: L'arte della guerra asimmetrica fra terrorismo e globalizzazione*. Gorozia 2001.

Reno, William. *Private Security Companies and Multinational Corporations*. Wilton Park Conference. London: International Alert, 2000.

Richards, Anna and Henry Smith. *Addressing the Role of Private Security Companies within Security Sector Reform Programmes*. London 2007.

Scahill, Jeremy. *Blackwater: The Rise of the World's Most Powerful Mercenary Army*. New York: Serpent's Tail, 2007.

Schreier, Fred and Marina Caparini. *Privatizing Security: Law, Practice and Governance of Private Military and Security Companies*. Genf, 2005.

Schwartz, Nelson D.: "The War Business. The Pentagon's Private Army." In: *Fortune*, 3. March 2003.

Shearer, David. *Private Armies and Military Intervention*. London: International Institute for Strategic Studies; Adelphi Paper, Nr. 316, 1999.

Silverstein, Ken. *Private Warriors*. New York: Verso, 2000.

Singer, Peter W. *Corporate Warriors: The Rise of the Privatized Military Industry*. Ithaca: Cornell University Press, 2003.

Singer, Peter W. "War, Profits, and the Vacuum of Law: Privatized Military Firms and International Law." In: *Columbia Journal of Transnational Law*, Frühjahr 2004, 521–549.

Spelten, Angelika. *Gewaltökonomie. Möglichkeiten und Grenzen entwicklungspolitischer Handlungsoptionen. Eine Frient Handreichung.* Bonn, June 2004.

Spicer, Tim. *An Unorthodox Soldier. Peace and War and the Sandline Affair.* Edinburgh: Mainstream Publishing, 2003.

Thompson, William. *The Grievances of Military Coup Makers.* Beverly Hills 1973.

Treverton, Gregory F. *Reshaping National Intelligence for an Age of Information.* New York: Cambridge University Press, 2001.

Uesseler, Rolf. "Neue Kriege, neue Söldner. Private Militärfirmen und globale Interventionsstrategien," *Blätter für deutsche und internationale Politik* 3 (2005): 323–333.

UNDP. *Human Development Report. Millennium Development Goals: A Compact among Nations to End Human Poverty.* New York 2003.

United Kingdom government. *Private Military Companies: Options for Regulations* (Green Paper). London 2003.

United Kingdom government. *Public Private Partnerships: Changing the Way We Do Business.* Elements of PPP in Defence. London 2004.

United Nations. *Human Security—Now. Commission on Human Security.* New York 2003.

United Nations. *In Larger Freedom: Towards Development, Security and Human Rights for All.* Report of the Secretary-General. New York 2005 (Document A/59/2005).

United States General Accountability Office. *GAO/NSIAD-00-107.* Washington 1997.

Unites States Senate. *Contractors Overseeing Contractors. Conflicts of Interest Undermining Accountability in Iraq.* Joint Report by Special Investigations Division. Washington, 18. May 2004.

Vaux, Tony et al. *Humanitarian Action and Private Security Companies.* London: International Alert, 2002.

VENRO. *Stellungnahme zum Aktionsplan Zivile Krisenprävention, Konfliktlösung und Friedenskonsolidierung der Bundesregierung.* Bonn, 9 September 2004.

Venter, Al J. "Market Forces: How Hired Guns Succeeded Where the United Nations Fails," *Jane's International Defense Review*, March 1998.

Vignarca, Francesco. *Mercenari S.p.A.* Milan: Rizzoli, 2004.

Weltbank. *Sicherheit, Armutsbekämpfung und nachhaltige Entwicklung.* Bonn 1999.

Wulf, Herbert. *Internationalisierung und Privatisierung von Krieg und Frieden.* Baden-Baden: Nomos, 2005. Also published in English as *Internationalizing and Privatizing War and Peace.* Hampshire, England: Palgrave MacMillan, 2005.

Wynn, Donald T. "Managing the Logistic-Support. Contract in the Balkans Theatre," *Engineer* (July 2000).

Zarate, Juan C. "The Emergence of a New Dog of War: Private International Security Companies, International Law and the New World Order," *Stanford Journal of International Law* 34, (Winter 1998): 75–156.

Rolf Uessler was born in 1943 in Dortmund, Germany and studied economy, psychology, and journalism. He has lived in Rome as a freelance writer and researcher since 1979. His work focuses on illegal activity in the world economy, organized crime, and shadow economies; privatization and de-democratization; and mafia and government in Italy. The author was active for more than a decade in the Italian antimafia movement and has developed tools for the analysis of money laundering and of illegal financial transactions. He has written numerous essays on this topic in German and Italian journals. His published books include: *Mafia, Myth, Power, Mora* (Bonn 1987), *Challenge Mafia: Strategies against Organized Crime* (Bonn 1993) (both books published in German). *Servants of War* was first published in German by Ch. Links Publishers in 2006.